Politics in the Russian Regions

Studies in Central and Eastern Europe
Edited for the International Council for Central and East European Studies by
Roger E. Kanet, University of Miami, USA

Titles include:

Graeme Gill *(editor)*
POLITICS IN THE RUSSIAN REGIONS

Roger E. Kanet *(editor)*
RUSSIA
Re-Emerging Great Power

Katlijn Malfliet, Lien Verpoest and Evgeny Vinokurov *(editors)*
THE CIS, THE EU AND RUSSIA
Challenges of Integration

Stephen Velychenko *(editor)*
UKRAINE, THE EU AND RUSSIA
History, Culture and International Relations

Forthcoming titles include:
Rebecca Kay *(editor)*
GENDER, EQUALITY AND DIFFERENCE DURING AND AFTER STATE SOCIALISM

John Pickles *(editor)*
GLOBALIZATION AND REGIONALIZATION IN POST-SOCIALIST ECONOMIES
Common Economic Spaces of Europe

John Pickles *(editor)*
STATE AND SOCIETY IN POST-SOCIALIST ECONOMIES

Stephen White *(editor)*
MEDIA, CULTURE AND SOCIETY IN PUTIN'S RUSSIA

Stephen White *(editor)*
POLITICS AND THE RULING GROUP IN PUTIN'S RUSSIA

Thomas Bremer *(editor)*
RELIGION AND THE CONCEPTUAL BOUNDARY IN CENTRAL AND EASTERN
EUROPE

Stephen Hutchings *(editor)*
RUSSIA AND ITS OTHER(S) ON FILM
Screening Intercultural Dialogue

Joan DeBardeleben *(editor)*
THE BOUNDARIES OF EU ENLARGEMENT
Finding A Place for Neighbours

Stanislav J. Kirschbaum *(editor)*
THE MEANING OF EUROPE, CENTRAL EUROPE AND THE EU

Studies in Central and Eastern Europe
Series Standing Order ISBN 0-230-51682-3 hardcover
(outside North America only)

You can receive future titles in this series as they are published by placing a standing order.
Please contact your bookseller or, in case of difficulty, write to us at the address below with
your name and address, the title of the series and the ISBN quoted above.

Customer Services Department, Macmillan Distribution Ltd, Houndmills, Basingstoke,
Hampshire RG21 6XS, England

Politics in the Russian Regions

Edited by

Graeme Gill
Government and Public Administration
The University of Sydney, Australia

First published 2007 by
PALGRAVE MACMILLAN
Houndmills, Basingstoke, Hampshire RG21 6XS and
175 Fifth Avenue, New York, N.Y. 10010
Companies and representatives throughout the world

PALGRAVE MACMILLAN is the global academic imprint of the Palgrave Macmillan division of St. Martin's Press, LLC and of Palgrave Macmillan Ltd. Macmillan® is a registered trademark in the United States, United Kingdom and other countries. Palgrave is a registered trademark in the European Union and other countries.

ISBN-13: 978-0-230-51686-1   hardback
ISBN-10: 0-230-51686-6   hardback

This book is printed on paper suitable for recycling and made from fully managed and sustained forest sources. Logging, pulping and manufacturing processes are expected to conform to the environmental regulations of the country of origin.

A catalogue record for this book is available from the British Library.

Library of Congress Cataloging-in-Publication Data

Politics in the Russian regions / edited by Graeme Gill.
        p. cm. — (Studies in Central and Eastern Europe)
    Includes bibliographical references and index.
    ISBN-13: 978-0-230-51686-1 (cloth)
    ISBN-10: 0-230-51686-6 (cloth)
        1. Central-local government relations—Russia (Federation)
    2. Business and politics—Russia (Federation) I. Gill, Graeme J.
JN6693.5.S8P65 2007
320.447'049—dc22
                                                        2007060070

10   9   8   7   6   5   4   3   2   1
16   15   14   13   12   11   10   09   08   07

Printed and bound in Great Britain by
Antony Rowe Ltd, Chippenham and Eastbourne

Contents

v

List of Tables

List of Figures

Preface by General Editor

When the International Council for Central and East European Studies (ICCEES) was founded at the first international and multidisciplinary conference of scholars working in this field, held in Banff, Alberta, Canada, on 4-7 September 1974, it was given the name International Committee for Soviet and East European Studies (ICSEES). Its major purpose was to propose was to provide for greater exchange between research centres and scholars around the world who were devoted to the study of the USSR and the communist states and societies of Eastern Europe. These developments were the main motivation for bringing together the very different national organisations in the field and for forming a permanent committee of their representatives, which would serve as an umbrella organization, as well as promoter of closer co-operation. Four national scholarly associations launched ICSEES at the Banff conference: the American Association for the Advancement of Slavic Studies (AAASS), the National Association for Soviet and East European Studies in Great Britain (NASEES), the British Universities Association of Slavists (BUAS), and the Canadian Association of Slavists (CAS).

Over the past three decades six additional Congresses have been held: in Garmisch-Partenkirchen, Germany, 1980; Washington, USA, 1985; Harrogate, UK, 1990; Warsaw, Poland, 1995; Tampere, Finland, 2000; and Berlin, Germany, 2005. The next Congress is scheduled for 2010 in Stockholm, Sweden. The original four national associations that sponsored the first congress have been joined by an additional seventeen full and six associate member associations, with significantly more than a thousand scholars participating at each of the recent congresses.

It is now a little over three decades since scholars felt the need to coordinate the efforts in the "free world" to describe and analyze the Communist political systems, their societies and economies, and East-West relations in particular. Halfway through this period, the Communist system collapsed, the region that was the object of study was reorganized, and many of the new states that emerged set out on a path of democratic development, economic growth, and, in many cases, inclusion in Western institutions. The process turned out to be complex, and there were setbacks. Yet, by 2004, the European Union as well as the North Atlantic Treaty Organization had welcomed those post-Communist states that had met all of the requirements for membership. Not all of the applicant states achieved this objective; but the process is ongoing. For this reason, perhaps even more than before, the region that encompassed the former Communist world demands study, explanation, and analysis, as both centripetal and centrifugal forces are at work in each state and across the region. We are most fortunate that the community of scholars addressing these issues now includes many astute analysts from the region itself.

Notes on the Contributors

David Cashaback is a Social Sciences and Humanities Research Council of Canada postdoctoral fellow at the School of Political Studies, University of Ottawa. His principal areas of research are comparative federalism, language policy and Russian politics, and his current work explores the links between federalism and territorial and nonterritorial linguistic minorities in Russia's regions.

Graeme Gill is ARC Professorial Fellow and Professor of Government and Public Administration at the University of Sydney. A Fellow of the Academy of Social Sciences in Australia, he has published widely in the field of Soviet and Russian politics, democratization, and the development of the state. He is currently working on symbolism in the Soviet Union and Russia.

Daniel Göler is assistant Professor in the Department of Geography in the University of Bamberg. He works on urban and population geography, post-socialist transformation, and rural areas and peripheries.

Andreas Heinemann-Grüder is a senior research analyst in the Bonn International Centre for Conversion. He is currently working on questions of the territorial management of conflict in ethnic federations, and has published widely on this topic.

Julia Kusznir is Director of the Koszalin Institute of Comparative European Studies in Koszalin, Poland and a member of the Research Centre for East European Studies in Bremen University. She works on political and economic elites, the Russian oil and gas industry, and political economy.

Oksana Oracheva is the programme director in Russia of the International Fellowships Program of the Institute of International Education, and Associate Professor, Department of Political Science and Political Governance, Russian State Academy of Civil Service under the president of the Russian Federation. She has been editor of the Russian regional bulletin published by the East–West Institute, and has published on federalism in both Russia and the West.

Rostislav Turovsky is a Lecturer at Moscow State University and the Higher School of Economics and a member of the Russian Association of Political Science. He works on regional policies, federalism, regional government and electoral geography, and is the author of three books and numerous articles.

Kerstin Zimmer is in the Institute for Sociology at Philipps University Marburg. She has worked on local government in Donetsk and regional development policy in eastern and central Europe. She is now working on migration from Ukraine to the European Union.

Introduction: Power and the Russian Regions

Graeme Gill

Scholarly attention on Russia in the period since the fall of the Soviet Union has tended to concentrate primarily on developments at the centre, in Moscow. This focus is understandable, both in terms of the importance of politics in the capital for both the country as a whole and the world, and of the intrinsic interest of Russian developments. However, there has also been a politics occurring in the regions, and increasingly scholars have been taking note of this. The course of such politics has been shaped overwhelmingly by two factors: the relationship with the centre, and the way power has been structured at the regional level.

One of the key factors shaping a country's administrative structure is size. But this works in several ways and in different dimensions. The greater the national population, the higher the demands for government services, but the larger the potential tax base from which such services may be funded, and vice versa. The greater the diversity within the national population, the more complex the demands on government are likely to be. The larger the territorial extent of the country, and the greater the geographical diversity within its borders, the more extensive the state's tasks in managing both the territory and the exploitation of its resources. In such circumstances, the actual structure of the state itself comes into play. No state can be run effectively from a single centre without some degree of decentralization of administrative power and process. Even states that are geographically small require some level of decentralization, even if this is just the allocation of part of the central authority to appointed agents for the fulfilment of a restricted number of administrative tasks, like tax collecting or the administration of justice. But in large states such decentralization usually needs to be more regularized, more permanent and to be organized on a territorial basis. A main issue for political analysts for a long time has been whether such decentralization has involved the

1

establishment of autonomous power centres in the regions. Where there has been no such autonomous power, regional and local authorities have been the instruments of the political centre, conducting rule on behalf of those in charge of the central state structure. The result has been a unitary system. Where autonomous power has been established at the regional level, and where regional authorities thereby possess power that is independent of the centre, a federal system exists.[1] Central and regional power coexist, each operating in different spheres of activity so that they, in theory, complement rather than contradict each other. Federalism, characterized by this division of powers, has often been seen as a suitable response to diversity within the society. But federalism has also been seen as a means of increasing the democratic nature of government by bringing government closer to the citizens. In Russia, where some form of decentralization was essential because of the size of the country, federalism was seen as an appropriate answer to both the diversity and the democracy issues.

Russian federalism and diversity

That federalism should be seen in this way is not a surprise. Formally the USSR had been a federal state and, within it, Russia had also been a federation, so when the Soviet Union collapsed, the formal constitutional infrastructure of a federal Russia was in place. Soviet Russia already consisted of federal units, and these could comprise the component elements of an independent federal Russia. But although Soviet Russia had formally been a federal republic, in fact the federal distribution of power had been undercut by the unitary nature of the Communist Party and by the way in which it was this institution that effectively ruled the Soviet Union, not the state structure. When the Soviet Union collapsed, the most important political elites in Russia[2] rejected the former Soviet system of rule and, at least rhetorically, embarked on the path of building a democratic political system. In doing so they rejected the model of a unitary political machine extending throughout the entire country, seeing the federal structure as a viable and attractive alternative.

What also made federalism appear to be an appropriate means of structuring the Russian state was the diversity that existed in the Russian Federation. Different parts of the country had very different demographic structures, economic profiles, geographical and climatic conditions, and varying levels of facilities and services. From the urbanized sophistication of Moscow and St Petersburg through the sparsity and bleakness of the northern mining settlements to the rural squalour of some of the farming regions, the range of circumstances in which people lived created a highly differentiated country with a diversity of different needs and demands. Some of this diversity is reflected in the different subjects of the federation. These units vary widely in terms of their basic characteristics. For example, the Republic of Sakha is 388 times the land area of the Republic of North Ossetiya, while Moscow has 443 times the population of the Evenkiya autonomous oblast (AO).[3] Levels of development vary widely, with some regions highly industrialized and others with barely any industry at all. This creates very different economic profiles; for example, per capita income in the Yamalo-Nenets AO in the mid-1990s was 178 times that in the Republic of Ingushetiya;[4] the budget in some regions (including Moscow city and oblast, St Petersburg, Khanty-Mansii AO and the Republic of Tatarstan) is a net donor to the federal budget, while between 80 per cent and 90 per cent of the regional budget of the Buryat AO and the Republic of Ingushetiya comes from federal transfers.[5] The differentiation between the federal units and the communities they encompass makes for a highly complex national state.

In addition to this socio-economic complexity, there is also political complexity. This stems from the federal structure as it has developed in Russia, a structure which, until the Putin reforms, was characterized by a significant level of political incoherence. The roots of such incoherence are to be found in the power regional leaders were able to claim in the early part of the 1990s, and the weakness and consequent inability of the Yeltsin-led centre to wind back those powers. A great stimulus for regional leaders to make extravagant claims for their power and autonomy came from the Russian Declaration of Sovereignty of 12 June 1990 which acknowledged the need to significantly extend the rights of the autonomous republics and the regions of Russia, and from Yeltsin's August 1990 encouragement of them to "take as much independence as you can."[6] The powers claimed by regional leaders, which were often embedded in the newly-introduced regional state constitutions, were very extensive, often including the claim to national sovereignty and the unilateral upgrading of the constitutional status of the political unit; for example, in July 1990 North Ossetiya declared itself a union republic. The centre tried to bring some order into the state structure by fostering a Federal Treaty, which was signed on 31 March 1992 by representatives of the federal government and most of the republics of the federation; only Tatarstan, which sought a bilateral treaty, and Chechnya, which declared itself to be independent, refused to sign. The Treaty generally accepted the powers claimed by regional authorities, including that of republican sovereignty.

The Treaty also accepted as the basis for federalism the bifurcated nature of the Soviet federal structure. This bifurcated nature consisted of the acceptance of two different principles for the federal units, ethnic and territorial. In practice, this meant that some of the units of the federation were formed along ethnic lines and others on a purely territorial basis. Of the 89 subjects of the federation, 32 are ethnically-defined: 21 republics, 10 autonomous okrugs (AOs) and one autonomous oblast; the other 57 are territorially-defined: six krais, 49 oblasts and two federal cities.[7] However, given that there are acknowledged to be some 128 different national groups in Russia, it is clear that the federal structure only in small part is a reflection of this ethnic diversity; indeed, some of the ethnic groups with their own administrative units are smaller than some national groups which lack such units.[8] This situation is further complicated by the so-called "Matryoshka" nature of Russian federalism whereby one subject of the federation (the AO) is politically and territorially part of another subject of the federation (the oblast or krai), thereby creating compound subjects of the federation.

The Federal Treaty was to be superseded by the new Constitution adopted in 1993. This declared that the federal Constitution and laws were paramount over all other constitutions and laws. It also declared that all subjects of the federation were to be constitutionally equal (Article 5), and listed a number of areas that were subject solely to federal jurisdiction and a number of areas subject to the joint jurisdiction of the federation and its subjects; residual areas were under the jurisdiction of the individual subjects. But the claimed equality has not been the case in practice, with greater powers generally being enjoyed by the 21 ethnic republics than the other subjects of the federation. The constitutional basis for this is Articles 11 and 78 of the Constitution which made provision for the establishment of bilateral treaties between the federal centre and the subjects of the federation. Between 1994 and 1996, 46 such treaties were signed;[9] eleven with republics, 26 with oblasts, eight with krais and autonomous oblasts, and one with St Petersburg; a forty-seventh treaty was signed with the city of Moscow in June 1998.[10] The terms of each of these treaties were different, with the result that the precise relationship between centre and individual subjects was different. Many of these treaties, and the secret agreements that were sometimes attached to them, gave the local authorities a range of economic and political benefits, including in the case of some of the republics the right to conduct their own foreign relations and establish national banks. The provisions of many of these treaties reflected the powers the republics arrogated to themselves in the first couple of years of the 1990s noted above. Throughout this treaty-making process, the treaties were a reflection of the power of the regional authorities compared with the centre. Under Yeltsin, the federal centre was unwilling to seek to exert central power too much, in part because of the circumstances of domestic politics at this time (and especially during Yeltsin's first term), and because of the partial vacuum at the heart of the political process resulting from Yeltsin's continuing health problems. The political asymmetry that developed was in large part a function of the weakness of the federal centre.

Asymmetry is not uncommon in federations, but what sets the Russian Federation apart from those elsewhere is the scale of that asymmetry; it has generally been much greater in Russia than in other established federations. The clearest instance of this is the very high number of regional laws and constitutional provisions which contradicted those of the federal centre.[11] This was clearly something that the new President Vladimir Putin sought to address. As Oksana Oracheva, Andreas Heinemann-Grüder and David Cashaback show, Putin has over his time in office set in train a series of changes to the federal structure designed to reduce political asymmetry and to reinforce the power of the centre. As the following chapters show, there were six major elements in Putin's reforms:

1. The creation in May 2000 of seven federal districts, each headed by a presidential envoy appointed by and responsible to the president. The new districts closely conformed to the existing military districts into which the country was divided, while five of the seven initial envoys came from a military or security background. The envoy had wide-ranging powers, including the monitoring of regional compliance with the Constitution, federal laws and presidential decrees, overseeing of the appointment and placement of personnel in the regional branch of the federal bureaucracy, the oversight of security issues, and the establishment and coordination of inter-regional economic programmes. While they were said to be responsible for coordinating the work of federal agencies in their districts, their role was clearly superior to that of the local elected governors,[12] and this therefore constitutes a direct attempt to bring regional authorities into line.[13] The creation of this position was accompanied by the elimination of the presidential representative in each of the regions established by Yeltsin in 1991.

2. The reform of the federal upper house, the Federation Council. From January 2002, the governors and chairs of regional assemblies lost their ex officio rights to sit in the upper chamber. They were to be replaced by a delegate selected by the governor (and approved by the regional

legislature) and one chosen by the legislature. This move removed the governors from an embedded position in the central decision-making apparatus, and also removed their immunity from prosecution.[14]

3. Creation of the State Council in September 2000 as a new advisory body to the president comprising all of the chief executives of the regions. It was scheduled to meet at three-monthly intervals.[15] It has no independent power, is purely advisory and, having been created by presidential decree, can be dissolved in this way as well.

4. In December 2004 in the wake of the Beslan tragedy, the president was given the power to appoint regional leaders. The presidential envoy, in consultation with regional leaders, civil society groups and public organizations, would make a recommendation to the president. The subsequent nomination was to be confirmed by the regional assembly. If that assembly twice declined to confirm that nomination, it could be dissolved by the president. This provision replaced an earlier one providing legal grounds for the removal of a governor by the centre, although this earlier provision did not enable the president to appoint a replacement; a new election was to be held within six months of the removal.[16]

5. The bringing of regional legislation into line with federal laws. This "harmonization" has involved pressure from the centre for the regions to bring their constitutions, laws, charters and decrees into conformity with the federal law, and is designed to create a single legal space.[17] Much of the legislation that had been adopted in the regions contradicted federal law, and this was designed to end this situation. Notions of republican sovereignty were also quashed by the Constitutional Court.

6. There was significant encouragement given to the subjects of the federation to consider mergers in order to reduce the number of units in the system. A case of this is discussed by Oksana Oracheva.

Putin has clearly sought to bring about more regularization in the federal structure, and to thereby eliminate much of the political asymmetry that has characterized Russian federalism. This has also involved the assertion of greater central control. This has implications for the question of the relationship between Russian federalism and democracy.

Russian federalism and democracy

The principal argument for federalism promoting democracy lies in the division of political power that the federal arrangement constitutes. Centres of power at regional levels are meant to act as restraints on the unbridled exercise of power from the centre, but it is not clear that regional authorities in Russia have acted consistently this way. In constitutional terms, it is only in those areas of joint responsibility or sole regional responsibility that the regional authorities have much scope for limiting the central government. In principle, this opens up significant scope for the restraint of central power. Among those areas defined in the Constitution to which joint jurisdiction applies and which could imply the imposition of restraints on central power are:[18] protection of human and civil rights and freedoms, issues relating to the ownership and use of all natural resources, delimitation of state property, environmental protection, education, the coordination of public health, social protection including social security, combating of disasters, the establishment of general principles of taxation and the levying of duties, personnel of judicial and law-enforcement bodies, protection of the traditional way of life of numerically small ethnic communities, establishment of the general principles for the organization of a system of bodies of state power and local self-government, and the coordination of the international and foreign economic relations of parts of the Russian Federation and fulfilment of international treaties. This is a considerable list of areas in which regional authorities have some constitutionally-based power, in addition to those residual areas that are solely under their jurisdiction. But it is not clear that this constitutional basis has been used very widely to limit central power.

The principal constitutional means whereby such restriction could be enacted is through the legislature. The lower house, or State Duma, is the primary law-making house in this structure, and although many of the deputies have at different times come together in factions to support different policy lines, such factions have generally not been organized along the lines of the federal units. Certainly some have been based in some of the federal units; for example, New Regional Policy in the first Duma and Regions of Russia in the second both had regional roots, but the basis of their unity was the economic interests they sought to represent rather than the territorial divisions of the federation. Following the Duma election of 2003, the pro-Putin United Russia party gained a dominant position in the chamber.[19] The construction of this party had involved the drawing in of many of the regional governors, a move which further undercut their capacity to exercise any independent role in the legislature. The more important house for the representation of regional interests was to be the Federation Council. Comprising two representatives from each subject of the federation (one each from the representative and executive bodies of state power), the Federation Council had the responsibility to examine and approve all laws adopted by the State Duma.[20] Initially, the representatives were popularly elected, but from 1995 this was changed to give ex officio membership of the Council to the heads of the legislative and executive branches of regional government. As indicated above, this was changed again in 2000 so that the heads of both branches sent deputies to represent them rather than enjoying membership themselves. While the governors and legislative heads were present in the Council, this seemed to be a body with significant political weight. However, because of their full-time responsibilities in the regions, many officials did not attend sessions of the Council on a regular basis. The difficulty in achieving a quorum often forced the Council to resort to postal voting. But in any case, the Constitution declares that a law will be deemed to have been passed if it is supported by more than half of the total number of members of the Council "or if it has not been examined by the Federation Council within fourteen days."[21] This provided significant scope for legislation to go through without review. Thus even when the Council should have been at its most powerful, between 1996 and 2000, it did not act as much of a check on central power. And given that prior to 1995 most governors were appointed by President Yeltsin while from 2002 the members of the Council were simply the deputies of regional officials, these people were not well placed to stand up to the exercise of central, especially presidential, power. The creation of the advisory State Council in no way compensated for this.

But federalism is likely to further democracy only if the regional governments are themselves democratic. Only if the government is democratically constructed and is responsible to the electorate can it be close to the people. But as Kerstin Zimmer shows, federalism does not guarantee democratic government at lower levels.

Regional regimes

The collapse of the Soviet regime was not accompanied by a broad-based commitment to democratic values either among political elites at the central or regional levels or by the mass of the populace. Accordingly, at regional and local levels, there was not an immediate overthrowing of the established power-holders and the emergence of new elites, unconnected with the former authorities. In many regions, incumbent leaders were able to hang on to power – if not alone, then in combination with newly emergent political forces. Although over time there has been the development of many of the procedural qualities of democracy, and therefore many of the regions have been characterized by the implementation of democratic procedures like multi-candidate elections and mass involvement in voting, in only a minority of the regions were regimes established that had clear and unambiguous democratic credentials. In many places democratic forms hide a more restrictive politics;[22] there has not been the widespread development of democratic regimes in the regions that many had hoped for.[23]

With the collapse of the Soviet Union, power in the regions lay in the hands of incumbent political and economic elites, based respectively in the politico-administrative structure and in the major economic enterprises in the region. Such elites were usually able to use the positions they occupied to strengthen their hold on power. This did not constitute the continuation of the Soviet-era political machines that dominated politics at these levels; rather, it represented new ways of organizing politics that accorded with the changed circumstances. Using the opportunities that flowed from the erosion of the centre's capacity to project its power into the regions and from assertion of local sovereignty, local elites were able to mould the development of the political system to serve their interests; the creation of a presidential system was one method often used to achieve this end. Similarly, the political authorities could structure economic reform in such a way as to benefit themselves and their local allies and hinder attempts by potentially hostile outsiders to gain an economic foothold in the region; the restriction of the privatization provisions to locals was an important means of doing this. Some local assets were even passed into the hands of regional administrations rather than being privatized, something which could mean significant economic potential and resources being at the governor's disposal.[24] Thus, through the manipulation of political and economic reform, local elites were often able to develop machines based on political and economic resources which they could use to consolidate their control in the region. Writing in relation to Omsk, Neil Melvin has referred to how "A powerful core grouping, formed from the merger of the local state apparatus and leading economic interests, dominated the key positions of power in the *oblast*."[25]

The consolidation of political machines has been a common feature at the regional level and, as Kerstin Zimmer shows, has been independent of the formal state structure; such machines have appeared in both federal and unitary systems. The basis of such machines is a combination of appointment, financial dependence and electoral interdependence. This is well illustrated in the case of Tatarstan, but the general principles apply widely throughout the Russian regions. First, appointment. Like their Soviet predecessors, regional political machines were heavily dependent upon the capacity of those who ran the machines to appoint allies or supporters to the principal positions in the hierarchy. This normally meant the leading political and administrative posts in the region, especially at the AO, raion and city levels. Second, financial dependence. The Russian constitutional system gave no financial autonomy to the lower levels of the administrative structure, with the result that the budget for each subordinate level was dependent upon what it was granted by superordinate levels. This gave significant power to those who ran the administration at these latter levels, a power which they could use to encourage political reliability and support among their counterparts on the lower rungs of the administrative hierarchy. In the case of oblast governors and republican presidents, their ability to garner economic assets for their administrations in the privatization process further enhanced their capacity to wield an economic weapon to keep members of their machine in line.

Third, electoral interdependence. Crucial in the survival of this sort of political machine is its capacity to mobilize votes. Given the democratic rhetoric of the post-Soviet period and the consequent need to meet the procedural requirements of democracy, elections have been a constant feature of political life at all levels of the country since 1993. But free elections for political office could upset the control of local machines, so those machines had to ensure that the elections were structured in such a way as not to challenge their positions. The manipulation of voting qualifications and of the nomination process, the elimination of electoral challengers, the manipulation of electoral dates and rules on turnout, gerrymandering, electoral pressure, and outright electoral fraud have all been used by incumbents to maintain themselves in power.[26] This has been a significant feature of politics in Tatarstan.[27] It is important for the consolidation of individual officials in power that they can organize their own election; indeed, Tatar president Mintimer Shaimiev forces all of those he appoints to administrative positions to stand for election as a deputy in the local assembly to ensure that they are able to both get out and deliver the votes.[28] But this is important not just for the local candidates; higher-level leaders also rely on such electoral support for their own positions. This sort of dependence stretches right up the structure to the position of the Russian president; just as Shaimiev relies on the lower levels of his machine to deliver him the votes in republican elections, so Putin relies on the governors to deliver him electoral support in national-level elections. The integration of the governors into United Russia is a reflection of this. The importance of this is reflected in the way in which, in the early 1990s when the dispute between Moscow and Tatarstan was at its height, Shaimiev's machine consistently refused to deliver the Tatar vote to Yeltsin.[29] This relationship between superiors and subordinates is essentially an exchange of patronage for electoral support, and this is a tie both within regional political machines and between these and central politicians.

Electoral control is thus one of the keys to the continuing power of the political machines. Such control is aided by a couple of other factors. Political parties are very weakly developed in the regions; they possess few members, have little in the way of infrastructure, and usually have access to only meagre resources. Furthermore, the regional press is rarely a vigorous exponent of freedom of speech, often being under the general control of the local authorities. Accordingly, the political arena within which local oppositionist forces can organize and mobilize to challenge existing elites is weak in most regions. This has enabled dominant elites to further consolidate their positions in power, using the infrastructure of democracy to achieve this end. But the other side of regional machines has been economic.

Central to regional power in many regions have been alliances between local political and private economic elites. This is a major focus of study in the chapters by Rostislav Turovsky and Julia Kusznir. Such an alliance can prove to be very beneficial to the local elites. For both political and economic elites, such an association can help to suppress potential challengers from within the region; the political authorities may use their administrative resources – such as taxation rates, control over local inspectors and government regulations – to hinder the development of companies competitive to their allies, while alliance with business can cut off possible funding and other sorts of resources from potential political challengers. For political elites, close business connections can provide them with access to the sorts of economic resources that will not only grease the wheels of their political machines, but facilitate their running of the local economy and thereby to appearing to be performing satisfactorily in the eyes of Moscow. Indeed, working closely with business can have very positive effects for the local economy. For economic elites, such an alliance can both facilitate their involvement in the local economy – providing them with benefits and privileges that may otherwise not have been available – and also assist them in fending off possible challenges to their position from competitor companies from outside the region.[30]

In practice, in most regions there have been three major potential partners to such alliances: regional political elites, regional economic elites, and central (Moscow-based) economic elites, or their representatives; in some regions, foreign companies have also played a part, while the establishment of presidential envoys has also potentially projected the federal political centre into regional affairs in an indirect fashion. The Soviet collapse had significant implications for the Russian regions. For some, as Daniel Göler shows, it has been catastrophic. But for others it seemed to foreshadow substantial opportunities for economic gains. Throughout most of the 1990s, regional economic actors were the main ones involved with the regional political elites. In these sorts of situations, the power and position achieved by economic elites was in large part a function of their importance in the regional economy. Where they were dominant in that economy, such as the diamond industry in Sakha and oil in Tyumen, local economic interests could play a prominent part in local governance, while in those areas without dominant economic interests, such as Penza and Tyva, local economic interests were less in evidence in the regional power structure. However, following the 1998 economic crisis, which made investment in Russia more profitable, and the weakening of regional political actors as a result of Putin's reforms, many large Moscow-based economic concerns have been more interested in penetrating the regions and in playing a part in regional power structures. The result has been a kaleidoscope of patterns of interaction at the regional level between political elites and regional and Moscow-based economic elites.[31]

In some regions, like Tatarstan and Bashkortostan, the political leaders have been able to keep a tight control over the economy and business accepts the administrative rules set by the governors in exchange for privileges and access to budget resources. In Tatarstan this has been helped by the central role played in the oil industry by people close to Shaimiev, and by the way that he has used his political resources to see off a potential challenge to Tatneft's position in the republic by Lukoil. In other regions, like Khanty-Mansii AO and Nizhnii Novgorod, there has been much more of a partnership between political and economic elites, with the governor effectively guaranteeing the arrangements and deals made between business groups in the region. In this case, the potential for economic competition seems to be greater than in the first one, and the political elites are therefore essential for ensuring overall stability. In yet other regions, like Chukotka and Kalmykiya, the economic elite, or a part of it, may seize political power and oversee the economic and administrative arrangements in the region in the economic interests of that elite itself. A prominent example of this occurred when the so-called "oligarch" Roman Abramovich became governor of Chukotka, and directed much of his business activities through that region. And, finally, there have been cases like Kirov oblast where there has been continuing conflict.

This could be between either the political and economic elite, or sections of the economic elite.

However, as Rostislav Turovsky points out, the balance of forces between political and economic elites and also within both can change, and therefore one pattern of power will not necessarily remain in evidence in any particular region. Nevertheless what is certain is that this interaction between political and economic elites is central to the structuring of power in the regions, both when that power is democratically organized and when the regime is more authoritarian in tone.

Conclusion

Thus, the main dynamics fuelling regional politics are the tension within the federal structure, and especially the relationship with the centre, and the relationship between actors at the regional level. It is this intersection of power from outside the region with power structures within the region that constitutes the principal defining force for regional politics. And with no region now closed to the federal government and to the economic power to be found in the major companies situated in Moscow, the interplay of these two sources of power is likely to become even more important. It is these sources of power and how they are unrolling that are the foci of the chapters, which were initially presented as papers at the VII ICCEES World Congress, in this book.

Notes

1 A qualification here is that even in unitary systems, the local level of government often enjoys a degree of autonomous power defined functionally; that is, they alone possess authority in certain spheres of life while the central state enjoys a monopoly of authority in other spheres of life.
2 But not in all parts of the former USSR.
3 Cameron Ross, *Federalism and Democratisation in Russia* (Manchester: Manchester University Press, 2002), p. 8.
4 Ibid., p. 9.
5 Ibid., p. 84.
6 Cited in John B. Dunlop, *The Rise of Russia and the Fall of the Soviet Empire* (Princeton: Princeton University Press, 1993), p. 62. He reaffirmed this during the treaty-making period. *Segodnia*, 31 May 1994.
7 These are listed in Jeffrey Kahn, *Federalism, Democratization, and the Rule of Law in Russia* (Oxford: Oxford University Press, 2002), p. 10.
8 For information about the ethnic populations within the Russian Federation and in each of the subjects of the federation, see V.A. Tishkov *et al.* (eds),

Narody rossii. Entsiklopediya (Moscow: Nauchnoe izdatel'stvo "Bol'shaya Rossiiskaya Entsiklopediya", 1994), pp. 433–41.

9   Ross, *Federalism and Democratisation*, p. 41, and Kahn, *Federalism*, p. 150.

10 Kahn, *Federalism*, p. 159. Kahn, *Federalism*, pp. 160–4 discusses why these particular units and not others received treaties.

11 For some figures on this, see the chapter by David Cashaback.

12 This term will be used generically to refer to the chief executive in the regions, even though in the republics this person has been called the president.

13 For one study of how this has worked in practice, see Peter Reddaway and Robert W. Orrtung, *The Dynamics of Russian Politics. Putin's Reform of Federal–Regional Relations. Volume 1* (Lanham: Rowman & Littlefield Publishers Inc., 2004). For the relevant presidential decree and the parliamentary resolution, see *Rossiiskaya gazeta*, 16 May 2001. On the districts and their presidential envoys, see Kahn, *Federalism*, pp. 241 and 243.

14 The law will be found in *Rossiiskaya gazeta*, 5 August 2000.

15 The presidential decree establishing the Council is in *Rossiiskaya gazeta*, 1 September 2000.

16 Paradoxically, this measure seemingly designed to reduce the governors' security of tenure coexisted with a January 2001 amendment to the law concerning the terms of governors which effectively allowed 69 incumbent governors to seek a third term and 17 a fourth. Richard Sakwa, *Putin: Russia's Choice* (London: Routledge, 2004), p. 153.

17 Associated with this was 2003 amendment of the joint jurisdiction provisions followed in 2005 by the handing back to the regions of some of these powers. See chapter by Cashaback.

18 The Constitution allocates joint jurisdiction on guaranteeing that the laws and other acts of the subjects of the federation accord with the Constitution and federal laws, but does not apply the same principle to federal laws. This is Article 72 of the Russian Constitution.

19 In the election itself United Russia did not gain a majority of seats (224 of 450), but when the Duma met, significant numbers of deputies joined its ranks.

20 Although any veto by the Council could be overturned by a two-thirds vote in the Duma or by the president.

21 Article 105.

22 For one attempt to chart levels of democratization in the regions, see Christopher Marsh, "Measuring and Explaining Variations in Russian Regional Democratisation", in Cameron Ross (ed.), *Russian Politics under Putin* (Manchester, Manchester University Press, 2004), pp. 176–97. Marsh (pp. 193–4) argues that, on a range of one to five, where five is the highest level of democratization and one the least democratic, and based on participation levels in gubernatorial elections and votes for candidates other than the winner, 6.4 per cent of regions scored five, 28.2 per cent four, 39.7 per cent three, 15.4 per cent two and 10.3 per cent one. These figures apply to 78 regions.

23 For some surveys, see Mary McAuley, *Russia's Politics of Uncertainty* (Cambridge: Cambridge University Press, 1997); Vladimir Gel'man, Sergei Ryzhenkov and Michael Brie, *Making and Breaking Democratic Transitions. The Comparative Politics of Russia's Regions* (Lanham: Rowman and Littlefield Publishers Inc., 2003); Kelly M. McMann and Nikolai V. Petrov, "A Survey of Democracy in Russia's Regions", *Post-Soviet Geography and Economics* 41, 3,

2000, pp. 155–82; and Nikolai Petrov, "Regional Models of Democratic Development", Michael McFaul, Nikolai Petrov, and Andrei Ryabov *et al.*, *Between Dictatorship and Democracy: Russian Post-Communist Political Reform* (Washington, DC: Carnegie Endowment for International Peace, 2004), pp. 239–67. Also see the references in Petrov, "Regional Models", pp. 335–6, note 1.

24 See Henry E. Hale, "Explaining Machine Politics in Russia's Regions: Economy, Ethnicity, and Legacy", *Post-Soviet Affairs* 19, 3, 2003, pp. 241–2.

25 Neil J. Melvin, "The Consolidation of a New Regional Elite: The Case of Omsk 1987–1995", *Europe–Asia Studies* 50, 4, 1998, p. 642. Italics in original.

26 For a survey of some of the ways in which this has been done, see Ross, *Federalism and Democratization*, ch. 9.

27 V.V. Mikhailov, V.A. Bazhanov and M. Kh. Farukshin (eds), *Osobaya zona: Vybory v tatarstane* (Ulianovsk: Kazanskoe Mezhdunarodnoi Pravozashchitnoi Assamblei, 2000), and V.V. Mikhailov (ed.), *Respublika Tatarstan:demokratiya ili suverenitet?* (Moscow, 2004).

28 Kimitaka Matsuzato, "From Ethno-Bonapartism to Centralized *Caciquismo*: Characteristics and Origins of the Tatarstan Political Regime, 1990–2000", *The Journal of Communist Studies and Transition Politics* 17, 4, 2001, p. 55.

29 For a discussion of this, see Matsuzato, "From Ethno-Bonapartism", pp. 59–60. In another context, see Henry E. Hale, "Machine Politics and Institutionalized Electorates: A Comparative Analysis of Six Duma Elections in Bashkortostan", *The Journal of Communist Studies and Transition Politics*, 15, 4, 1999, pp. 70–110.

30 For discussion of a celebrated case of this, see Peter Kirkow, "Regional Warlordism in Russia: The Case of Primorskii Krai", *Europe–Asia Studies* 47, 6, 1995, pp. 923–47.

31 For a regional breakdown of dominant economic interests, see Robert W. Orrtung, "Business and Politics in the Russian Regions", *Problems of Post-Communism*, 51, 2, March–April 2004, pp. 52–4. For another analysis, see S. Peregudov, N. Lapina and I. Semenenko, *Gruppy interesov i rossiiskoe gosudarstvo* (Moscow: Editorial URSS, 1999), ch. 5. On regional alliances between local representatives of the organs of power, major regional bureaucrats and representatives of new business being known as the "party of power", see V.N. Berezovskii, *Politicheskaia elite sovestskogo proshlogo i rossiiskogo nastoiashchego priemy i metody konkurentnoi bor'by* (Moscow: Tsentr politicheskoi kon'iunktury Rossii, unpublished, March 1996), p. 26.

1
Russia's Ethnofederalism: Under-Institutionalized, Not Self-Sustaining

Andreas Heinemann-Grüder

Contemporary Russia: unitary in all but name

Observing the de-federalization efforts under President Putin raises the old issue of what conditions contribute to the sustainability and (self-) enforcement of federations. How does de-federalization occur in general and what does this tell us about the sustainability of a multi-ethnic federation in particular? Against the backdrop of Putin's recentralization policy, I will discuss the prerequisites of federal sustainability with a particular focus on the entitlements of ethnic groups and on ethnic federalism. Among the determinants of de-federalization under Putin I highlight particularly three: under-institutionalization, shifting power configurations between the centre and regions, and the non-democratic character of regional regimes.

As with the assorted varieties of "democracy", there is a wide range of understanding as to what a "federation" implies – or should imply. Ivo Duchacek once distinguished "ten yardsticks" of federalism, which largely generalized the US model.[1] My own list is shorter. Accordingly, a full fledged, ideal-type federation must meet five criteria. These are: firstly, two independently legitimized levels of government (central and regional), which are, secondly, capable of autonomously making authoritative and substantive decisions in their sphere of authority; thirdly, meaningful representation and co-decision capacity by the regions at the federal level; fourthly, substantial areas of joint jurisdiction; and fifthly, institutionalized mechanisms of federal, i.e., non-partisan, conflict regulation. Some authors have chosen to include in the definition factors such as third-party enforcement, the quality of democracy, symmetry, or an integrative party system.[2] However, prerequisites for a federation's survival should not be mixed up with its features.

Ethnic federations or "ethnofederations" are a subtype of the over-arching concept of a "federation". The concept of ethnic federation is relatively new: it is used for multi-ethnic federal states such as the former Soviet Union, Yugoslavia, Ethiopia, Nigeria, India or Russia. In ethnofederations the constituent units are formed – at least in part – on ethnic grounds or they are supposed to represent specific ethnic groups. It is of secondary importance whether these ethnic groups actually exist as self-conscious and somehow associated groups, whether they actually represent the groups in whose name they act or merely embody a symbolic label or elite interests. The origin and legitimacy of the constituent units of an ethnic federation can be traced back to a specific ethnic group's historical claims on or settlement patterns within a distinct territory. In ethnofederations the representation of the regions at the federal level also involves ethnic principles. Ethnic federations are additionally characterized by a substantial degree of de jure asymmetry. Finally, ethnofederations are often characterized by a party system that labels, mobilizes, channels, and represents ethnic affiliations. In real life, ethnic federations differ according to the dominance of one or another dimension or a specific combination thereof. However, the demarcation between ethnic federations and territorial ones is amorphous. Ethnic units may exist in parallel with purely territorial ones; ethnicity and territoriality rarely coincide; historic groups may have assimilated or otherwise lost their distinctness. Furthermore, the concept of ethnicity may simply reflect a discursive label, but not an observable pattern of group behaviour. Yet ethnic federations serve, at least in theory, a specific purpose if compared to purely territorial federations – they should eliminate the need for separate nation-building.

Applying the fundamental federal criteria to Russia's contemporary regime, it is questionable whether Russia can still be categorized as a federation. It seems more appropriate to characterize it as a unitary system with federal remains rather than as a "federation with deficits". Russia resembles a unitary state in all but title. With the abolition of independent and direct elections for chief executives in the regions (justified as a reaction to the terrorist kidnapping in a school in Beslan in September 2004), the levels of government are no longer independently legitimized. Whereas the "reforms" before the terror attacks in Beslan could be interpreted as a power balance shift favouring the central government, the nomination of governors by the Kremlin administration has destroyed an essential element of federalism. Independent sources of regional legitimacy, as well as autonomous spheres of decision-making, are critically undermined by the appointment of governors by the Russian president, by the formal and informal interference of the seven presidential envoys into regional politics, and by the factual homogenization of regional political regimes.[3] The regions are no longer immune from the elimination of their constitutional autonomy and identity. Formally, the different levels of government are separate and responsible in their spheres of competence, but *de facto* there are no legal constraints on the interference and control by the president's federal envoys and inspectors in the regions. The reformed Federation Council – no longer consisting of either directly elected senators (1993–1995) or of the heads of the regional executives and legislatures – mostly represents Moscow-based lobbyists, but it is no longer a powerful representation of the regions capable of balancing the State Duma.[4] By transforming the constitutionally provided "joint competencies" into the sphere of federal supremacy, the concurrent decision-making capabilities are also substantially limited. The constitutional concept of "joint competencies" has turned into a federal prerogative. The federation is superior whenever it claims legal territory. Finally, the norms and institutionalized vetoes for protecting multi-ethnicity have became a matter of mere convenience and opportunism.

The question why there was no substantial resistance to Putin's re-centralization deserves more attention because it provides answers about the basis of Russia's federalism and perhaps about federalism in general. The ease with which Putin reversed decentralization and federalization under Yeltsin requires further explanation. Transitology does not fully explain Putin's reversal. It does not fit with the prominent paradigm of a regional "power grab" (why was it so easy to grab this power back?), the erosion of legal space under Yeltsin (how was it possible to "harmonize" thousands of legal discrepancies in a matter of weeks?), ethnic mobilization and separatism (why was there no resistance to ethnic demobilization?), or the opposite thesis of relative institutional stability. Misinterpretations betray flawed paradigms. I would claim that most analyses were too institutionalist, formalistic, ideological, or constructivist – official policy declarations, constitutions, legal acts, and formal regulations were overestimated as indicators of federal relations, while power relations were underrated or exclusively perceived from a centralist conviction ("strong regions are bad, a strong centre is good"). The symbolic, declarative, often virtual character of formal regulations and their regulative importance was overestimated while the federal process itself rarely became the subject of thorough empirical study. The obsession in the 1990s with the prospect of disintegration and allegedly unconstrained federal bargaining blinded the eyes to a greater danger: the open door for a presidential power grab.

Under-institutionalization of the federal structure

Multi-ethnic federations often face recurring challenges. Ethnic, linguistic, religious or tribal group affiliations can be strengthened at the expense of an overarching national or constitutional consensus. The allocation of ethnic representational rights and the protection of ethnic diversity may constrain the rights of (democratic) majorities, of non-entitled ethnic groups and of individuals. Ethnicity and territoriality may also find expression in an ethnically and regionally fragmented party system. Furthermore, ethnic federations tend to (re-)distribute taxes, subsidies, grants, or other forms of assistance in an unequal manner – often in favour of ethnically defined regions. On the other hand, central governments frequently react to politicized heterogeneity or regionalist movements with tough centralization measures, direct rule, military governments, or emergency tactics, undermining thus the federal idea of "shared rule and divided rule". To put it crudely, federalism is commonly seen as causing too much diversity or too much unity, too much regionalism or inviting counter-centralism, thus being in a constant conflict of centrifugal and centripetal forces. The ascribed incentives are contradictory, at least far from unanimous. Therefore, one should be cautious when ascribing institutional effects to federalism or ethnofederalism per se. The contextual environment is key.

How a federation copes with its centrifugal or centripetal challenges is affected by power configurations, structural factors as well as institutional arrangements – more specifically among these arrangements is the "type" and "quality" of the political regime. It makes a difference whether a federation is based on a democratic or non-democratic regime or whether it interacts with a presidential, semi-presidential, or parliamentary regime.[5] Yet while there exists a vast body of literature on the interdependencies between political regimes, electoral systems and party systems, federal arrangements have been mainly treated in isolation of these factors, or examined as a mere "add-on". Any understanding (or analysis) of the recent dynamics of Russia's federalism must keep these interdependencies in mind.

Most approaches to Russian federalism fit within the institutionalist or the political economy strand. From an institutionalist perspective, it was argued that federalism under Yeltsin had been market-distorting, anti-democratic, weak at the centre, and threatening to the integrity of the country.[6] The political economy literature – while some of it descriptive, some operating with rational choice deductions – claimed that centre–periphery relations provided incentives for mere rent-seeking and maximalist regionalism. This view basically held the idea that federal frameworks were simply instruments for other ends. Ethnofederalism, in particular, had been used as a bargaining chip, as a means for the power preservation of communist leaders of titular ethnic groups, for the control over the electoral space and clientelistic elite selection, and for the control over natural resources. Two main lines of argument are discernible in these interpretations – the mismatch between institutional prescriptions and actor preferences, and an institutional incentive structure, which is dysfunctional for preserving the federation itself. Indirectly, the mismatch between institutions and actor preferences could be interpreted as a reflection of weak institutional constraints, too. Actors would prefer acting outside the institutional framework because compliance would not pay off while non-compliance would not be sanctioned.

The indecision of the Constitution over key principles left space for federal bargaining and flexibility, but due to the ill-defined margins, the constitutional order opened room for transgressing these boundaries as well. The constitutional ambiguities probably served integrative purposes only for a transitional period.[7] Russia's post-Soviet constitutional order and federal practice had institutionalized a combination of five contradictory principles: constitutional and contractual federalism; presidential power concentration and federal power division; ethno-federal and territorial federalism; symmetry and asymmetry; and executive as well as legislative federalism. The Russian Constitution of 1993 embodied tensions and contradictions which reflected the institutional and symbolic legacy of Soviet federalism: divided interests concerning key constitutional principles, unstable power configurations between the centre and the regions, and compromises built into the Constitution itself. The abolition of the Soviet state apparatus and of many public services it had provided, combined with a dominant ideology of market liberalism, created opportunities for weakly restrained clashes over power redistribution between the federal and sub-national levels of government. With hindsight, the combination of constitutional and contractual federalism, of symmetry and asymmetry, and of ethnic and territorial federalism was neither stable nor functional. I would argue that it was not conscious disobedience to the federal government as such, but the constitutional order itself that allowed for transgressions.

The contradictions between the federal and regional constitutional order, well established during the 1990s, could be traced back to the clash of founding principles in the Federation Treaties of 1992 and the Constitution of 1993. The most typical forms of regional-legal acts contradictory to the Russian Constitution consisted of the sovereignty claims of republican constitutions, the regulation of secession, and infringements on the rights and freedoms of Russian citizens. Many regions adopted laws limiting the implementation of federal laws in their respective regions, assumed competencies belonging to the federal government, adopted laws regulating the presence of migrants on their territory, or limited the electoral rights of Russian citizens on their territory. The most blatant legal contradictions pertained to the sovereignty of the Russian Federation versus the right of self-determination; the equality claim of the Constitution versus the asymmetrical status of the "subjects" of the federation; the territorial and ethnic principles of representation; the presidential prerogatives versus federal sharing and division of powers; the supremacy of the Russian Constitution and federal laws versus opposite claims in the constitutions of the republics; the provision of unity of the governmental system versus the right of the "subjects" to determine their own regional state system; the supremacy of the Constitution versus the possibility to determine competencies by means of bilateral treaties; and the wide range of "joint competencies" and the confusion over how they should be shared or divided in practice. These "transgressions" actually reflected a situation of weak institutionalization. The constitutional ambiguities made "order" vulnerable and provided fertile ground for later re-centralization.

One could argue that the prescriptive power of constitutions should not be overrated, as they reflect a minimal consensus at the time of their writing, leaving space for interpretation, negotiation, and adjustment. Applying this to Russia, however, one could say that many of the features of "republican sovereignty", "self-determination", and asymmetry were of a symbolic, almost phantom-like nature.[8] This is definitely the case, but the Constitution ill defined too many key concepts. The legal regulation of national or ethnic policy remained highly deficient. The national (or ethnic) policy of the federal government also lacked an authoritative and continuous coordinating body. The Ministry for the Affairs of the Federation and Nationalities was several times re-organized, temporarily dissolved, and it always failed to assign competencies clearly. Finally, conflict regulation was under-institutionalized: the court system did not function as a neutral "third party" that enforced rule obedience.

Ill-defined ethnic group rights

The status of ethnofederal region (republic, autonomous okrug and autonomous oblast) was the result of institutional inertia from Soviet times rather than substantial criteria. It was never properly defined which of the ethnic groups were of such a specific collective nature that would justify preferential treatment. The problem of who is or should be the subject of ethnic group rights in the Russian Federation is not confined to the definition of ethnic regions. The ambiguous assignment of rights to ethnic groups in the constitutional order is in part to blame for the conflicts between group rights and between these and individual rights.

In Russia, three types of ethnic groups are subjects of collective rights: "peoples", "minorities", and "indigenous peoples". However, the question of which groups, based on what characteristics, should be entitled to some kind of rights, is far from clear. Which group forms a "people" in comparison to a "minority" is dubious. All non-Russians could be seen as minorities, but this would contradict the notion that there are several peoples inhabiting Russia. Minorities could be all those without an ethno-territorial unit of their own, but even those groups nominally a majority in a region could be in a minority position in another region. Ethnic Russians could also be treated as a minority, at least in all those regions where they represent a demographic minority. Whereas the contemporary language usage prefers to speak of peoples (narod) and minorities, the older Soviet distinction between nation and nationality may give a clue as to what is meant by the difference. The distinction goes back to the concept of ethnic hierarchy under Stalin. Nations were then ascribed a right to statehood and "self-determination", whereas nationalities were not. A commentary on the Russian Constitution by Irina Umnova treats "peoples" as a group that represent a politico-territorial unit that is a subject of the Russian Federation. This view would de-ethnicize the concept of "peoples" – "peoples" would be all those living in a certain region, regardless of their ethnic make-up. [9] But why should people that are mere inhabitants or citizens of a certain federal unit be entitled to self-determination – the de-ethnicization of regions would equalize nominally ethnic regions with purely territorial ones and thus undermine the very meaning of distinct peoples.

Russia's Declaration of Sovereignty of 1990 announced that one of the goals of the sovereignty of the RSFSR would be to guarantee every people the right to self-determination in either a "national-state" or "national-cultural" form.[10] It was never spelled out who the bearer of sovereignty or self-determination should be – the population (citizens) of a republic, a certain ethnic group, or several named ethnic groups. If the inhabitants of a republic form the "people" (narod) – the Tatar or Chuvash "people", for example – then the question is begged as to whether the titular ethnic group – the ethnic Tatars or Chuvash – are entitled to privileged treatment vis-à-vis non-titular groups living in the same territory. Some republican constitutions enlist several ethnic groups, thus allegedly forming a common multi-ethnic people, but are those not mentioned thus excluded by implication? The preamble of the Russian Constitution is equally confusing, as on one hand it speaks of the "multinational people of the Russian Federation", but then on the other the "equality and self-determination of the peoples" – does Russia consist in constitutional terms of one people, although of a plurality of component groups, or a multiplicity of constituent groups each entitled to "self-determination"? What so-called "national-cultural autonomy" (NCA) was supposed to embody remains unclear even now. A law from 1992 ("On Principles of Legislation of the Russian Federation on Culture") declared that the Russian state would "guarantee" the right of all ethnic communities to establish a national-cultural autonomy for those with a compact settlement pattern but living "outside their national-state formation and not having their statehood". This could have meant that the NCA is only offered to the diasporas of ethnic groups living outside their federal unit, such as Tatars living outside Tatarstan. But it could have also meant that only groups without an ethno-territorial region of their own would be entitled to form a kind of non-territorial autonomy.[11] Some politicians, for example Valerii Tishkov, saw the NCA as a political alternative to the ethnofederal build-up, as a means to de-federalize ethnicity. In this perspective, the NCA was not just meant to organize folkloristic events, but to participate in elections and to represent ethnic groups in governmental bodies. Yet, this view did not gain the upper hand.[12] The law on political parties of 2001 explicitly forbids the formation of political parties on grounds of profession, race, ethnicity and religion.

Both the Russian Constitution and the constitutions of the republics also utilize fuzzy language. Variations on the concept of *demos* are frequently mixed in the same document. Republican constitutions talk of "the population" (*naselenie*) of a certain republic, the "people" of a certain republic (for example, the people of Tatarstan), the "multinational people" (*mnogonatsional'nyi narod*), a multiplicity of ethnic groups (*etnicheskaya obshnost'*), enumerated ethnic groups, a single specific ethnic people (like the ethnic Tatars), a specific nation (*natsiya*), a nationality (*natsional'nost'*, *narodnost'*), in addition to references to small nations, indigenous peoples, or "other peoples".[13] The conception of the "people" (*narod*), frequently used in more recent legal documents, assumes an overarching community based on territoriality and their belonging to a specific constitutional order – for example, "the people of Tatarstan". Conceptions with multiple or specifically named ethnic groups assume communities based on ethnic markers instead – for example, "ethnic Tatars". Two elements stand out in the Russian conception of "minority": their relatively small number and their non-dominant status.[14] National minorities can establish associations on a local, district, regional, or federal level. The status of national minorities is at times treated as if it means a kind of internal diaspora – ethnic groups living outside territories of compact settlements of the same group. In this sense, it could be interpreted as a supplement to "national-territorial", or federal, autonomy.

The law "On state support for small indigenous peoples of the Russian Federation" of 1999 mandated the government to protect indigenous traditions, to represent indigenous people in local government, and to hear their concerns. There are 40 to 60 small indigenous groups who maintain their traditional ways of life in Russia, amounting to almost 25,000 people who are officially recognized as the Small Indigenous Peoples of the North, Siberia and Far East of the Russian Federation. The economic sustainability of these ethnic minorities largely depends on federal and regional assistance.[15]

According to the 2002 census, the overall number of indigenous people actually increased throughout the 1990s by more than one per cent per annum. However, there are some uncertainties with respect to the accuracy and completeness of this data. At times, the records mixed up ethnic minorities with similar denominations; additionally, the problem of plural identities was not taken into account. The Russian Census of 2002 brought another surprise – about forty groups were "discovered" which the previous censuses had never identified, among them Chelkans, Chulym, Kamchadal, Kerek, Kumandin, Soyot, Tazi, Telengit, Teleut, and Tubalar. Other ethnic groups were treated as mere subgroups of larger groups and thus had "disappeared" from the census.[16] Since socioeconomic support depends on belonging to a recognized and registered ethnic group, some ethnic minorities may have registered under a false name in order to be entitled to governmental assistance.

The law "On national-cultural autonomy" of 1996 defined self-determination and ethnic development in purely cultural terms.[17] It entitled ethnic associations at different levels with the right to "personal autonomy".[18] Voluntary societal (non-governmental, but officially registered) associations of citizens, who belong to an ethnic minority in a given territory, and whose activities pertain to the preservation of traditional lifestyles, language development, education, and national culture are entitled to receive assistance from regional or local governments, yet only on a case-by-case basis for concrete projects.[19] However, it is not clear how an association of a "national minority" must be established – as a voluntary association of a certain number of individuals belonging to or

actively identifying with a certain group or as a representation of a statistically established, but otherwise unorganized group? De facto, the
local, regional and federal "national-cultural autonomies" represent one
form of association among many other non-commercial associations. A
more recent commentary treats the NCA as a supportive measure only
for those groups facing "objective" difficulties in solving their "national-
cultural tasks" and being permanent citizens of a certain territory, exclud-
ing thus internally displaced persons or migrants.[20] This would limit the
national-cultural autonomy to those who could convincingly claim a
sort of deprivation. Registered national-cultural autonomies should contribute to the preservation of lifestyles (*samobytnost'*), language development, education, national culture, and the coordination of local ethnic
policies. With respect to the national-cultural autonomy of ethnic minorities, the Russian Constitutional Court decided that only one association
per ethnic group would be officially registered in a given region. A multi-
plication of national-cultural autonomies was thus constrained.[21]

In contrast to those people entitled to a right of self-determination,
the "Law on Societal Associations" of 1998 forbids national-cultural
associations' engagement in political activities; they are not allowed to
participate in elections.[22] Most of the regions themselves treat the NCA
as a supportive mechanism for somehow already established ethnic minorities, national groups or people, thus limiting the possibility of voluntary
association.[23] In practice, registered associations receive project-related
support, but there is very limited accountability on how these subsidies
are spent and whether they are spent on "cultural" measures at all. Osipov
comes to the conclusion that, taking together all the legislative amendments and constraints, it is much harder to form a "national-cultural
autonomy" than other societal associations.[24] In reality, the "national-
cultural autonomies" do not function as organizations channelling or
coordinating political claims of ethnic groups: they are a means to de-
politicize ethnicity, to prevent autonomy in any politically meaningful
sense. Thus, the "national-cultural autonomy" does not form a viable
alternative to the shortcomings of ethnic federalism, but rather seems to
put ethnicity in a cage in order to deter political claims based on ethnic
concerns from being mounted.

In practice, "cultural rights" mostly pertain to regional or local support for the publication of books and journals, TV programmes and
other mass media, but first of all to language rights. Language rights of
non-Russians, titular groups or "minorities" are supported in all types of
regional units. About 80 minority languages are taught or used as the
language of introduction in primary and secondary schools throughout

the country. The federation formally "guarantees" every citizen the right to use his or her native language and the free choice of deciding the language of communication, education, schooling, and in arts. The law "On languages of the peoples of the Russian Federation" (1991 and 2002) additionally declares that all languages are on equal legal footing.[25] However, the only allowed official script is Cyrillic. Language support is usually organized in areas of compact settlement.

The approach of regional authorities to non-Russian groups varies, depending on geographic location, the number of immigrants, and the individual propensity of their governors. Mukomel' discerns four patterns in the way Russian regions deal with their minorities: a policy of estrangements and denial; a policy of confrontation with particular ethnic groups; a balancing policy; and a policy of constructive cooperation.[26] Support programmes for ethnic minorities were adopted by some regional governments, among them Kabardino-Balkariya, Komi, Udmurtiya, Krasnoyarsk krai, the regions of Amur, Volgograd, Orenburg, Perm, Samara, Tver, Tomsk, and Tula. Although much of the "national policy" seems to be a mere declaration, Mukomel' observes a broadening of the approaches in the regions, from organizing symbolic or folkloristic events to the support for minority education, minority languages, mass media for non-Russians, and minority associations.[27]

Summing up this section one can say that the concept of ethnic groups is not specified – neither as a structural unit, a collective subject of rights nor as a collective actor in societal interactions. All related attempts might end up in artificially "essentializing" or "reifying" group identities that hugely differ in practice; a call for identifying generalizable group rights might be futile from the outset. Consequently, the definition of ethnic group rights is opaque, arbitrary, and – with the exception of welfare entitlements of small indigenous peoples – without regular material or financial underpinnings for their implementation. The support of the federal government or of regional governments, except in resource-rich ethnic regions, for the preservation and development of ethnic distinctness is mostly symbolic. It is a policy of wordy, but vague recognition while unaccountable and nontransparent in practice. It might be principally impossible to codify such a dynamic, evolutionary and fluid concept as ethnic group. But what happened in Russia since the end of the 1990s is an official containment and tightening of socially organized expressions of non-dominant ethnic identifications.

The quests for support among ethnic groups may vary, as do different degrees of self-consciousness and organization. Whereas the post-Soviet state- and nation-building began with a multiculturalist, polyethnic, non-assimilationist imagery, the transition from the Yeltsin to the Putin era has been marked by a focus on the ethnic Russian "core" nation, a latent shift from ethnic markers to religious ones, particularly among Muslims, and – after a time of ethnic demobilization in the second half of the 1990s – symptoms of renewed ethnicization countering the official "Russification of Russia".[28]

Ambiguities of matryoshka federalism

Post-Soviet Russia led by Yeltsin was keen to create a state image different from the Soviet one, based on multi-ethnicity instead of one that imposed assimilation or merger into a supranational, socialist nation and of a federal, non-centralist state, seeing ethnic "self-determination" also as a means of subnational democratization. During the 1990s, the Russian federation fostered the inherited Soviet "institutionalization of ethnicity" by awarding alleged "statehood" to republics based on the "self-determination" claim of the people inhabiting them.

The ethnofederal structures of the Russian Constitution were a legacy of the Soviet Union, rekindled in order to legitimize the post-Soviet order. With few exceptions, the autonomous republics, autonomous okrugs, and autonomous oblasts of the Russian Federation retained the classifications assigned to them in the 1920s or 1930s. In 1992, the government changed the term "autonomous republic" to simply "republic". However, according to the 1989 Soviet census, in only 15 of the thirty-one ethnically designated republics and other autonomous regions were the titular ethnic people the largest group. Of the twenty-one republics existing in Russia in the mid-1990s, nine fell in this category, with the smallest percentages of ethnic Russians (or the largest share of non-Russians) in Chechnya, Dagestan, Ingushetiya, and North Ossetiya.

Not abolishing ethnofederalism may have offered "meaning" to the post-Soviet federation by helping to prevent a Yugoslavian scenario, but its structural underpinnings were flawed and its institutional prescriptions highly contradictory. The demographic composition of the ethnic republics and other autonomous regions barely justified a territorial autonomy of "titular" or "indigenous" populations. Only few of the ethnic groups entitled to a republic or autonomous okrug demonstrated an "essentialized" collective identity different from other non-dominant groups or ethnic Russians. Civil society movements asking for a "revival" of old traditions or a retention of Soviet support for folklore and language teaching often found themselves in a minority position.[29] The social basis for claiming ethnic group rights differed among non-Russian groups, but it usually proved quite weak among the indigenous Siberians, the Finno-Ugrian people, and even the non-Russians along the Volga. Indigenous claims were usually rooted in a predominantly rural populace. Minority groups can be divided into pluralistic, assimilationist, secessionist, and militant ones. Pluralistic groups seek to keep their identity and to gain acceptance of their distinctness, while assimilationist groups desire absorption into the dominant group. The latter two types were the dominant behavioural pattern among non-Russian ethnic groups.[30] The North Caucasian people are an exception to this.

Radical changes in the political economy, such as the privatization of state property, mobility of the workforce from rural to urban areas, socioeconomic decline, and the infringements of "big business" into regional economic protectorates also affected the political orientations of ethnic regions. Although the post-Soviet period was at times portrayed as "post-colonial", the representatives of non-dominant ethnic groups – mostly intellectuals in social decay – often looked to Soviet cultural ideals and practices "as a means for anchoring their communities with a sense of collective belonging in the post-Soviet era".[31] However, the identity concerns of non-dominant groups had to be weighed against costs and practicality. The debate over the status of the ethnic republics and autonomous regions and okrugs has therefore been, with few exceptions such as Tatarstan, Bashkortostan and some North Caucasian republics, about issues of control over natural resources, not about the rights of titular ethnic groups or indigenous peoples. The political and economic elites of the autonomous regions (republics and autonomous okrugs) often only bolstered autonomy rights as a means to protect political, financial, and economic interests. In particular, Russian oil companies took a strong interest in resource-rich autonomous regions – for example, by influencing elections in oil-exploiting republics and autonomous okrugs.

The legal position of autonomous okrugs has been dubious from the outset. On the one hand the Constitution portrays them as equal members of the federation and autonomous in the sense that they have their own charters, budgets, and systems of state power. On the other hand, they are essentially dependent on interaction with the surrounding oblast. From the autonomous okrug's perspective, the conflict is more with the surrounding oblast than with the Moscow government; the okrugs may even need the central government in order to bolster their position vis-à-vis the oblasts. Regulations of the surrounding oblasts affect the okrugs. The statute of Tyumen oblast, for example, states that citizens of the autonomous okrugs can participate in the election of the Tyumen oblast governor.[32] But, as Wilson notes with regard to the two autonomous okrugs inside Tyumen oblast, "the most significant source of conflict between the okrugs and the oblast' concerns the fate of the region's lucrative resource industry. Changes in the allocation of resource revenues, coupled with disagreements over the role of the oblast' government in the management of the resource industry in the okrugs, have sparked heated debates over future development of the resource sector".[33] Legally, the matter is still not satisfactorily regulated. Whereas the Tyumen oblast statute claims that the legislation of the oblast and the autonomous okrugs regulates the use of natural resources in accordance with federal legislation, the Russian Constitution considers natural resources only to be a matter of concurrent jurisdiction between the federal government and the government of the region in which the resources are located, i.e., it does not ascribe a right of co-determination to the oblast surrounding the autonomous okrug.

Some ethnic regions are deeply divided over whether their status as a republic or autonomous okrug should be preserved. The Republic of Adygeya, for example, is split over whether it should fuse with Krasnodar krai. The ethnic organizations of the Adygeyans and the government are in favour of preserving the republic, while most non-Adygeyans are in favour of a merger. In 2005 Perm oblast and Komi Permyak autonomous okrug had already merged and Krasnoyarsk krai voted to merge with the Taimyr autonomous okrug and Evenkiya. The Buryats – potential candidates for another merger – are distributed over three ethnic regions: the Ust-Orda Buryatiya autonomous okrug (surrounded by Irkutsk), Agin-Buryatiya, which belongs to Chita, and the Republic of Buryatiya. Ust-Orda Buryatiya will hold a referendum on merging with Irkutsk oblast into one region, but Buryats from neighbouring regions are agitating against the fusion. Some Buryat activists in Ust-Orda are also mobilizing against a merger.[34]

Observing these institutional ambiguities, it is obvious that the effects of "institutionalizing ethnicity" are far less consistent than often assumed.[35] The motivations for retaining or not retaining the status of an ethnic region are mixed and disparate: they vary inside and among the regions, depend on the demographic composition, the prevalence of a rural–urban cleavage, age structure, elite composition, and resource endowments. With the temporary exception of Chechnya, no "nationalizing" project is discernable among the ethnic regions; ethnofederalism per se has thus not been an institutional resource for ethnic mobilization. The institution of an ethnic region alone did not pre-determine elite strategies and mass identifications; it is only one power resource among many, and not necessarily the most pertinent one.

The benefits of republican status also vary. As Donna Bahry found: "In 1997, 12 of the Russian Federation's 21 republics had a poverty rate of 30 per cent or more, compared to just nine of 58 Russian regions. (The average rate for the Russian Federation as a whole was 20.8 per cent.) Of the 11 regions in the Federation with the highest poverty rates (40 per cent or more of the population living below the poverty line), eight were republics".[36] Socioeconomic discrepancies are very severe not only among the regions in general, but among the republics in particular. Tatarstan belongs to the three regions (apart from Moscow and Tyumen oblast) that have a Human Development Index (HDI) of more than 0.800, whereas the Republic of Tyva has an HDI of 0.634 (close to Nicaragua and Gabon) and the Chukotka autonomous okrug of 0.696.[37]

In general, predominantly Russian-populated regions and large ethnic regions offer quite equal education opportunities to children and young people. However, Chechnya, Ingushetiya, and small-sized and thinly populated autonomous areas in the North and East of Russia show low educational coverage (or opportunities).[38] Other indicators of the Human Development Index show that infant mortality is especially high in some republics in the North Caucasus and the Republic of Tyva, as well as in the autonomous areas of the Far North, where small groups of indigenous people live. The high infant mortality rate is mainly related to the dearth of stable sources of income and high poverty rates. Regardless of the economic growth over recent years, the socioeconomic discrepancies among the regions are not diminishing. In 2003 Zubarevich concluded that the "ethnic factor does not dominate human development in Russia's regions. Among the ten regions with the highest HDI are three of the most advanced republics (Tatarstan, Komi, Bashkortostan); among ten of the least developed regions there are four Russian regions (oblasti)."[39] However, some multi-ethnic regions with low Millennium Development Goal indicators are in underdeveloped republics and autonomous okrugs as well as in territories populated by indigenous people of the Far North. Among the ethnic regions with a very high degree of dependence on the federal budget (figures for 2001) include Tyva (87 per cent), Dagestan (83 per cent), Ingushetiya (79 per cent), the Jewish autonomous oblast (74 per cent), the Altai Republic (59 per cent), the Chukotka autonomous okrug (55 per cent), Marii-El (48 per cent), and Buryatiya (47 per cent).[40] The main insight from these findings is that playing the ethnic card by itself does not change socioeconomic status. Over time, structural discrepancies are the key to the relative share of federal transfers, not ethnic mobilization.

Effects of ethnofederal arrangements

Russia's ethnofederalism has fostered certain conflicts – over the constitutional order, status, over group rights versus individual rights, and in some cases between titular and non-titular ethnic groups. However, the proliferation of overt conflicts still seems modest in comparison to the Nigerian claims for ethno-linguistic statehood, the frequent division of states in India along ethno-linguistic lines, or the conflicts over the status of autonomies in Spain, particularly in the Basque country. Extra-institutional conditions have informed the low intensity of conflicts within ethnic regions, among them ethno-demographic factors, poor natural resource endowments, multifaceted ethnic self-perceptions, and non-nationalist governing elites.

During the 1990s, republics had asked for additional rights, as did economically strong territorial regions (oblasts and krais) in order to resist centralist tendencies, or "to avert the consequences of frequently crude reform policies devised without proper consideration for their special historical, geographical, cultural and linguistic conditions."[41] Regardless of highly diverse resource endowments, structural conditions and ethnic composition, the status of republic increased their bargaining power vis-à-vis the central government, at least among those republics less reliant on federal subsidies.[42] However, the asymmetrical status per se did not translate into a privileged bargaining position. Natural resource endowments were seen as equally essential, if not more important; richer republics received bilateral treaties earlier and on better terms.[43] Treisman suggested a link between voting patterns in the first half of the 1990s and political outcomes in the area of fiscal federalism, a claim subsequently questioned by Popov and Kitty.[44] De Bardeleben found instead "a mix of strategies has been pursued by both central and regional authorities in each region, an expression of the ad hoc and bargaining nature of Russian federalism" and that "a governor pursuing an oppositional stance is not likely to convince his public that this will be an effective tool for dealing with Moscow."[45] Apart from resource endowments, the potential for ethnic mobilization and a bargaining position vis-à-vis the central government was informed by the percentage share of the titular ethnic group in a given ethnic region – the fewer "titulars", the lower the mobilization capacity. Additionally, some ethnic groups were better organized and more politicized than others.[46] All in all, a mixture of threats and signals of cooperation was paying off. Interestingly, socio-demographic factors like ethnic composition were either not used as variables for explaining republican privileges or, when used, did not significantly explain variances in pro- or anti-federal stances in the regions.[47] The "most ethnic" did not necessarily get the best bilateral treaties in the 1990s. However, the degree of mobilization of ethnicity explains some of the differences in receiving preferential treatment from the federal government. Obviously, Tatarstan, the North Caucasian republics, and Tyva played the ethnic card more successfully than other republics such as Komi, Kareliya, Khakassiya and Kalmykiya.[48]

According to polls conducted by the Institute of Ethnology and Anthropology of the Russian Academy of Sciences, in 1994 few people saw themselves to be discriminated against because of their ethnicity.[49] These polls, conducted more than ten years ago, need updating in order to establish whether respective perceptions continue to be valid. Although the evidence is scattered, privileging ethnic regions during the 1990s did not cause a visible rejection among the disfavoured ethnic Russians or non-titular groups. Polls conducted in Tatarstan suggest that non-titular groups, among them many Russians, identified with Tatarstan as a republic due to its economic policy and bargaining power vis-à-vis Moscow.[50] The exclusion of non-titular groups from authoritarian rule in the republics was probably tolerated as long as the leaders were able to deliver public goods to the republican clientele at large.[51] During the 1990s it seemed "rational" for many citizens of resource-rich ethnic republics, regardless of their belonging to a titular ethnic group, to support "regionalization" or "sovereignization". It was probably seen as a means to increase leverage vis-à-vis the central government and to protect a region against incursions by outside business interests. But since the turn of the century this trend seems to have been reversed, although the data are not fully comparable and inconclusive. Based on polls conducted by VTsIOM one can discern a marked increase in ethnic self-awareness among ethnic Russians. From 1998 to 2002, the number of those supporting the slogan "Russia for the Russians" increased from 45 per cent to 55 per cent; only 19.6 per cent did not see a threat from people of non-Russian ethnicity living in Russia.[52]

Over time, the behavioural pattern of republican leaders has changed, as did the reaction patterns of the federal government. The popular imagery of confrontation and disintegration was clearly exaggerated. The decline of ethnic associations even in the strong republics like Tatarstan, Bashkortostan, or Sakha illustrates that important segments of the titular ethnic groups began to see ethnic issues as a distraction from more tangible concerns such as unemployment, living conditions, wage payments, or pensions. Most nationalist movements had a weak social basis, were fragmented, or were partially incorporated by the republic's president.[53] A factor that also affected the intensity of ethnic claims is the dominance of old communist elites among republican leaders. Old indigenous communist leaders usually opted for the incorporation of moderate nationalists, but were against mass mobilization.

During the Yeltsin era the presidents of the republics had gained legitimacy, influence, and political capital by expanding their competencies and control over resources vis-à-vis the central government. Since the implementation of Putin's "reforms", the republican presidents have adopted a different strategy – self-containment and consolidation inside the republics. However, such a consolidation was only possible as long as authoritarian leaders controlled the political and economic space. Only few were capable of doing so – President Shaimiev in Tatarstan and President Rakhimov in Bashkortostan, but not the weaker presidents of Komi or Sakha. Only those who could consolidate their regional power were able to protect themselves against the re-configuration of the regional elites following outside interference. Tatarstan, for example, could retain some autonomy because of its control over the oil industry in the republic. However, most of the regions are no longer closed. Not only the federal government, but also national business penetrates the regions. National companies that plan to expand into certain regions employ various kinds of pressures in order to influence chief executives in the regions, ranging from support of the incumbent, electoral support for a more convenient candidate, or the nomination of a business candidate of their own.[54]

Putin's de-federalization and the submission of ethnic regions

According to general prosecutor V. Ustinov's assessment, there were so many illegal decisions and normative acts at the turn of the century that the legal area "represented a patchwork of legal medley. There emerged a very real danger of a dissolution of the country into separate fiefdoms."[55] It is hard to distinguish these assessments from political rhetoric. In an interview given in the autumn of 1999, Vladimir Putin, then still prime minister, replied to a question about a looming disintegration of Russia: "I categorically contradict that there are tendencies in the regions to distance themselves from Moscow. The danger of disintegration was very real in 1991 and 1992."[56] Instead of falling into the official propaganda trap Nikolai Petrov interprets the de-federalization as the application of methods that suited very well the logic of the security services rather than a response to a looming disintegration. "Their mentality saw no need for a lengthy coordination of different interests, for a complex balancing of forces, or for nuances. Rather, there was either something that was 'our' and fully under their control, or something that was 'not ours' ".[57] However, in 2000, federal politicians – from the left and right of the spectrum – were united in the claim that the existing federal system was the main source of instability. A hegemonic discursive field emerged that welcomed Putin's so-called "federal reforms" as a necessary step towards the consolidation of the state's stability.[58] Discussions mostly centred on the efficiency of implementing the reforms; very few commentators saw Putin's reforms as anti-federal and anti-democratic.[59]

Most observers highlight the discontinuity from Yeltsin to Putin. However since the mid-1990s, presidential decrees, the Constitutional Court, and the June 1999 law "On principles and the order of dividing competencies (predmetov vedeniia) and prerogatives" prepared the ground for Putin's later re-centralization. Since 1994, the Constitutional Court has ruled in several cases (for example, on the Komi Republic in 1994 and 1999, Udmurt Republic in 1998, Kursk in 1999, North Ossetiya-Alaniya in 1999, and Khakassiya in 1999), in favour of local self-governments, in contrast to the provisions of republican constitutions which made local government a dependent administrative organ whose heads are nominated or otherwise controlled by the regional state executive.[60] A presidential decree of 12 March 1996 (No. 370) had already stated that the principles of dividing competencies between the central government and the regions would be determined by federal law.[61] In 1998, the Constitutional Court stated the supremacy of federal law and ruled out the position that bilateral treaties delegated federal competencies to individual regions.[62] This law substantially minimized the scope and significance of the bilateral treaties.[63]

The most decisive step for unifying regional regimes was probably the October 1999 law "On the general principles of organization of the legislative (representative) and executive organs of state power of the subjects of the Russian Federation". From 2000 onwards, the State Procurator questioned the legality of some 10,000 legal acts in the regions which contradicted either this law or the Constitution. Some 6,000 "anti-constitutional" acts were replaced or modified following formal requests by the procurator. Some 3,000 legal acts were declared invalid.[64] All in all, 60 republican constitutions and statutes of other regions were "aligned" with the Russian Constitution. Most of the *de jure* and *de facto* privileges and asymmetries of the ethnic republics have been curbed, among them sovereignty claims, the choice of their governmental system, prerogatives in governing "joint competencies", favourable bilateral treaties, tax exemptions and export licenses, a certain independence in foreign economic relations, ownership of natural resources, the appointment of federal officials in their regions (especially judges and prosecutors), and republican citizenship. Provisions of the republican constitutions pertaining to the formation of the executive and legislative branches of government had to be adjusted to all-Russian standards. Particular ethnic groups were no longer allowed to label themselves as bearers of republican "sovereignty". There is no longer separate citizenship of the republics. The heads of local government will be elected in future and thus not merely be subordinate officers of the republics. The so-called "power ministries" in the republics once again became departments of the respective Russian ministries.[65] Claiming an extensive scope of prescription, the Russian Constitutional Court basically determined that the regions were no longer allowed to have other than a presidential (or semi-presidential, but not parliamentary) form of government. Only language and cultural rights remain as the specific rights of ethnic regions.[66]

"Harmonization" has meant, with few exceptions, enforced obedience by the regions. Apart from federal legislation, the Constitutional Court, the Supreme Court, the State Procurator, and pressures exerted by the presidential envoys played the most decisive role in shaping this outcome. Republics like Tatarstan, Bashkortostan, Adygeya, Ingushetiya, North Ossetiya, and Sakha filed appeals against the Constitutional Court's decisions in order to get time for adjustment, but ultimately without achieving any success. The mechanism for regulating conflicts between competing legislation became the Constitutional Court and Courts of General Jurisdiction. Republics such as Tatarstan, Sakha, and Bashkortostan fought defensive judicial battles. In the course of forcing the republics to comply with the Russian Constitution and federal laws, even dependent republics like Buryatiya or Tyva tried to withstand the pressure from the Russian president. It was therefore not just economic power or the degree of "indigenization" that informed their initial intransigence.[67] However, instead of protesting with extra-constitutional means, the republics turned to the Constitutional Court as the ultimate decision-maker. The Parliament of the Republic of Sakha, as well as the President of Chuvashiya, filed a case at the Constitutional Court questioning the constitutionality of certain provisions of the aforementioned federal law "On general principles of the organization of legislative (representative) and executive organs of state power of the subjects of the Russian Federation" (6 Oct. 1999, revised 8 Feb 2002). The Constitutional Court was asked to determine the constitutionality of three aspects of Putin's reforms – the right to dissolve regional parliaments, the right of the president to express a warning against a regional parliament or the regional chief executive, as well as the right to temporarily dismiss a regional chief executive in cases where regional authorities did not implement court rulings. The Constitutional Court rejected Sakha's objections on all three counts.[68]

The president of the Republic of Buryatiya turned to the Constitutional Court because he felt that the constitution of Buryatiya would unduly limit his competencies as a directly elected president. In this sense he approached the Constitutional Court of Russia as an arbiter or judge in an inter-organ conflict inside his republic. The Buryat president was asking for a limitation of his accountability vis-à-vis the republican legislature – a request that was rejected by the Russian Constitutional Court because this matter belonged to the sphere of regional competencies.[69] The Parliament of Bashkortostan questioned the constitutionality of the right of the federal president to nominate the judges of federal courts and of arbitrage courts acting on the territory of the regions. The Bashkir Parliament claimed that decisions on the personnel of courts were in the area of "joint competencies". However, the Constitutional Court flatly rejected a regional right to co-participation in the process of installing federal judges.[70] In a case on the law of the Koryak autonomous okrug providing for the right of the regional parliament to express a vote of no confidence towards members of the executive, the Russian Constitutional Court decided that such a right would undermine the concept of "checks and balances" and would thus contradict the Russian Constitution.[71]

The Constitutional Court was not the only federal body to seek to bring about "harmonization". Tatarstan's State Council decided on 15 September 1999 to introduce the Latin alphabet by September 2011. The Russian State Duma reacted harshly at that time, arguing that the Latin alphabet would undermine the common cultural space, and some even expressed fears of a threat to national security.[72] In 2002, the State Duma claimed the exclusive right to determine the alphabet for the "state languages" used in Russia and its constituent parts.[73] Even in the realm of language laws in the republics, the federal government challenged bilingualism requirements for presidential candidates and the adoption of the Latin script in Tatarstan. It also banned Muslim women from wearing headscarves in their passport photographs.[74]

Federalism and democracy

To understand the de-federalization process under Putin, the debate on federalism and democracy is of particular importance. Here we find two opposite views. One camp sees federalism as a relative of democracy. Federalism would be a seedbed of democracy, as it would allow for more

participation and accountability, stimulate civil society, add access channels for political participation, broaden sources of legitimacy, limit the
"terror of the majority", broaden citizenship by institutionalizing multi-
ethnicity and provide for subnational competition, thus stimulating
local self-governance, innovation and efficiency. The counter-argument
holds that federalism institutionalizes regional overrepresentation and
undemocratic veto positions, preserves sub-national authoritarianism,
promotes ethnocratic instead of democratic rule, exacerbates regional
disparities, undermines the rule of law, and facilitates the rise of dema-
gogues rather than encouraging democracy.[75] But if one looks at the
empirical evidence in diverse settings, there is no inevitable link among
democracy, federalism, and the degree of sub-national autonomy. Especially
in emerging and multi-ethnic federations, the integration of sub-national
units or groups often took precedence over democracy. Two imperatives
usually compete in these cases – integration and democracy. Federations
generally tend to overrepresent territorial units or ethnic groups on the
federal level and thus contradict the democratic principle of "one man
one vote". Regional autonomy may protect non-democratic regimes too,
although federal democracy may cascade downwards as well. Federalism is
probably a far too multi-faceted regime to attribute to it common effects.

Empirically, there are more authoritarian regimes among the republics
and autonomous okrugs than among the purely territorial regions of the
Russian Federation. The most critical cases are Bashkortostan, Kalmykiya,
Chuvashiya, North Ossetiya, Kabardino-Balkariya, followed by Tatarstan,
Buryatiya, and other republics.[76] In particular, the republics were very
slow in the early 1990s in establishing post-Soviet, democratic regimes.
Old elites effectively survived by virtue of holding positions in the unre-
formed Supreme Soviets in the republics. "They acquired political resources
that enabled them to remain in control of local power hierarchies after
the communist party and its mechanisms of political integration collapsed.
A shift to directly elected presidencies, which occurred in the majority of
the republics, did not elevate new elites to power either. Rather, they
institutionally redefined the incumbent heads of republics and the existing
power hierarchies."[77] Initially, the retention of ethnofederalism thus
inhibited democratization of the republics.

Gordon Hahn implies that the authoritarian variant of ethnofederalism
may have stabilized the regions, whereas democratization could have
sparked ethnic mobilization. Hahn argues that

> the harmonization policy's abrogation of republican constitutions'
> sovereignty clauses and other elements of the national republics'

autonomy and self-rule, by advancing regional democratization, are also facilitating ethnic mobilization and oppositional activity. To be sure, other Putin policies are also sparking ethnic and Islamic mobilization in Muslim national republics, including Tatarstan and Bashkortostan. Such mobilization, however positive from the point of view of mobilizing civil society as a counter to state-dominated institution building, could prove to be not only a democratizing factor but also a destabilizing one to the extent it mobilizes simultaneously several nationalities with conflicting interests in the regions.[78]

Hahn's argument sounds "unconventional" by portraying past authoritarianism as a source of stability whereas Putin's alleged "democratization" is seen as a potential source of instability. By implication one could assume that authoritarian ethnic federalism provides stability, whereas an equalization of the regional status and "democratization" Putin-style holds the prospect of ethnic mobilization and instability. Hahn suggests that ethnic mobilization might become an unintended consequence of Putin's re-centralization. However, Hahn's argument is flawed in at least three ways. First, it associates authoritarianism with stability. Yet the authoritarian rule in the ethnic regions is inherently unstable, because it is exclusive, dependent on the continuous provision of clientelistic favours and it feeds corruption, extractive behaviour, and kleptocratic rule. These conditions have already been a fertile breeding ground for fundamentalist movements in other world regions.[79] Second, Hahn identifies Putin's recentralization with democratization, particularly due to the expected increase in voter mobilization – an unfounded postulation, because with the nomination of governors, the most meaningful elections in the regions were abolished. Third, the argument implicitly repeats the old, empirically unproven claim that democracy is impossible in divided societies.[80] However, Hahn might be correct with his prediction that Putin's re-centralization will spark a revival of ethnic mobilization and especially Islamism, but this would be due to his policy of duplicative administrative control, creating dependencies, of equalization and encroachment into regional affairs, and "securitizing" federal-regional disputes.

The imposition of uniform rules under Putin's presidency could be interpreted as a strengthening of the rule of law and of checks and balances. The appointment of local chief executives by the governors has, for example, been abolished as has the representation of appointed executives in regional legislatures. Republican presidents are no longer immune from prosecution. The legislative power of municipal parliaments has been formally enhanced, and the usurpation of local self-government by regional governments constrained.[81] In Autumn 2002, the electoral law of Tatarstan had to be amended in order to observe the 10 per cent range of maximum difference in the size of the electorates. The precedent established in Tatarstan affected the electoral law in Komi as well. Gordon Hahn adds to this list another hopeful observation: "The federal government's efforts to end regional leaders' independent control over law enforcement agencies in their regions have led to added protections of civil and minority rights in the national autonomies ..."[82] The set-up of interregional human rights commissions and the establishment of human rights ombudsmen in the regions may enhance the protection of minority and civil rights. The argument in favour of re-centralization ultimately holds that only a single authoritative centre providing for rule of law, effective state administration, and determining the competencies and functions of the state could create the prerequisites for democratization.[83] However, the empirical record of more than five years of re-centralization does not confirm the expected strengthening of rule of law, neither in terms of local self-government nor in terms of a protection of individual rights by the federal envoys acting as monitors and policy coordinators on Putin's behalf.[84]

Putin's re-centralization is based on the assumption that democracy and federalism are mutually exclusive. However, the substitution of regionally based authoritarianism by direct rule over the regions is unlikely to become a panacea for authoritarianism and ethnocracy. As Filippov and Shvetsova note, it is not only "fundamentally inconsistent with democratic competition" but "equally inconsistent with the non-democratic political competition which, even if democracy is abandoned, will arise sooner or later."[85] In Soviet times centralism and authoritarian integration only functioned as long as the centre could enforce its policy and influence subnational policy with ideological levers. Given the low degree of incorporation of non-Russian elites into the central government it is unlikely that non-Russian groups will *in toto* abandon their aspirations for self-preservation and territorial representation. Great-power chauvinism and xenophobia among ethnic Russians and parts of the Moscow elite may additionally estrange non-Russians and lead, at least in parts, to radicalization instead of the pluralistic sentiments or assimilation that prevailed in the first post-Soviet decade.

Putin's policy does not just curb the authoritarian policy styles of governors or republican presidents – it undermines the prerequisites for democratization. With the abolition of the federal power division, Putin undermines democratic institutions. De-federalization and de-democratization are mutually conducive. The equalization disempowers regional politics, reduces the division of powers, minimizes the representation and access channels of the regions in the federal system, increases executive accountability at the expense of democratic accountability, and identifies the "centre" with the federation. The president nominates chief executives of the regions, the regional Duma will rubber-stamp the nominee, and if not, the president may install an "acting governor" and threaten to dissolve the regional Duma. The president will have the right to fire a governor, but the regional Duma will not. Critics have pointed out that this practice will violate articles 1, 3, 5, 10, 11, 32, 71, 72, and 73 of the Constitution, as well as several Constitutional Court rulings in which the court held that only the direct election of regional leaders can be considered to satisfy the requirements of the Constitution. However, the Constitutional Court, contrary to the opinion of leading Russian specialists on constitutional law, approved the presidential nomination procedure for governors. The chief executives in Chechnya and Ingushetiya have already given a preview of presidential appointees lacking legitimacy in the regions; one could even go as far as to say that Putin's reforms follow a model of Chechenization of federal-regional relations: additional control layers and buffer zones, and rule on the ground by proxy.

The past mix of confrontation and cooperation has changed as a result of the impact of Putin's re-centralization. The republics are more adaptive and cooperative, and less confrontational. However, Putin's policy not only consists of intimidation and confrontation; he has also offered informal deals such as allowing the incumbent president to stay in power for a third term. In practice, Putin's "dictatorship of the law" follows double standards. A law on regional bodies of government, adopted in October 1999, allows governors to run for a third and even fourth term – *de facto* in return for not obstructing the implementation of the Russian president's policy. The legal two-term limit only begins with the adoption of the law in 1999. The repenting presidents of Tatarstan (Shaimiev), Bashkortostan (Rakhimov), Kabardino-Balkariya (Kokov), Kalmykiya (Ilyumzhinov), and Dagestan (Magomedov) were allowed to run for a third term because they promised loyalty and offered favourable electoral outcomes for United Russia or Putin's second term as president. In these cases Putin preferred continuity of leadership and loyalty to the "rule of law". Less submissive or subservient republican presidents – such as Nikolaev in Sakha and Spiridonov in Komi – were forced to leave office or were not allowed to run for a third term. In some of the Muslim republics of the North Caucasus, on the grounds of countering fundamentalism or preventing Islamist counter-reactions, the federal government tolerated legislation contradicting federal laws or the Constitution. In Karachaevo-Cherkessiya, for example, a law was accepted on the grounds that it was supposed to counter Wahhabi fundamentalism. In Ingushetiya, a law allowing polygamy and elements of traditional justice was not rescinded. In Chechnya's constitution, even the notion of sovereignty and republican citizenship was permitted.[86]

A loss of the Russian president's confidence may in future justify firing a governor. This opens up ample space for subjective judgement; it contradicts the conception of due process. The term of an appointed governor is no longer specified. The Russian president can nominate those who have already served two or even three gubernatorial terms – and this is the carrot which makes incumbents give in. The appointed governors may take back some of the duties transferred to the federal districts and thus be compensated for their loss of an independent source of legitimacy.

Putin's appointment of governors will restrict political access and expression, diminish popular control and accountability. It will provide institutional incentives for nepotism and corruption, and it is therefore likely to revive resentment and frustration.[87] Added to the changes in electoral and party laws, the political space open for contestation has been substantially reduced. If performance and efficiency depend on competition over strategies and outcomes, they must perforce suffer because loyalty trumps competition. Governors will no longer have to search for a local base, but instead demonstrate obedience and seek access to the presidential administration. The appointment of governors will change the whole architecture and patterns of political regimes in the regions. The predictable estrangement of regional chief executives from their constituencies will cause disengagement and frustration. Furthermore, in the long run the Kremlin alone will be held responsible for mischief in the regions.

Key features of federalism abolished by Putin also include the multiple electoral laws in the regions. In the aftermath of the dissolution of regional assemblies in October 1993, Yeltsin had already suggested the adoption of a single "first-past-the-post" system in single-member districts throughout Russia's territory. But the regions opted for a variety of systems.[88] Putin's reforms standardize electoral laws in the regions. In May 2002, the State Duma voted to alter the various electoral systems of the regional parliaments so that they resemble the mixed system for the State Duma.[89]

Putin destabilizes centre–region relations because there is no confidence that the game will be repeated. Putin's recentralization is based on distrust and constant reshuffling of ill-defined institutional innovations. According to Nikolai Petrov, Putin's reforms are weakening all institutions apart from the presidency: they replace the basic rule of institutions "by substituting bodies that resemble them in function but lack independent legitimation and that are tied to the president".[90] The current system allows the federal authorities to constantly overstep the constitutionally or otherwise legally prescribed authority of the regions. There is no consensus over the definitions of constitutionally prescribed or legitimate authority. The regions are left without effective representation in the centre. This may ultimately foster individualism instead of cross-regional bargaining and co-responsibility for stability.

"Federalism" is reduced to the jurisdictional subordination of subnational units. Key yardsticks of federalism are no longer being met in Russia. The component units are no longer immune to the elimination of their constitutional autonomy and identity. The factual heterogeneity is no longer protected; residual powers are minimal. The court system, including the Constitutional Court, is not independent from the presidential executive; it is not a neutral arbiter. No longer does Russia have independent layers of government which are independently elected. Putin's restructuring constrains the space for federal bargaining and for allocation of responsibilities. In sum, the regions are no longer part of a federal partnership.

Causal explanations

Russian observers and democratic politicians trying to understand their defeat vis-à-vis Putin highlight the popular disenchantment about the 1990s, the split among the democrats, the preference for economic growth, the legacy of personalism, the frustration over crony capitalism, poor campaigning by the democrats, and Putin's ability to capitalize on the fear of terrorism. Very few interpret Putin's anti-federal reforms as part of an authoritarian regression.[91]

Post-Soviet federalism in Russia has been described as a mix of Soviet legacies and a function of power configurations between the centre and the regions. However, the debate about formal aspects of centre–region relations was not systematically linked to the political economy of federal relations. The so-called "power grab" of the regions had obviously resulted more from the weakness of the centre rather than strong regional or ethnic identities. Consequently, Putin could recentralize power without significant resistance once "the centre" again commanded crucial power resources. One institutional reason for the ease of Putin's restructuring is the amassing of executive competencies in the presidency. The executive-legislative power-distribution is heavily biased and thus detrimental for sustaining federalism. The chief executive is constitutionally far too strong for a truly federal balance.

National politicians, including the opposition parties (left and right) turned against federalism – with only rare exceptions – and welcomed Putin's "reforms" once they believed federalism would not increase their prospects of winning desired outcomes. The national parties lacked region-specific agendas, and with the exception of the CPRF, territorial influence in them was weak.[92] The party system itself is not federal, but national, and the national parties have no interest in sustaining federalism; they have no stable base in the regions.

However, it was not just the instrumental approach to federalism that opened up opportunities for re-centralization. The semi-authoritarian or authoritarian regimes in many, if not most, regions and the bias in favour of the executives, made regional power vulnerable. Regional authoritarianism was based on informal communication and redistribution mechanisms, not formal rules. Authoritarian leaders in the republics depended on their clientelistic networks, patronage, and ability to deliver public goods. Yet changes of national and regional government make informal rules highly vulnerable because with a loss of power by the incumbent, his or her informal exchange networks may also disappear. The massive shift of power to senior executive office holders in the regions, who were mostly subjected to direct, yet party-less election, minimized the mobilization power of the regions vis-à-vis the central government. Regional elites in general, and those of ethnic units in particular, did not rely on the mobilization of regional or ethnic parties. With the new law on parties, the incentive and ability to form regional parties almost disappeared.[93] The governors had neither parties of their own nor powerful legislatures that they could rely on in order to withstand and counteract Putin. The political resources of the governors depended on personal qualities, "massaging" electoral laws and media control, but not on party machines. The majority of Russia's governors gave in to Putin's policy. Among the governors and republican presidents, we discern a Stockholm syndrome – the regional elites try to assuage their hostage taker and pay the ransom. Collective action and opposition would have been costly, particularly as long as the president remains popular.[94] Most incumbent governors may speculate about being appointed forever, being freed of accountability to voters, and avoiding criminal investigations. Putin's tactic consists of "give up some of your powers 'voluntarily' or you will lose them altogether."[95]

Some observers go as far as to claim that federalism had no roots at all. Clearly, societal and economic pluralism – the underpinnings of federalism – were much weaker than assumed. Judging on the basis of indicators like ethnic voting, the "sovereignization" of the 1990s was an elite endeavour, a bargaining chip, but not based on mass mobilization – the social and cultural support for ethnicization was minimal. The Russian Federation was evidently a federation without a sufficient number of convinced federalists. Specifically in relation to institutional arrangements, I assume that the disruptive potential of ethnic federalism needs containment by a constitutional consensus over the federal allocation of rights to ethnic groups, the protection of basic civil rights, and accepted (formal and informal) mechanism of conflict regulation.

Conclusions

Against the backdrop of the transformation of ethnic politics, as well as of ethnic federalism, some authors claim that the "national question" no longer exists or that it merely exists insofar as it is "constructed", "institutionalized", or "ontologized".[96] The idea that a certain territory – due to historical or contemporary settlement patterns or respective political claims – "belongs" to a specific ethnic group or that the "statehood" of ethnic regions is an expression of "self-determination", are difficult arguments to sustain on demographic, socio-economic, or liberal grounds. Ethnic regions are heterogeneous, and ethnic groups themselves are heterogeneous too. Institutional arrangements for multi-ethnic societies need to be flexible, adaptive to changes in ethnicity and capable of adjusting to various needs – ethnic federalism is therefore no "holy cow" by itself. The under-institutionalization of Russia's ethnic federalism reflects more than transitional or "bad" politics: it tries to fix conceptions of the ethnic self that do not necessarily correspond to the realities on the ground. The question is, then, whether there is any lasting meaning to "ethnic federalism" in Russia. Paradoxically, there are more conflict-related, cost-benefit ratio arguments in favour of retaining ethnic federalism rather than democratic or liberal justifications:

1. There is the Constitution itself – it recognizes the republics as the statehood of peoples. To revise the Constitution in this respect would undermine one of the founding myths of post-Soviet Russia, namely to distance it from the Tsarist and Soviet nationality policies of Russification, assimilation and supranational merger. The constitutional recognition of multi-ethnicity and an ethnofederal makeup might be seen as mere symbolic politics, but they are for many non-Russians a hallmark of non-assimilative politics.
2. Given the miserable record of "national-cultural autonomy," ethnic federalism grants political veto powers to non-Russian titular ethnic

groups, which they would not have otherwise. Despite the formal equalization under Putin, many ethnic republics still perceive their status as a means for being at least heard by the federal government.[97] The collapse of the Soviet Union deprived minorities of important channels of political representation and upward social mobility, which is only partially compensated by the indigenization of elites in the republics.[98] Ethnic federalism might be thus a protective device for non-dominant groups as long as the central government is undemocratic.

3. There is the history of Russian chauvinism and the lasting fear of homogenization pressures among non-Russians. Dmitri Glinski rightly argues that it is not just the Chechen wars but the intolerance, Islamophobia, Asiaphobia, claims of superiority, the official politics of favour for Russian Orthodoxy, and the pro-American or pro-European stance of the "Moscow establishment" that have resulted in an unintended force of Islamization.[99] Religious identity, Glinski further claims, was "discovered as a weapon and as an ideology of protest against exclusion."[100] Ethnofederalism may thus contribute to contain a turn from secular national aspirations to religious identification among non-Russians. This is not to argue that nationhood or nationality is or should be "essential", regardless of assimilative, modernizing or de-modernizing episodes; it is a dynamic category of experience and practice.

4. Certain politicized markers of ethnic identity among non-Russians are likely to last – highly symbolic attachments to an indivisible territory, language policies, and religious identification.[101] The denial or conscious marginalisation of ethnic distinctness by the dominant ethnic group is a very likely source of actually "essentializing" the absorbed or denied identity. Ethnofederalism may thus constrain fundamentalist revulsion because of its symbolic meaning.

5. There is an additional practical argument in favour of preserving the heterogeneous ethnic regions: forming homogeneous ethnic regions may create dangerously dense populations that are usually prone to later secession.[102]

However, it is hard to predict how ethnic relations will develop further. Adopting a broader view on the ups and downs of indigenization, ethnic mobilization, and de-mobilization since the foundation of the Soviet Union, it would be premature and naive to declare the current stage of ethnic de-mobilization and re-centralization to be the end of history. The contemporary unification process, combined with a crisis of authoritarian regimes in the ethnic regions, may instigate fundamentalist movements, which are different from the ethnonationalist movements of the first half of the 1990s. It seems likely that equalization and uniform rule will feed suspicion and discontent among non-Russian ethnic groups.

Compared to the Yeltsin era between 1993 and 1999, Putin's policy is characterized by a permanent rebuilding of institutions. Yeltsin caused instability by a permanent reshuffling of personnel, but Putin causes unpredictability by introducing half-baked institutions with ill-defined functions. Recentralization is not identical with viable institutions. We may infer that hierarchical nepotism, informal networks, government racketeering, corruption, the role of regional brokers, instrumental use of bureaucracies and security agencies will all continue to increase. We may also infer that the social contract – growth and stability in exchange for acquiescence – will fade away once Putin's system can no longer deliver its promised order and moderate increase in welfare. At the margins, especially in the North Caucasus, ethnic unrest or Islamic fundamentalism may increase the costs of upholding the centralist system. There is already evidence of a rise of political Islam in the North Caucasus responding to the growth of corruption and mismanagement despite Putin's "reforms". Political Islam tends to substitute for ethnic identification and responds to the growing delegitimization of official Islam.[103] The consensus among the Moscow-based elites on centralism may additionally erode. Parties of power like United Russia may fragment over time like the other "parties of power" in Russia.

We can only speculate about the impact of future democratization on ethnic mobilization, as there are many intervening variables. Voting does not necessarily lead to violence.[104] It might well be that ideas that go back to Yevgenii Primakov's time as prime minister, like the abolition of ethnic regions, will be implemented over the course of the next few years, although there seems to be insufficient support for such a move in the government for the time being. A referendum could be held on revising the Constitution with no qualified majority needed by the ethnic regions. The ongoing process of unifying regional regimes may proceed with the merger of some regions, particularly the further absorption of some autonomous okrugs by their surrounding regions (*oblasti*), or the downgrading of some republics to mere territorial units. Over time, the seven federal districts may assume a more powerful coordinating and integrative role, absorbing even more functions from the regions. The current stage of federal-regional relations is still dynamic; it would be premature to assume that the institutional reshuffling will come to a halt soon.

Looking back at the last 15 years of post-Soviet federalism we evidently need a more dynamic model that combines institutionalism with political economic perspectives. We should probably better examine the under-currents of federal relations in order to avoid two pitfalls: a religious belief in institutions, and inferring actors' characteristics and preferences by merely looking at their location and resources. Institutions are as strong as the interests they are serving, and interests or preferences are often unstable, unpredictable, malleable, depending on shifting actor configurations.

Federalism is not a self-sustaining system as such: it requires self-enforcing institutions as well as supportive second-order institutions such as inclusive, regionally as well as nationally based, multi-dimensional, and cross-cutting parties. Democratic federalism needs, in order to survive, auxiliary institutions, ensuring that federal institutions are not equated with short-term outcomes. Federalism – like democracy – is likely to survive only if it is seen as an end in itself, not a means to other ends. Federal stability is therefore not only defined by legal or constitutional provisions. One does not need federalism for democracy to survive, but one evidently needs democracy for federalism to survive. Russia should look at the sobering experiences of the former Yugoslavia, the Soviet Union, Ethiopia, Nigeria, and at times India with substituting key federal arrangements by authoritarian, direct presidential or military rule over the regions. The survival rate of non-democratic federations, particularly multi-ethnic ones, is lower than democratic ones. Authoritarian federalism is inher-ently unstable, maybe only an intermediary situation – it may either turn into authoritarianism without federalism or federalism without authoritarianism.

Based on democratic theory and theories of federalism, we may expect that Putin's regime will be confronted with diminishing support and a legitimacy crisis once Putin's charisma begins to fade and the authoritarian paternalism is no longer able to deliver the promised goods. However, we do not know when this is going to happen. Agency is pivotal. It would therefore be naïve to assume that when Putin steps down in 2008, democracy and federalism will be instantly restored.

Notes

1 Ivo Duchacek, *Comparative Federalism: The Territorial Dimension of Politics* (Lanham: University Press of America, 1987).
2 William H. Riker, *Federalism: Origin, Operation, Significance* (Boston: Little Brown 1964); Mikhail Filippov, Peter Ordeshook and Olga Shvetsova, *Designing Federalism: A Theory of Self-Sustainable Federal Institutions* (Cambridge: Cambridge University Press, 2004).

3   Peter Reddaway and Robert W. Orttung (eds), *The Dynamics of Russian Politics: Putin's Reform of Federal–Regional Relations*, vol.1 (Lanham: Rowman & Littlefield Publishers Inc., 2004); Lynn D Nelson and Irina Y. Kuzes, "Political and Economic Coordination in Russia's Federal District Reform: A Study of Four Regions", *Europe-Asia Studies* 55, 4, 2003, pp. 507–20.

4   See Margarete Wiest, *Russlands schwacher Föderalismus und Parlamentarismus. Der Föderationsrat* (Münster, Hamburg, London: LitVerlag, 2003).

5   Cameron Ross, *Federalism and democratisation in Russia* (Manchester: Manchester University Press, 2002).

6   D. Slider, "Russia's Market-Distorting Federalism", *Post-Soviet Geography and Economics* 38, 8, 1997, pp. 445–60; Stephen L. Solnick, "Federal Bargaining in Russia", *East European Constitutional Review*, 4 (4, Fall) 1995, pp. 52–8; Stephen L. Solnick, "The Political Economy of Russian Federalism: A Framework for Analysis", *Problems of Post-Communism* 43, 6, 1996, pp. 13–25; Stephen Solnick, "Russia over the Edge: Explaining the Failure of Liberal Statebuilding", *East European Constitutional Review* 7, (4, Fall), 1998, pp. 70–2; K. Stoner-Weiss, "Central Weakness and Provincial Autonomy: Observations on the Devolution Process in Russia", *Post-Soviet Affairs* 15, 1, 1999, pp. 87–106; J. Moses, "Political-Economic Elites and Russian Regional Elections, 1999–2000: Democratic Tendencies in Kaliningrad, Perm and Volgograd". Paper presented at the annual meeting of the American Association for the Advancement of Slavic Studies, Crystal City, VA, 2001. On undemocratic practices in the republics, see J. Alexander and J. Grävingholt, "Democratic Progress Inside Russia: The Komi Republic and the Republic of Bashkortostan", *Democratization* 9 (4, Winter) 2002, pp. 77–105; Richard Sakwa, *Putin: Russia's Choice* (London, New York: Routledge, 2004).

7   Andreas Heinemann-Grüder, *Der heterogene Staat. Föderalismus und regionale Vielfalt in Russland* (Berlin: Berlin Verlag Arno Spitz, 2000).

8   Nataliya Varlamova, "Konstitutsionnaya model' rossiskogo federalizma", in H.V. Varlamova and T.A. Vasileyevoi (eds), *Rossiskii federalizim: konstitutsionnye predposylki i politicheskaya real'nost'. Sbornik dokladov* (Moscow, 2000), p. 52.

9   Irina A. Umnova, *Konstitutsionnye osnovy sovremennogo rossiiskogo federalizma* (Moscow: Delo, 2000), p. 159.

10 "Declaration of Sovereignty of the RSFSR", 12 June 1990, Russian version printed in: Ramazan Abdulatipov and Lyudmila Boltenkova (eds), *Federalizm* (Moscow, 1993), vol. 3, part 2, pp. 35ff.

11 Aleksandr G. Osipov, *Natsional'no-kul'turnaya avtonomiya. Idei, resheniya, instituty* (St Petersburg: Tsentr nezavisimykh sotsiologicheskikh issledovanii, 2004), p. 66.

12 Ibid., p. 72.

13 S.V. Sokolovskii, "Kontseptual'izatsiya etnonatsional'noi politiki v tekstakh respublikanskikh konstitutsii", in N.A.Voronina and Markus Galdi (eds.), *Pravo i etnichnost v sub'ektakh Rossiiskoi Federatsii* (Moscow: TACIS Project on "Promotion of Tolerance and Improving Interethnic Relations, Russia", 2004), pp. 14ff.

14 S.V. Sokolovskii, *Perspektivy razvitiia kontseptsii etnonatsionnal'noi politiki v Rossiiskoi Federatsii* (Moscow: Privet, 2004), pp. 80ff.

15 Valery V. Stepanov, "The Russian Experience with Ethnic Statistics on the Small Nations of the North", UN Department of Economic and Social Affairs,

Workshop on Data Collection and Disaggregation for Indigenous Peoples, New York, 19–21 January 2004.

16 Ibid. p. 26.

17 Federal'nyi zakon "O natsional'no-kul'turnoi avtonomii" (22 May 1996, with amendments from 21 March 2002, 10 November 2003, 29 June 2004).

18 Valery Tishkov, "Population Census and Changing Identities in Russia". Paper presented at the "Russian Census Workshop", Watson Institute, Brown University, March 2002.

19 Osipov, *Natsional'no-kul'turnaya avtonomiya*, p. 129.

20 Ibid., pp. 116 and 120.

21 Postanovlenie Konstitutsionnogo Suda RF po delu o proverke konstitutsionnosti chasti tret'ei stat'i 5 Federal'nogo zakona "O natsional'no-kul'turnoi avtonomii" v sviazi s zhaloby grazhdan A.Kh. Dittsa i O.A. Shumakher ot 3 marta 2004 g., *Vestnik Konstitutsionnogo Suda* 2/2004, pp. 57–70.

22 "Federal'nyi zakon o vnesenii izmenenii i dopolnenii v federal'nyi zakon 'Ob obshestvennykh ob'edineniyakh' ", 19 July 1998, No.112–F3.

23 V.V. Stepanov, "Natsional'no-kul'turnaia avtonomiia v Rossii kak ideia i pravovaia norma", Voronina and Galdi, *Pravo i etnichnost*, p. 108ff.

24 Osipov, *Natsional'no-kul'turnaya avtonomiya*, p. 131.

25 *Vedomosti RSFSR*, No. 50, 1991, p. 1740.

26 V.I. Mukomel', "Politika po otnosheniyu k etnicheskim men'shistvam v sub'ektakh severnogo kavkaza i drugikh regionakh Rossii: Pozitivnye praktiki", in Voronina and Galdi, *Pravo i etnichnost*, p. 245; Emil Pain, "Reforms in the Administration of the Regions and Their Influence on Ethnopolitical Processes in Russia, 1999–2003", in Peter Reddaway and Robert W. Orttung (eds), *The Dynamics of Russian Politics: Putin's Reform of Federal-Regional Relations, vol. II* (Lanham: Rowman & Littlefield Publishers Inc., 2005), pp. 341–70.

27 Mukomel', "Politika po otnosheniyu", p. 256.

28 Pain, "Reforms in the Administration", p. 351ff.

29 Gary N. Wilson, "'Matryoshka Federalism' and the Case of the Khanty Mansiysk Autonomous Okrug", *Post-Soviet Affairs*, 17, 2, 2001, pp. 167–94; Seppo Lallukka, "Finno-Ugrians of Russia: Vanishing Cultural Communities?", *Nationalities Papers*, 29, 1, 2001, pp. 9–39; Eszter Ruttkay-Miklian, "Revival and Survival in Iugra", *Nationalities Papers*, 29, 1, 2001, pp. 153–70; Aleksandr Shkliaev and Eva Toulouze, "The Mass Media and the National Question in Udmurtia in the 1990s", *Nationalities Papers*, 29, 1, 2001, pp. 97–108; Antti Laine, "Where East Meets West: The Last Stand of Finns and Karelians in Contemporary Karelia?", *Nationalities Papers*, 29, 1, 2001, pp. 53–67.

30 Seppo Lallukka, "Finno-Ugrians of Russia: Vanishing Cultural Communities?", *Nationalities Papers*, 29, 1, 2001, p. 16.

31 Alexia Bloch, *Red Ties and Residential Schools. Indigenous Siberians in a Post-Soviet State* (Philadelphia: University of Pennsylvania Press, 2004), p. 187.

32 Wilson "'Matryoshka Federalism'" p. 181.

33 Ibid., p. 183.

34 Russian Regional Report, vol. 11, No. 7, 19 March 2006.

35 Rogers Brubaker, *Nationalism Reframed: Nationhood and the National Question in the New Europe* (Cambridge: Cambridge University Press, 1996); Valerie Bunce, "Federalism, Nationalism, and Secession: The Communist and Post-communist Experience", in Ugo Amoretti and Nancy Bermeo (eds), *Federalism*

and Territorial Cleavages (Baltimore: Johns Hopkins University Press, 2004), pp. 417–40.

36 Donna Bahry, "Ethnicity and Equality in Post-Communist Economic Transition: Evidence from Russia`s Republics", *Europe-Asia Studies*, 54, 5, 2002, p. 674.

37 Natalia Zubarevich, "Russia: Case Study on Human Development Progress Toward the MDGs at the Sub-National Level", United Nations Development Programme. Human Development Report Office, Occasional Paper, 2003.

38 Ibid., p. 8ff.

39 Ibid., p. 26.

40 Ibid., p. 29.

41 Ildus G. Ilishev, "Nation-building and Minority Rights in Post-Soviet Russia: The Case of Bashkortostan", in Yaacov Ro'i (ed.), *Democracy and Pluralism in Muslim Eurasia* (London: Frank Cass, 2004), p. 308.

42 M. Filippov and O. Shvetsova, "Asymmetric Bilateral Bargaining in the New Russian Federation – A Path-dependence Explanation", *Communist and Post-Communist Studies*, 32, 1, 1999, p. 65.

43 Jessica Griffith Prendergast, "There Are Republics and Then There Are Republics: Who Matters?" Working Paper No. 2, Department of Geography, University of Leicester, May 2004, at: www.le.ac.uk/geography/research/RussianHeartland/index.html; M. Nicholson, *Towards a Russia of the Regions* (Oxford: Routledge, 2005), p. 25.

44 Daniel Treisman, "The Politics of Intergovernmental Transfers in Post-Soviet Russia", *British Journal of Political Science*, 26, 1996, pp. 299–335; Daniel Treisman, "Russia's 'Ethnic Revival'. The Separatist Activism of Regional Leaders in a Postcommunist Order", *World Politics*, 49, 2, 1997, pp. 212–49; Daniel Treisman, "Deciphering Russia's Federal Finance: Fiscal Appeasement in 1995 and 1996", *Europe–Asia Studies*, 50, 5, 1998, pp. 893–906; Daniel Treisman, "Fiscal Redistribution in a Fragile Federation: Moscow and the Regions in 1994", *British Journal of Political Science*, 28, 1998, pp. 185–222; Kitty Stewart, "Are Intergovernmental Transfers in Russia Equalizing?", *Innocenti Occasional Papers*, EPS 59, Florence: UNICEF, 1997; Vladimir Popov, "Fiscal Federalism in Russia: Rules Versus Electoral Politics", found at: www.nes.ru/public-presentations/Papers/Popov.htm.

45 Joan DeBardeleben, "Fiscal Federalism and How Russians Vote", *Europe-Asia Studies*, 55, 3, 2003, p. 360.

46 Dmitry Gorenburg, *Minority Ethnic Mobilization in the Russian Federation* (Cambridge: Cambridge University Press, 2003).

47 DeBardeleben, "Fiscal Federalism", pp. 339–63.

48 Prendergast, "There Are Republics", p. 14.

49 Project "National Consciousness, Nationalism, and Conflict Resolution in the Russian Federation", Institute for Anthropology and Ethnology of the Russian Academy of Sciences, Moscow 1997.

50 Rozalinda N. Muzina, "Etnokonfessional'nye osobennosti i faktory formirovaniya grazhdanskoi identichnosti". Seminar "Etnicheskii faktor i federalizatsii v Rossii", 18 January 2001, Kazan, found at: *http://federalmcart/ksu.ru/conference/seminar3*.

51 Jörn Grävingholt, *Pseudodemokratie in Russland. Der Fall Baschkortostan* (Bonn: Deutsches Institut für Entwicklungspolitik, 2005).

52 VTsIOM survey, Express 7 (July 26–29, 2002), at: *www.wciom.ru.*
53 Rafik Mukhametshin, "Post-Soviet Tatarstan: Democratic Strains in the Ideological Evolution of the Tatar National Movement", Ro'i (Democracy and Pluralism), pp. 287–305; Dmitry Gorenburg, "Regional Separatism in Russia: Ethnic Mobilization or Power Grab?", *Europe–Asia studies,* 51, 2, 1999, pp. 245–74.
54 Zubarevich (Russia), p. 115.
55 Cited by B.N. Toropin, *Konstitutsiia Rossiiskoi Federatsii. Stabil'nost' i razvitie obshestva* (Moscow, 2004), p. 32.
56 Interview with Vladimir Putin, *Die Zeit,* Nr. 47/1999.
57 Nikolai Petrov, "The Security Dimension of the Federal Reforms", in Reddaway and Orttung, *The Dynamic,* vol. II, p. 12.
58 Among others see Gordon M. Hahn, "The Impact of Putin's Federative Reforms on Democratization in Russia", *Post-Soviet Affairs* 19, 2, 2003, pp. 114–53; Leonid Smirnyagin, "Federalizm po Putinu ili Putinu po federal-izmu: Zheleznoy pyatoy", Moskovskiy Tsentr Karnegi, Brifing 3, Moscow, March 2001.
59 Nikolai Petrov, "Russia under Putin: Consolidating the Centralized State, Weakening Democracy and the Federal System", *East–West Institute, Russian Regional Report,* 6, 23, 19 June 2001.
60 *Vestnik Konstitutsionnogo Suda* 2, 2000, pp. 13–18; *Vestnik Konstitutsionnogo Suda* 1, 2000, pp. 43–47; *Vestnik Konstitutsionnogo Suda* 1, 1999, pp. 23–9; *Vestnik Konstitutsionnogo Suda* 3, 1999, pp. 25–33; *Vestnik Konstitutsionnogo Suda* 2, 2001, pp. 20–30.
61 *Sobranie zakonodatel'stva RF,* 12, 1996, p. 1058.
62 *Sobranie zakonodatel'stva RF,* 26, 1999, p. 3176.
63 Varlamova (Konstitutsionnaya), p. 58.
64 N.A. Voronina, "Normativnoe regulirovanie federativnykh otnoshenii v Rossii i regional'noe zakonodatel'stvo", Voronina and Galdi, *Pravo i etnichnost,* p. 63.
65 V.A. Kovalev, "Respublika Komi", in Matsuzato Kimitaka (ed.), *Fenomen Vladimira Putina i rossiiskie regiony. Sbornik statei* (Sapporo: Slavic Research Centre, Hokkaido University), Slavic Eurasian Studies No. 1, 2004, pp. 220–66.
66 Prendergast, "There Are Republics".
67 The point that the defense of republican identities was not reducible to gain maximization had already been made by Gorenburg, *Regional Separatism* p. 259.
68 *Vestnik Konstitutsionnogo Suda* 5, 2002, pp. 3–37. Minority opinions questioned the constitutionality of charging the Russian president with law enforcement and the limits to his discretionary powers.
69 *Vestnik Konstitutsionnogo Suda* 3, 2001, pp. 53–8.
70 *Vestnik Konstitutsionnogo Suda* 3, 2004, pp. 20–3.
71 "Opredelenie Konstitutsionnogo Suda RF po zarposu Gubernatora Koriiatskogo avtonomnogo okruga o proverke konstitutsionnosti punkta 4 stat'i 7 Zakona Koryatskogo avtonomnogo okruga 'O poriadke soglasovaniya Dumoi Koryatskogo avtonomnogo okruga otdel'nykh dolzhnostnykh lits Administratsii Koryatskogo avtonomnogo okruga dlya naznacheniya na dolzhnost' i prini-atiya resheniya o nedoverii im' ot 6 iiunia 2003 g.", *Vestnik Konstitutsionnogo Suda,* 3, 2004, pp. 3–6.
72 N.M. Mukharyamov and L.M. Mukharyamova, "Tatarstan v usloviyakh ret-sentralizatsii po-putinski", Kimitaka, Fenomen, p. 359.

73 Zakon, "O yazykakh narodov Rossiiskoi Federatsii", November 2002.
74 Prendergast, "There Are Republics", p. 23.
75 On the latter view see Riker, *Federalism*, p. 111.
76 Kelly M. McMann and Nikolai V. Petrov, "A Survey of Democracy in Russia`s Regions", *Post-Soviet Geography and Economics* 41, 3, 2000, pp. 155–82.
77 Grigorii V. Golosov, *Political Parties in the Regions of Russia. Democracy Unclaimed* (Boulder: Lynne Rienner Publishers,2004), p. 163.
78 Hahn, "The Impact", p. 142.
79 Herbert Kitschelt, "Origins of International Terrorism in the Middle East", *Internationale Politik und Gesellschaft*, 1, 2004, pp. 159–88.
80 M Steven Fish and Robin S. Brooks, "Does Diversity Hurt Democracy?", *Journal of Democracy* 15, 1, 2004, pp. 154ff.
81 Hahn "The Impact", p. 123ff.
82 Ibid., p. 131.
83 Ibid., p. 148.
84 Pain "Reforms in the Administration", p. 356 and Tomila Lankina, "President Putin's Local Government Reforms", in Reddaway and Orttung, *The Dynamics*, Vol. II, pp. 145–77.
85 Mikhail Filippov and Olga Shvetsova, "Fedaralism and Democracy in Russia". Paper prepared for the conference "Postcommunist State and Society: Transnational and National Politics", Syracuse University, 30 September–1 October 2005, p. 19ff.
86 Prendergrast, "There Are Republics", p. 31ff.
87 Robert Bruce Ware, "Russian Democracy", *Johnson's Russia List no* 8395, 4 Octobar 2004.
88 Bryon J. Moraski, "Electoral System Design in Russian Oblasti and Republics: A Four Case Comparison", *Europe–Asia Studies*, 55, 3, 2003, p. 439; Darrell Slider, "Elections in Russia's Regional Assemblies", *Post-Soviet Affairs*, 12, 3, 1996, pp. 253–4.
89 Moraski, "Electoral System Design", pp. 437–68.
90 Petrov, "How Have the Presidential Envoys", p. 55ff.
91 Michael McFaul, Nikolai Petrov and Andrei Ryabov, *Between Dictatorship and Democracy: Russian Post-Communist Political Reform* (Washington, DC: Carnegie Endowment for International Peace 2004); Gabriele Gorzka and Peter W. Schulze (eds), *Wohin steuert Russland unter Putin? Der autoritäre Weg in die Demokratie* (Frankfurt/Main: Campus, 2004).
92 Golosov *Political Parties*, p. 74
93 Ibid., p. 261.
94 It seems easier (as Leonid Smirnyagin in 2001 reported of a conversation with a member of the Federation Council) "to lick one boot than to clean 400,000", see Julie A. Corwin, "Why Are so Many Elected Leaders in Russia Ready to Give up on Elections?", *RFE/RL Russian Political Weekly* 4, 36, 16 September 2004.
95 Nikolai Petrov, "Putin's Centripetal Reform", *Moscow Times*, 7 June 2004.
96 This point is made by Valery Tishkov, *Chechnya: Life in a Wartorn Society* (Berkeley: University of California Press, 2004), p. 8ff.
97 Interviews by the author in December 2005 with the heads of permanent missions of ethnic regions in Moscow (Tatarstan, Chuvashia, Komi, Mari-El, Khanty-Manzii autonomous okrug).

98 Dmitri Glinski, "Russia and its Muslims: The Politics of Identity at the International-Domestic Frontier", *East-European Constitutional Review*, 11, 1/2, 2002, p. 75.

99 Ibid., p. 73.

100 Ibid., p. 77.

101 Malashenko, *Islamskie orientiry: Severnogo kavkaza* (Moscow: Moscow Carnegie Center), p. 16.

102 Monica Duffy Toft, *The Geography of Ethnic Violence: Identity, Interests, and the Indivisibility of Territory* (Princeton: Princeton University Press, 2003).

103 Paul Goble, "Window on Eurasia: Russia is Losing the North Caucasus", *Johnson's Russia List* no. 9220, 9 August 2005.

104 For the opposite view see Edward D. Mansfield and Jack Snyder, *Electing to Fight: Why Emerging Democracies Go to War* (Cambridge: MIT Press 2006).

2
Federalism and Defederalization in a Country in Transition: the Russian Experience

Oksana Oracheva

Federalism as a political model for a country in transition

There appears to be a consensus that federalism as a political institution is the most appropriate solution to the internal ethnic, regional, cultural or religious diversity in a country. A federal structure allows the accommodation of demands for regional autonomy within the same territorial unit. "Politics of accommodation"[1] is usually seen as a distinguishing feature of federalism. Furthermore, "federalism is also a way of decentralizing conflict and isolating continuous regional issues so that they do not 'bubble up' to disrupt national politics."[2]

Federalism is understood as "the linkage of individuals, groups and polities in lasting but limited union, in such a way as to provide for the energetic pursuit of common ends while maintaining the respective integrities of all parties."[3] Federalism is based upon spatial power distribution and shared sovereignty. These basic principles of federalism could be seen as an additional remedy against concentration of state power that could lead towards the restoration of authoritarian rule. According to Daniel J. Elazar, "the intimate and vital connection between federalism and democracy, which is so often overlooked in the democracies of the West, even those organized federally, because it is taken for granted, is being demonstrated in new, highly visible and convincing ways in those countries now in the process of turning toward democracy."[4] As Ivo Duchacek argues, true federalism "can never accommodate fascism or communism – and vice versa. Federalism is simply a territorial expression of the core creed of democracy, that is respect for and management of political pluralism both within and among the territorial components of a nation-state."[5] Duchacek metaphorically compares federalism and democracy with twin brothers, and states that federalism is more dependent on democracy than democracy on federalism.[6]

We can identify certain essential federal features that could support the successful transition to democracy and then the consolidation of that democracy:

1. constitutionally guaranteed spatial power distribution;
2. constitutionally guaranteed territorial representation and bicameralism;
3. existence of the system of checks and balances in centre–region relations;
4. acknowledgment of diversity of interests and protection of ethnic minorities and territorial communities;
5. incorporation of federation subjects in decision-making and policy implementation and decentralization of political control;
6. institutionalization of relations between federation subjects.

However, federalism *per se* is not a guarantee that a political regime will be democratic. Although federalism can contribute to the establishment of political stability in a country characterized by ethnic and regional diversity, the emergence of political stability is not guaranteed. Moreover, federalism has some built-in weaknesses that could limit the success of democratic consolidation. Among such characteristics of federalism are:

1. federalism does not eliminate social conflicts but "allows for conflicts to emerge and be politicized";[7]
2. there is no institutionalized guarantee against possible centre expansion and return towards over-centralization;
3. a decentralized decision-making process implies certain limitations on policy implementation;
4. under the circumstances of uncertainty, institutionalization of territorial diversity could be one of the factors leading towards development of centrifugal tendencies or, even more, state disintegration.

The strong state of uncertainty caused by democratic transition could consequently reinforce the internal weaknesses of federalism. However, this does not prevent countries in transition from adopting federal practices. Moreover, federalism as a political argument is often used by political regimes for justification of two opposite tendencies: enforcement of democratic rules and procedures in governance and civil society, and for stepping back to the authoritarian rule and/or unitary type of spatial configuration.

The latter could be illustrated by the modern history of Russian federalism. Since the collapse of the Soviet Union, Russian political elites regularly play the federal card whenever political or social conflict arises.

It is possible to highlight three major approaches adopted in Putin's Russia towards state development that could to some extent be associated with federalism or have an impact on its development:

1. the reconfiguration of territorial communities on the basis of a need to resolve economic and social conflicts and to stabilize political democracy;
2. the elimination of ethnic elements of federalism and the introduction of pure territorial constituent units, again on the basis of a need to resolve ethnic conflicts and establish political stability;
3. the reshaping of the federal structure by changing power distribution in favour of the centre.

The first two approaches towards federalism could have both positive and negative effects on the outcome of the transition. However, the Russian case demonstrates that any reconfiguration reinforces administrative practices and limits democratic decision-making. The third approach clearly indicates the regime's choice for authoritarianism. Some of these points will be elaborated and illustrated below.

The reconfiguration of territorial communities in Russia: changing the number of federation subjects

Contemporary Russia primarily inherited its administrative and territorial structure from the Soviet past. The former Soviet Union represented the coexistence of different types of territorial communities within the same country. The Soviet Federation was a multilayered state with a federation within the federation. The Soviet federation was concurrently based upon two different principles – territorial and ethnic.[8] The Russian Federation largely took over this complexity, adopting mixed principles for the formation of the federation: ethnic republics coexist with territorial units. This complexity is deepened by another inherited factor: the existence of compound federation subjects, where one subject of the federation (the autonomous okrug) is territorially and politically part of another subject of the federation (the oblast or krai). Not surprisingly, Russian federalism is widely compared with the traditional Russian doll, "matryoshka", in which the large doll contains smaller ones. As well as these administrative and territorial boundaries, modern administrative structures have been inherited from the Soviet past. The country's administrative structure has remained almost unchanged since the last period of parcelling out (1943–1954) followed by some insignificant steps back towards unification in 1957.[9] The distinctive feature of this system is the full domination of vertical ties over horizontal ones within the regions. With very few exceptions (for example Vologda, Kemerovo and Samara regions), all regions are mono-centric.[10]

The other factor that had a significant impact on the development of Russian federalism was political – that is, the struggle between the late Soviet Union as a state and the Russian Federation as its constituent unit. This struggle was personified in the first Soviet president, Mikhail Gorbachev, and the first Russian president, Boris Yeltsin. Both leaders needed support from territorial communities and their leaders, contributing to the growing movement for territorial autonomy within the Soviet state. President Yeltsin's appeal to federation subjects to take as much sovereignty as they can swallow,[11] led in the end to the "parade of sovereignty" in Russia that resulted in change in the form of regional institutionalization and gave a start to the new period in centre–region relations as well as in the development of Russian federalism. Almost all autonomous republics adopted their own declarations of sovereignty. Some of them went even further, proclaiming the supremacy of their laws over those of the Russian Federation. The great majority of autonomous republics immediately proclaimed their ownership of, and therefore control over, all industrial and mineral resources, land, water and likewise. Four autonomous oblasts – Adygeya, Gorny Altai, Karachaevo-Cherkessiya and Khakassiya – upgraded their status in the federation and proclaimed themselves republics. Autonomous okrugs decided also to upgrade their status within the federation and Chukotka even completely broke away from its home region, Magadan oblast.

Therefore, the fundamental problem confronting the Russian Federation through the process of transition is that of the extraordinary complexity of its administrative structure that must accommodate both ethnic and regional diversity as well as the interests of federal and regional political leaders. Two strategies for reshaping the subjects of the federation have become evident.

The quest for the optimal number

The 1993 Constitution established the country's current administrative and territorial structure. Russia is a compound of 21 republics formed according to the ethnic principle, six krais and 49 oblasts (purely territorial in character), 10 autonomous okrugs and one autonomous oblast (all ethno-territorial in nature).[12] While the Constitution reinforced the federal structure of the Russian state, the system designed was and still is asymmetrical. First, both the Federal Treaty signed in March 1992 by all except two constituent units (Republics of Tatarstan and Chechnya) as well as the Constitution approved of significant symbolic differences between republics and other regions. Secondly, while the republics and regions were granted certain powers, the Constitution allows considerable changes in power distribution between the centre and the regions as well as in regional representation without changing the Constitution itself. Although the process of institutionalization of centre–region relations started more than a decade ago, it has not yet been completed.

Almost from the very existence of the contemporary Russian state, the issue of the number of federation subjects has been on the political agenda. Russian state formation started from an increase in the inherited number of its constituent units due to the breakaway of autonomous okrugs, which became fully-fledged federation subjects. However, soon after the territorial status quo was institutionalized, Russian politicians initiated discussions on reshaping the state's structure and reducing the number of constituent units. Vladimir Shumeiko[13] and Sergei Shakhrai,[14] who were considered the spokesmen of regional policy in early and mid-1990s Russia, frequently discussed the idea of changing the country's territorial structure. The former St Petersburg mayor Anatolii Sobchak was more specific and suggested unification of the city of St Petersburg and Leningrad oblast, resulting in the creation of a North-West region. The issue of unification became an important one during the Leningrad oblast gubernatorial elections in 1996. The Moscow mayor (Yurii Luzhkov) made similar declarations about the unification of Moscow city and Moscow oblast. The Sverdlosk oblast governor (Eduard Rossel) put forward the idea of unifying three Urals oblasts – Sverdlovsk, Chelyabinsk and Kurgan – to form the Urals republic. Regional leaders saw unification as another way to increase significantly their power as heads of much bigger and stronger federation subjects.

One of the first leaders to officially articulate the idea of reshaping territorial communities was the former prime minister Yevgenii Primakov. In January 1999, at the All-Russia discussion meeting on development of federal relations, Primakov raised the question of the review of the adopted federal principles, including the possibility of regional enlargement. According to Primakov, it was time to make all federation subjects equal, to restore the efficiency of governance, and to build the power vertical. This enlargement project could be based on the boundaries of eight interregional economic associations.[15] Primakov consequently justified his enlargement project and presented it at the meetings of regional associations. In doing so in early 1999, Primakov echoed statements repeatedly made earlier by some of the Russian governors (including

Eduard Rossel of Sverdlovsk, Dmitrii Ayatskov of Saratov, Viktor Kress of Tomsk, and Konstantin Titov of Samara), following the August 1998 economic crisis, on the necessity to review the current territorial boundaries and to enlarge some of the federation subjects. However, as Mikhail Afanasev argues, Primakov's statements were more a part of a political campaign and an examination of public opinion than a real political project.[16]

In May 2000, with the establishment of seven federal districts, the issue of reshaping territorial communities was reopened. As this was the first major initiative of the newly elected President Vladimir Putin, it immediately restarted discussions on reduction of the number of federation subjects from 89 to seven or so. Even though the establishment of seven federal districts did not change the territorial structure of the state, it was seen as a first step towards regional enlargement. The major difference from the previous projects was in the basis of reconstruction. If the eight interregional economic associations were not artificial institutions but shared a background for potential unification, the boundaries of the newly created federal districts were difficult to justify from either an economic or a geographic point of view. As Boris Rodoman points out, "federal okrugs are not practical as federation subjects" for a number of reasons: they have too many regions inside their boundaries, their boundaries and names do not correspond with traditional geography, and more important, they are far away from real federalism.[17] Moreover, at the time of their establishment, the goal of regional enlargement could not be seen as a major objective of the federal centre.[18]

Nonetheless, the presidential representatives formally and informally supported the discussions about possible unification. In December 2003 the presidential representative in the Far East, Konstantin Pulikovskii, justified his support of enlargement projects. First, unification should be economically cost-effective and lead towards better living conditions for people who live in those territories that decided to merge. Second, the merger of larger and smaller federation subjects would resolve the problems of shortages of qualified administrative personnel in smaller federation subjects where there are not enough qualified specialists to occupy all administrative positions.[19] In May 2005, responding to journalists' questions, Konstantin Pulikovskii repeatedly acknowledged the fact that regional enlargement should be seen as a positive development of the Russian Federation leading towards simplification of state governance, reduction of state bureaucracy and regularization of the administrative institutions.[20] The presidential envoy in the Northwest federal district, Iliya Klebanov, made similar supportive statements about the unification of Pskov with Novgorod oblast, and Arkhangelsk oblast with Nenets autonomous okrug.[21] However, Aleksei Makarkin argues that Klebanov's statements may have been aimed at supporting his image as a federal political leader after a number of failures during gubernatorial elections.[22]

Despite a long period on the political agenda, actual implementation of the idea of reducing the number of federation subjects only took place with the merger of Perm oblast and Komi-Permyak autonomous okrug into the newly-created Perm krai in December 2005.[23] However, then presidential envoy in the Volga federal district, Sergei Kirienko, pointed out that one should not generalize this positive experience, because any unification should be based only on full support of the population of the respective regions expressed through a referendum. Moreover, while unification could be a solution for compound regions when one subject of the federation is a part of another one, in other cases one should be very careful with any mergers or unifications, as the country already has about 2,000 territorial disputes and any possible changes of territorial communities could provoke serious social conflicts.[24]

Kirienko's cautious approach towards unification is echoed in opinion polls conducted in 2003 by the Foundation for Public Opinion. In a survey, 29 per cent of respondents said that unification would be more positive than negative, 17 per cent believed the opposite, and 22 per cent thought that nothing would change. At the same time, when people were asked how they felt about possible unification of their region with the neighbouring one, the answers were much more pessimistic: 22 per cent believed that the population of their region would not benefit from unification, 21 per cent that the region would be better off and 18 per cent felt nothing would change. People doubt the value of merger projects for a number of reasons. 10 per cent were afraid of administrative disorder due to the big territory to be governed, and of increases in the level of bureaucracy and corruption. 11 per cent thought that the living conditions of the population of their region would worsen as economically depressed regions would merge with those better off; only 5 per cent believed that there would be some positive outcome of unification, namely that bureaucracy would decrease and the governance process would be simplified.[25]

As support for unification projects is not overwhelming, there is a clear need for information campaigns to build acceptance in different groups and communities. Perhaps more common is the economic argument that unification projects would be successful as more developed regions merge with less developed ones. However, one should also consider the existence of strong regional (not necessarily based on ethnicity) identity that would be undermined by mergers.

Nevertheless, having started with Perm krai, the process is accelerating and becoming another political campaign that could draw people's attention from more significant social transformations. This tendency manifests itself not only in a growing number of almost meaningless statements made recently by federal and regional politicians, but also in proposals for unification projects as one of the major goals to be accomplished by presidential envoys during 2006. The "Rodina" faction leader in the State Duma, Dmitrii Rogozin, who is now viewed as one of those who articulates the most provocative political initiatives of the Kremlin administration, announced that starting in 2006 presidential envoys would concentrate on issues of regional enlargement in order to reduce the number of federation subjects from 89 to 30–40 territorial units.[26]

Ethnofederalism and territorial reconfiguration

The other strategy for reshaping federation subjects in Russia is to introduce a purely territorial structure regardless of the ethnic diversity of the country. The political elites at the start of the transition rejected this solution totally. During a time of uncertainty, the federal government was afraid of creating large territorial units that could demand independence at some point in the future. Moreover, the federal political elite was seeking the support of strong republican leaders who led the "parade of sovereignty" and managed to receive special status within the federation for their subjects. However, once political elites embarked on the path of reconsidering and reshaping the federal structure, the issue of changing the nature and boundaries of current federation subjects came back on the political agenda. Unification could be seen as another away of eliminating the ethnic basis of the federation and replacing it with a purely territorial structure.

Currently six different types of constituent units are in the federation. Three of those types – republics, autonomous okrugs and autonomous oblasts – are based on ethnic principles. Of the 89 subjects of the federation, 32 are based on what Rogers Brubaker calls institutionalized ethnicity. According to Brubaker, institutionalized ethnicity "constituted a pervasive system of social classification, ... a standardized scheme of social accounting, an interpretative grid for public discussion, a set of boundary-markers, a legitimate form for public and private identities, and ... a ready-made template for claims to sovereignty."[27] But such institutionalized ethnicity is part of Russia's federal asymmetry. As Russia is a multiethnic society with more than a hundred different ethnic groups, federalism cannot serve the interests of all ethnic communities. Some received an institutional "homeland" and others did not. This is one of the indicators of an asymmetrical approach towards ethnicity, one that enjoys strong support from republican elites and some federal politicians.

Transition and the period of uncertainty encouraged regional political elites to demand equal power and privileges with republican leaders, and some analysts see a new conflict dimension appearing, caused by institutionalization of ethnicity and asymmetry of the federation. Leonid Smirnyagin points out that "added to federalism the nationalities issue significantly decreases the state's sustainability and increases the danger of state disintegration. The match of territorial boundaries with social ones reinforces the significance of such boundaries."[28]

One of the most ambitious projects for reshaping the subjects of the federation has originated from the Council for the Study of Productive Resources, and is known as the concept of Aleksandr Kazakov (the member of the Federation Council from Rostov oblast) and Aleko Adamesku. According to this proposal, Russia should be reorganized into 28 regions, as shown in Table 2.1.

As one can see from Table 2.1, the proposed structure of the Russian state would be based solely on the territorial principle, with ethnic elements eliminated even from all proposed regional names. Moreover, only two current republican capitals (Kazan and Ufa) would retain their capital status, but within bigger non-ethnic regions. The main idea of this project, according to the Council for the Study of Productive Resources, is that "the reform of Russia's administrative and territorial structure should be based upon economic expediency first, then territorial and social suitability comes in and only after that one should take into consideration national and cultural differences of the region."[29] However, analysis of the proposed mergers clearly demonstrates that elimination of the ethnic element in Russian federalism is a very important part of the concept. Otherwise it is difficult to explain the list of regions to be merged.

Nonetheless, the proposed concept has not received support from either the population of the regions to be merged or from political scientists. A number of regional newspapers and information agencies have measured public opinion on the issue of unification in terms of the proposed 28 regions. Not surprisingly, the majority of interviewees do not support this idea for both economic and cultural reasons. For example, the regional newspaper *Severnyi Kurier* published typical responses of residents of the Republic of Kareliya and Murmansk oblast on the question of possible unification: "Kareliya should keep its republican status; this is the only way for the Kareliyans to keep their unique original culture"; "It is not rational – geographically we are neighbours, but historically Murmansk region and Kareliya have been developing in a different way."[30] The concept

Table 2.1 Regional structure proposed by the Council for the Study of Productive Resources

Proposed name	Regions to be merged	Proposed capital
Central region	City of Moscow, Moscow oblast	Moscow
Western region	Bryansk, Kaluga and Smolensk oblasts	Smolensk
Upper Volga region	Tver and Yaroslavl oblasts	Yaroslavl
Volga-Oka region	Vladimir, Ivanovo and Kostroma oblasts	Ivanovo
Oka region	Ryazan and Tula oblasts	Tula
West Black Soil region	Belgorod, Kursk and Orel oblasts	Kursk
East Black Soil region	Voronezh, Lipetsk and Tambov oblasts	Voronezh
North-West region	City of St. Petersburg, Leningrad, Kaliningrad, Novgorod and Pskov oblasts	St. Petersburg
Kareliya-Murmansk region	Republic of Kareliya and Murmansk oblast	Murmansk
Northern region	Komi Republic, Arkhangelsk and Vologda oblasts	Arkhangelsk
Volga-Don region	Republic of Kalmykiya, Astrakhan, Volgograd and Rostov oblasts	Rostov-on-Don
Black Sea region	Republics of Adygeya and Karachaevo-Cherkessiya, Krasnodar krai	Krasnodar
North Caucasus region	Republics of Dagestan, Ingushetiya, Kabardino-Balkariya, North Ossetiya and Chechnya, Stavropol krai	Stavropol
Middle Russia region	Republic of Mordoviya and Nizhnii Novgorod oblast	Nizhnii Novgorod
Volga-Vyatka region	Republics of Mari-El and Chuvashiya, Kirov oblast	Kirov
Volga-Kama region	Republic of Tatarstan and Ulyanovsk oblast	Kazan
Middle Volga region	Penza, Samara and Saratov oblasts	Samara
West Urals region	Republic of Udmurtiya and Perm oblast	Perm
Southern Urals region	Republic of Bashkortostan and Orenburg oblast	Ufa
Eastern Urals region	Kurgan, Sverdlovsk and Chelyabinsk oblasts	Yekaterinburg
Ob-Irtysh region	Tyumen region and Khanty-Mansii and Yamalo-Nenets autonomous okrugs	Tyumen
West Siberia region	Novosibirsk, Tomsk and Omsk oblasts	Novosibirsk
South Siberia region	Altai Republic, Altai krai, Kemerovo oblast	Kemerovo
East Siberia region	Tyva and Khakassiya republics, Krasnoyarsk krai	Krasnoyarsk
Baikal region	Republic of Buryatiya, Irkutsk and Chita oblasts	Irkutsk
Amur region	Khabarovsk krai, Amur oblast, Jewish autonomous oblast	Khabarovsk
Pacific region	Primorskii krai, Kamchatka and Sakhalin oblasts	Vladivostok
North-East region	Republic of Yakutiya, Magadan oblast, Chukotka autonomous okrug	Yakutsk

has also been challenged by ethnic political elites. For example, Chairman of the "Kareliyan Congress" Anatolii Grigoriev strongly believes that "if the republic merges with any other region this would lead towards elimination of traditional Kareliyan culture."[31]

Even though Kazakov and Adamesku argue that their unification project is based upon pure economic expediency, their reasoning appears doubtful. As Nataliya Zubarevich argues, in the majority of regions to be merged, administrative costs would increase significantly as, for example, neighbouring regions lack sufficient communications networks.[32] Additionally, after the transition period was over, the donor region that is merging with the recipient one would need to provide full financial support to the merging underdeveloped subject. Moreover, new regional capitals with their concentrations of institutions would be less accessible for the regional populations because of greater distances. The head of Pskov oblast branch of the party Yabloko, Lev Shlosberg, argues that if Pskov loses its status as oblast centre through the merger with neighbouring regions, the Pskov population would be more distant from major political institutions, including those traditionally associated with defense of human rights (regional courts, for example). The economic situation could become worse, as the economically weaker region would be even less competitive. Important civil society institutions (regional branches of political parties, etc.) would also move to the new centre.[33]

Although the Kazakov/Adamesku project has not been implemented, the unification of ethnically-based autonomous okrugs with pure territorial regions could be seen as the first step towards eliminating ethnic institutionalization. Autonomous okrugs were considered to be a good platform for such an experiment. Historically, autonomous okrugs were created in the areas inhabited by small indigenous peoples of the North, Siberia, and the Far East. They do not have a history of strong and well-developed nationalist movements. With few exceptions, the indigenous peoples who provided the okrugs' names do not constitute majorities in their areas. Moreover, the autonomous okrugs (with very few exceptions) are economically depressed and fully dependent on subsidies from the federal budget. Therefore, one could assume that the unification of the okrugs with their respective regions would not cause any serious "ethnic" opposition. However, as current unification projects demonstrate, mergers can facilitate a revival of ethnic identity, or at least interest towards ethnic culture and language. Even if the majority of the population of Taimyr and Evenkiya autonomous okrugs fully supported unification with Krasnoyarsk krai through a referendum, indigenous political and cultural elites still express their concerns about the preservation of indigenous cultures and languages, seeing it as unclear how these issues would be resolved within the new territory.

The situation with economically developed and rich okrugs such as Khanty-Mansii and Yamalo-Nenets autonomous okrugs is even more complicated. The okrugs are economically better off than Tyumen oblast, but once a merger was completed, they would become part of a less developed Tyumen oblast. In May 2004, the expert political information agency "UralPolit.Ru" conducted an interactive survey on the possible unification of Tyumen oblast with Khanty-Mansii and Yamalo-Nenets autonomous okrugs. More than a thousand people expressed their opinion, and the results clearly demonstrated that support for proposed unification was very limited: only 25.37 per cent were in favour of unification, while 73.85 per cent disagreed with it and 0.78 per cent did not have an opinion.[34]

Nonetheless, unification campaigns have been developing rapidly. By the end of 2005 more compound federation subjects decided to merge. Appropriate referenda took place in Krasnoyarsk krai, Taimyr and Evenkiya autonomous okrugs (April 2005), Kamchatka oblast and Koryak autonomous okrug (October 2005). The merger of Kamchatka region and Koryak autonomous okrug, where all negotiations about a merger were completed in a few months and the referendum was held in the shortest possible time, is the best illustration of the campaign approach to mergers. The Perm oblast and Komi-Permyak autonomous okrug merger leading to the founding of Perm krai in December 2005 is considered to be a model of successful unification. Therefore, it is important to analyse how the merger occurred and what goals were pursued by the different parties involved.

Changing federalism in Russia: the case of Perm krai

Komi-Permyak autonomous okrug was founded in 1925. In 1938, when Perm oblast was restored, the okrug became part of it and has kept this status until now. Komi-Permyak okrug never broke away completely from its "mother" region; however, according to the 1993 Constitution it became a subject of the Russian Federation. In 1994 the okrug adopted its Charter reconfirming its status within the Federation: article 1 of the Charter stated that Komi-Permyak autonomous okrug was a fully-fledged subject of the Russian Federation.[35] At the same time, article 8 proclaimed that Komi-Permyak autonomous okrug was an integral part of the Perm oblast. Relations between the okrug and the oblast are regulated by the federal Constitution, the Federal Treaty, federal law, and special bilateral treaties between Komi-Permyak autonomous okrug and Perm oblast.[36]

Perm oblast Charter also states that Perm oblast acknowledges the rights of the people of Komi-Permyak autonomous okrug, their right for self-determination and development of language and culture, respecting their traditions and customs (article 6, part 1).[37] The Charter declares that the region would not interfere in the okrug's internal affairs (article 6, part 3),[38] and the only instrument that institutionalizes relations between okrug and oblast is the bilateral treaty (article 6, part 2).[39] The Perm oblast law "On the administrative-territorial structure of the Perm oblast" also confirmed that administratively the Komi-Permyak okrug was an integral part of the oblast and that administrative boundaries between okrug and oblast are set as of 1992.[40] In 1996 a triple agreement between Komi-Permyak autonomous okrug, Perm oblast and the Russian Federation was signed to define their spheres of competence and responsibility.[41] Therefore, one could argue that by the mid-1990s oblast–okrug relations were finally institutionalized. Being part of the oblast, Komi-Permyak okrug was always involved in oblast politics: the okrug had 2 deputies in the Perm oblast assembly and participated in the Perm oblast gubernatorial elections. Traditionally Komi-Permyak okrug and the oblast have very strong political, economic and cultural ties that were not destroyed by the fact that the okrug became a fully-fledged subject of the Federation. Moreover, the okrug political elite was always oriented towards the oblast.

In 1997 the author interviewed members of the Perm oblast assembly, including those who represented Komi-Permyak autonomous okrug. Questions were asked on centre–oblast relations, on oblast–okrug relations, and on their prospects for the future. It was interesting to observe the differences in approach towards prospects of closer relations between the okrug and the oblast or even the okrug's reintegration into the oblast. A majority of deputies, who represented different districts within the oblast, demonstrated indifference towards the issue, satisfaction with the current status of their relations, or were not supportive of any administrative changes. At the same time leaders of the Perm oblast assembly believed that greater cooperation between the okrug and the oblast would be beneficial not only for the economically depressed okrug but for the oblast as well. Not surprisingly, deputies representing Komi-Permyak autonomous okrug strongly supported greater oblast integration into the okrug's economic affairs and believed that the okrug would definitely benefit economically from the merger.

Oblast and okrug elites, politicians and business people had all discussed the idea of reintegration before it became a part of the nationwide political

agenda. In 2000, Yurii Trutnev, during his successful gubernatorial electoral campaign, made it one of his key initiatives. Nevertheless, the implementation of this initiative was not possible without involvement of the
federal centre. Two subjects of the federation could not merge without
changing the relevant federal legislation. Article 66 (5) of the Russian
Constitution states that "the status of component of the Russian Federation
can be changed by mutual consent of the Russian Federation and the
component of the Russian Federation in accordance with federal constitutional law."[42] However, the required constitutional law "On the
Process of Accession to the Russian Federation and Foundation of a New
Constituent Unit of the Russian Federation" was adopted only in
December 2001.[43] This law regulates the conditions and procedures for
such a merger. According to the law, only neighbouring federation subjects could initiate a merger. There could be two possible outcomes of
such merger – two federation subjects (A and B) could merge and create
a new subject of the federation (A + B = C), or one subject of the federation incorporates another without creating a new subject (A + B = A).
The law also requires that federation subjects interested in a merger should
hold a referendum, but only the President could place the draft law before
the State Duma. Thus, the adoption of the constitutional law allowed
the Perm political elite to start the process of merger.

On the surface Perm and Komi-Permyak elites initiated the process of
unification, but one could argue that this initiative was encouraged by
the presidential administration. President Vladimir Putin offered uncon-
ditional support to the process as the merger fully fitted his major goal –
the building of the power vertical, with regional enlargement as part of
this process. Moreover, Putin openly demonstrated his support and he
even visited Kudymkar (the capital of Komi-Permyak autonomous okrug)
in October 2003. Putin's visit raised the significance of the political campaign held before the referendum. The governor of Perm oblast, Yurii
Trutnev, confirmed this fact, and even more clearly expressed his opinion
on how this support should be used: "We have a very unique moment.
The president and his administration are interested in unification and
we should use their incentive for our own good. We could get additional
financial support for the implementation of unification."[44]

According to the referendum that was held on 7 December 2003, about
90 per cent of those who took part in the referendum in Komi-Permyak
autonomous okrug voted in favour of unification with the oblast, while
in Perm oblast about 85 per cent of voters supported the idea of
merger.[45] Such support for unification did not come as a surprise. The
unification campaign had actually been maintained for quite a long period

of time, even though it had officially started only one month before the referendum. But as analyses of the regional press demonstrated, only those who fully supported the merger were represented in the different mass media. One would have expected at least some opposition in the okrug that was losing both its political independence and institutionalized ethnic territorial community. However, such opposition was very weak and little heard. Even one of the opposition leaders, the former chairman of the okrug legislature, Ivan Chetin, did not fully disagree with the concept of unification, but insisted that the full conditions of the merger, including the okrug's special status, should be clarified from the very beginning. The low level of opposition could be explained by a number of factors. First, the pro-unification campaign was very pro-active, if not to say aggressive, and gave very little chance to fight against the mainstream – press, TV, radio, visits of federal politicians, discussion clubs, cultural events, show business star tours, etc. – everything was working for unification. The campaign even became part of the education process – schoolteachers were asked to talk about the common history and culture of peoples living in the Perm oblast and Komi-Permyak autonomous okrug, so children would be aware of the coming unification and referendum and talk about it at home.[46] Secondly, one should consider that the political culture of the Komi-Permyak rural population is dominated by passive loyalty to government and is hardly compatible with an openly expressed opposition to official power. Thirdly, the propaganda in favour of unification almost entirely rested on economic arguments – the public everywhere came across general figures of the supposed economic gains while all other themes were kept outside the discussion. In the face of such a campaign, the opposition could gain little hearing.

Thus, long before the referendum there was a general consensus that the population of both the oblast and the okrug would support the merger. Approval of the merger required 50 per cent plus 1. The regional elites were more concerned about a possible low turnout; a sufficient level of participation could hardly be achieved through a propaganda campaign alone. Therefore, regional elites actively utilized administrative resources in a way that clearly violated people's right to free expression of their opinion. The Perm Oblast Human Rights Centre summarized and publicized such violations. In particular, employees were required to present a written confirmation of participation in the referendum at their workplace, hospitals refused to admit people for regular treatment without an absentee ballot, the day of the referendum (Sunday) was made a working day and all employees were obliged to come to their workplace with an absentee ballot to vote collectively, etc.[47] Such techniques enabled regional elites to control the process of voting and to ensure that enough people would come to the polling stations.

The referendum in fact completed the process of negotiations that had started earlier. A number of very important agreements were made between oblast and okrug political elites on the one hand, and the federal centre on the other. Those agreements include, but are not limited to, preservation of special administrative status for Komi-Permyak okrug, maintenance of special bonuses for living in the North territories for the okrug population, establishment of a transition period and maintenance of federal transfers. Moreover, it was agreed that in 2004–2006 the federal budget would support a number of very important infrastructural projects, including construction of the railway between Grigorievskaya station and Kudymkar (so far the okrug has no rail connection with any other regions), the building of roads as part of the North corridor connecting Perm, Kudymkar and Syktyvkar, including the bridge over the Kama river, and the building of the gas pipeline from Ocher (Perm oblast) to Kudymkar.[48]

One could argue that despite all the economic justification for unification, this merger was more of an elite project. The Komi-Permyak political elite completely rejected the merger before certain guarantees were received. For example, in 2002 Komi-Permyak governor Gennady Saveliev initiated the campaign for driving signatures against the referendum and about 15,000 signatures were collected. However, later he denied his personal responsibility for the initiative[49] and headed the process of unification in the okrug. The Perm oblast elite finally got okrug support through negotiations, with certain very important concessions being made:

1. The more democratic merger formula (A + B = C) was adopted. In comparison, Krasnoyarsk krai, and Taimyr and Evenkiya autonomous okrugs chose a different formula of unification (A + B + C = A) without founding a new subject of the federation.
2. The okrug legally confirmed its special status within the region. However, the form of this special status remains unclear. According to the Perm researcher V. Kochev,[50] there are two possible scenarios for how this special status could be realized. The first scenario is based upon a two-layer government system, with the first layer being a state power and the second one being local self-government. This scenario is less favourable as it would lead to the unnecessary duplication of functions. The second scenario is characterized by a one-layer government system, as Komi-Permyak okrug becomes a unified municipality.

In this case the state functions would be realized at the krai level and okrug status would lose its special meaning. Moreover, the new Perm oblast governor, Oleg Chirkunov, who was then appointed the first governor of the Perm krai, only adds uncertainty to the issue of the okrug's status within the new subject of the federation because his statements imply different possible scenarios of the former okrug's status and future development within the krai.[51] Even though the law states that the okrug would form the municipal district, the manner in which it would be formed is not specified.

3. Oblast and okrug executive power effectively restricted the rights of the oblast and okrug legislatures. During the transition period neither legislature could adopt new laws or any other legal norms or initiate the process of the governor's dismissal. The okrug administration also received the right to appoint members of the okrug administration without consultation and approval from the okrug assembly. Therefore, the okrug elite was able to keep its power at least during the transition period.

4. The okrug would continue to receive both direct and special transfers directly from the federal budget in 2006, but through the Perm oblast budget in 2007–2008, until in 2009 the joint budget of Perm krai would be formed.[52]

To conclude, the negotiations were successful for the okrug and the oblast as both parties managed to gain significant benefits from support for unification. Former Perm oblast governor, Yurii Trutnev, who pushed the merger, was appointed the federal minister of natural resources at the time when the unification process had become irreversible.

Meanwhile, there is neither law nor agreement that clearly determines the scope and the content of guarantees and mechanisms for protection and further development of Komi-Permyak ethnic identity, language and culture. A series of interviews with members of the okrug administration and those working in education, including the okrug institute for the retraining of schoolteachers, conducted by the author in December 2004 and November 2005, demonstrates serious concern about the future of the Komi-Permyak language, development of ethnic culture and the practical substance of the okrug's special status within the region. The existing program on the development of inter-ethnic relations in the Perm region allows certain activities to support ethnic culture, such as regular monitoring of ethno-social problems, conducting ethnological, linguistic and folklore research in the okrug, foundation of the Institute of Language, Culture and History of Komi-Permyak People in Perm.

However, the suggested activities demonstrate that the Komi-Permyak people would be considered to be just one of the ethnic groups that live on the territory of Perm krai and they would not enjoy any special treatment compared with those other minorities (Tatars, Bashkirs and others). One may assume that the ignoring of ethnic issues in the process of unification was not accidental because the entire nationwide campaign of regional unification seems to aim at the goal of eliminating the ethnic element from Russian federalism.

Additionally, as all laws related to unification were passed with amazing speed, there was no opportunity to review them closely in order to ensure that all legislation is consistent with the Constitution and existing legal norms. As Milena Gligich-Zolotareva points out, if one considers the foundation of Perm krai as a model project that should be followed by other cases of unification, "then it is quite possible that they will sooner or later reach constitutional and legal deadlock. One should not reform federative relations on a basis that is defective from the constitutional point of view."[53] Two years after the adoption of the federal law that legally founded the new subject of the federation, it already required changes, including new mechanisms for the appointment of governors.

Indeed, the pilot unification process has not proved as flawless as the federal centre has tried to suggest. Certain commitments that were crucial at the time of the initial negotiations have still not been met. The situation of bridge construction over the Kama river clearly illustrates this argument – at the end of 2005 there was little evidence of progress in bridge construction and it is very unlikely that the project would be completed by the end of 2006 as initially agreed. The okrug's population is dissatisfied with the slow pace of changes in the economic situation and the rapid increase in the degree of uncertainty. Even okrug elites express their anxiety about the merger. Gennady Saveliev (at the time of writing still the governor of Komi-Permyak okrug) articulated these fears during Prime Minister Mikhail Fradkov's visit to the region in September 2005. As a local paper concluded, "neither for him [Saveliev] nor for the okrug's population does the unification of the two regions look very optimistic any more."[54]

Reshaping Russian federalism – federation without federalism (instead of a conclusion)

The reshaping of a federal structure in order to strengthen the central government could be a stabilizing factor in a country in transition. This option presupposes the withdrawal of some competences traditionally belonging to the federation subjects and transfer of them back to the central government. However, during the transition period, the adoption of this strategy could lead to defederalization and, more importantly, to the restoration of the authoritarian regime in one form or another. The recent political developments in Russia demonstrate that the country is undoubtedly moving in this direction.

Starting with the introduction of seven federal districts, President Putin has constantly been decreasing regional power and representation at the federal level. It is possible to specify a number of steps made in this direction:

1. Reconfiguration of the Federation Council and replacement of the heads of regional executive and legislative power by their representatives, whose legitimacy does not come from elections.
2. Foundation of the State Council that consists of governors, but is only a consultative body without any real power or possibility for effective regional representation.
3. Legal possibility of dismissing those governors who do not satisfy the political objectives of the Centre.
4. The actual appointment of governors after the Beslan tragedy in September 2004 and therefore making the Federation Council formation even more meaningful.
5. Changing the governor's role in the region, even though this new (old) role contradicts previous decisions – appointed governors should coordinate federal agencies in the regions.
6. Reshaping the territorial structure to clear space for loyal regional political leaders, dismiss undesirable regional leaders and/or allow those who remain loyal to stay in power beyond the second term.
7. Adoption of authoritarian practices in centre–region relations, including those associated with unification.
8. Redistribution of power initiatives in unification projects from the regions to the centre, from regional legislative bodies to the executive ones.

As one can see, President Putin is trying to replace federalism by the power vertical and a *de facto* unitary state. The actions being taken are minimizing the independence of regional governments and changing the system of checks and balances that usually protects federation subjects from excessive central intervention.

One of the arguments used to justify defederalization in Russia is to increase regional power accountability. However, the belief that the accountability of appointed governors towards the centre is greater than of those being elected is no more than another myth. The current appointment system has not really guaranteed changes, because a majority of governors have kept their offices. The presidential administration has a shortage of people who could be appointed to replace the governor whose personality or policy is not acceptable to the centre. The other way to replace those governors who for one reason or another do not meet federal centre expectations is to start the unification process; the case of the Kamchatka–Koryak unification is a good illustration of this approach.

Moreover, the centre is also trying to cut down regional independence and to base the level of independence not on the actual division of power, as federalism presupposes, but on the level of federal subsidies received. According to the federal representative in the Southern federal district, Dmitrii Kozak, "the level of a regions' independence should be proportional to subsidies received. The more money the federal centre gives, the less regional power there should be."[55] This view effectively leads to the establishment of temporary financial administrations. However, temporary financial administrations are no more than one form of federal intervention mechanisms, and could be seen as a redistribution of power from the regions back to the federal centre.[56]

The merger of more developed oblasts with less developed autonomous okrugs fits very well with this logic. The federal centre just shifts financial support, and therefore responsibility, for further economic development from the federal level to the regional level. The Perm oblast–Komi-Permyak autonomous okrug merger that is considered the pilot unification project is an illustration of such a switch of responsibility for regional economic development. And the Perm krai governor, Oleg Chirkunov, reconfirmed this in one of his interviews: "It is not profitable for the country to have a federation subject that is a recipient one. The country is more interested in having one donor region instead of two subjects, one of which is a recipient."[57]

It is indicative that the regional elite sees the unification project not only as something desired by the population of merging regions, but as the federal centre's business project. In this view all financial arrangements, privileges and transfers are seen as the price the federal centre pays for a more prosperous region agreeing to merge with a less developed subject.[58] Based on the Perm–Komi-Permyak unification experience, the law "On the Process of Accession to the Russian Federation and Foundation of a New Constituent Unit of the Russian Federation" was changed to ensure greater representation for both the federal centre and the regional executive power in the process; for example, a referendum on unification cannot now be held without presidential approval, as the president needs to issue a decree to start it, while the role of regional assemblies in the process of unification has significantly decreased as the governors of the merging regions are those who should put the project on the political agenda. Because governors are no longer elected, the newly introduced changes have put the regional population further away from the decision-making process that concerns their future, and made future unifications into projects exclusively for elites.

The adoption of practices of regional unification based upon elite agreements with little attention being given to the population's actual needs, the use of administrative resources to ensure hoped-for outcomes in centre–region relations, the playing of the federalism card and widely introducing mostly meaningless discussions on regional enlargement to draw people's attention from more important social reforms – all of this leads to the conclusion that Russia today is a federation without federalism.

Notes

1 Graham Smith, "Mapping the Federal Condition", Graham Smith (ed.), *Federalism: The Multiethnic Challenge* (London and New York: Longman, 1995), p. 7.
2 Peter C. Ordeshook and Olga Shvetsova, "Russia, Federalism and Political Stability", Social Science Research Council, Politics Workshop, 1995, p. 14.
3 Daniel J. Elazar (ed.), *Federal Systems of the World. A Handbook of Federal, Confederal and Autonomy Arrangements* (London: Longman, 1994), p. xv.
4 Daniel J. Elazar, "Federal Democracy in a World Beyond Authoritarianism and Totalitarianism", in Alastair McAuley (ed.), *Soviet Federalism, Nationalism and Economic Decentralization* (Leicester: Leicester University Press 1991), p. 3.
5 Ivo D. Duchacek, *The Territorial Dimension of Politics: Within, Among and Across Nations* (Boulder: Westview Press, 1986), p. 96.
6 Ibid., p. 96.
7 Alain G. Gagnon, "The Political Uses of Federalism", in Michael Burgess and Alain G. Gagnon (eds), *Comparative Federalism and Federation: Competing Traditions and Future Directions* (New York: Harvester Wheatsheaf, 1993), p. 18.
8 "The Soviet state not only passively tolerated but actively institutionalized the existence of multiple nations and nationalities as constitutive elements of the state and its citizenry". Rogers Brubaker, *Nationalism Reframed: Nationhood and the National Question in the New Europe* (Cambridge: Cambridge University Press, 1996), p. 23.
9 "Administrativno-territorial'noe Delenie Rossii XVIII-XX Vekov", *Otechestvennye zapiski*, 6, 7, 2002. http://strana-oz.ru/print.php?type=article&id=294&numid=7
10 Boris Rodoman, "Skol'ko Sub'ektov Nuzhno Federatsii?", *Otechestvennye zapiski*, 2, 17, 2004. http://strana-oz.ru/print.php?type=article&id=827&numid=17

11 This appeal was made in August 1990 as a part of Yeltsin's campaign against the power of the centre.

12 In the early twenty-first century the territorial structure of the Russian Federation has started to change. Some constituent units decided to merge through referenda, thereby decreasing the total number of subjects of the federation. This issue will be discussed later in this paper.

13 In 1994–1996 Vladimir Shumeiko was the Chairman of the Federation Council.

14 In 1991–1992 Sergei Shakhrai was the Deputy Prime Minister in charge of nationalities and regional policy; in 1993–1994 he was the minister of nationalities and regional policies.

15 Oksana Oracheva, "Rossiiskii Federalizm: Novoe v Politike Tsentra?", *Rossiiskii Regional'nyi Byulleten*, 1, 1 February 1999, pp. 5–6.

16 Mikhail Afanasev, "Chto Stoit za Initsiativami po Ukreplenyu "Vlastnoi Vertikali", *Rossiiskii Regional'nyi Byulleten*, 1, 8 March 1999, pp. 3–5.

17 Rodoman, "Skol'ko".

18 For analysis of seven federal districts, see, for example, Oksana Oracheva, "The Dilemmas of Federalism: Moscow and the Regions in the Russian Federation", in Yitzhak Brudny, Jonathan Frankel and Steffani Hoffman (eds), *Restructuring Post-Communist Russia* (Cambridge: Cambridge University Press, 2004), pp. 185–94.

19 Informatsionnyi Server "Bankfax", 25 December 2003 http://www. bankfax.ru/page.php?pg=22523.

20 "Polpred Odobryaet Ukrupnenie Regionov", *Moi Gorod*, 12 May 2005. http://www.moigorod.ru/news/details.asp?n=2146370999.

21 Aleksei Makarkin, "Polpred Klebanov Uvleksya Ideei Ukrupneniya Regionov", *Novyi Region* 25 August 2005. http://www.nr2.ru/policy/36707.html.

22 Makarkin, "Polpred Klebanov".

23 The history of this merger is very illustrative and will be analysed later in this chapter.

24 See, for example, "Kirienko ne khochet ob'edineniya Regionov", *Sekretnye materialy Rossii*. http://www.informacia.ru/2005/news715.htm.

25 Fond Obshchestvennoe Mnenie, 14 November 2003. http://www.fom.ru/topics/195.html.

26 Marina Shumilova, "Ukrupnenie regionov stanovitsya real'nost'yu nashei politicheskoi zhizni", *Bashinoform*, 19 October 2004. http://www.bashinform.ru/index.php?id=17590.

27 Brubaker, *Nationalism Reframed*, p. 23.

28 "Etnicheskie aspekty federalizma. Kruglyi Stol", *Fond Liberal'naya Missiya* 20 August 2003. http://www.liberal.ru/sitan.asp?Num=395.

29 "Ukrupnenie Regionov – Uravnenie s dvumya neizvestnymi: N Regionov cherez N Let?" *Rosbalt* 22 June 2004. http://www.rosbalt.ru/2004/9/24/167215.html.

30 *Severnyi Kurier*, 29 November 2002. http://kurier.karelia.ru/archive/issue213/politica/view4206.html.

31 "Velikoi Karelii ne ozhidaetsya", *Kurier Karelii*, 6 July 2005. http://petrozavodsk.ru/news/view.html?id=232919.

32 Expert opinion of Nataliya Zubarevich, 23 June 2004. http://kreml. org/opinions/58509825?user_session=e63cef80bb86255448778c99d0c03240.

33 "Ukrupnenie regionov sozdast ne 'Vertikal Vlasti, a Gorizontal Zapustenia' – Mnenie Pskovskogo analitika", *Regnum* 3 June 2003. http://www.regnum.ru/news/122376.html.
34 "Tri chetverti protiv", *UralPolit.Ru*. 25 May 2004. http://www.uralpolit.ru/tumen/?art = 4258.
35 "Ustav Komi-Permyatskogo avtonomnogo okruga" (Charter of Komi-Permyak autonomous okrug). Adopted 19 December 1994. Chapter 1. http://www.legislature.ru/ruconst/komiperm.html#1.
36 Ustav Komi-Permyatskogo avtomnogo okruga.
37 Ustav Permskoi oblasti (Charter of Perm region). Adopted 6 October 1994. Chapter 1. http://parlament.perm.ru/laws/ustav.html.
38 Ustav Permskoi oblasti.
39 Ustav Permskoi oblasti.
40 Zakon "Ob Administrativno-territorialnom delenii Permskoi oblasti". Adopted on 22 February 1996. Changed on 7 May 1997. http://www. permreg.ru/region/laws/?document=42.
41 "Dogovor o razgranichenii predmetov vvedeniya v polnomochii mezhdu organami gosudarstvennoi vlasti Rossiiskoi Federatsii i organami gosudarstvennoi vlasti Permskoi oblasti v organami gosudarstvennoi vlasti Komi-Permyatskogo avtonomnogo okruga ot 31 maya 1996 g.", *Rossiiskie vesti* 25 July 1996.
42 I quote the English translation of the Russian 1993 Constitution, Richard Sakwa, *Russian Politics and Society* (London: Routledge, 1996), pp. 395–429.
43 "O poryadke prinyatiya v Rossiiskuyu Federatsiyu i obrazovaniya v ee sostave novogo sub'ekta Rossiiskoi Federatsii", 17 December 2001. http://vff-s.narod.ru/fz/kz/01_06.html.
44 Valerii Tsygankov, "V Permskii krai zamanivayut rublem", *Nezavisimaya gazeta*, 27 June 2003.
45 *Rossiiskaya Gazeta*, 9 December 2003.
46 *Radio Svoboda*, 22 November 2003. http://www.svoboda.org/programs/CH/2003/CH.112203.asp.
47 "Pravozashchitniki zhdut ot vlastei publichnogo vystuplenia", http://www.prpc.ru/actual/komi/nw031203.shtml.
48 "Prognoz sotsial'no-ekonomicheskih posledstvii ob'edineniya Permskoi oblasti i Komi-Permyatskogo avtonomnogo okruga. 15 February 2003. http://krai.perm.ru/doc/doc_03_06_13.asp.
49 See, for example, http://rvs.perm.ru/numbers/3_04/3_sav.htm.
50 V.A. Kochev, "Obrazovanie novogo sub'ekta RF – Permskogo kraya: Pravovye aspekty", in L.A. Fadeeva (ed.), *Politicheskii al'manakh prikamia* (Perm: Izdatel'stvo "pushka", 2005), pp. 228–41.
51 See, for example, Oleg Chirkunov, "Mogu pozvolit sebe roskosh govotit pravdu", *Novyi Kompanion*, 2 August 2004. http://www.krai.perm.ru/pressa.asp?id = 666.
52 For more details, see the federal law "On Foundation of A New Subject in the Russian Federation As a Result of Unification of Perm Region and Komi-Permyak Autonomous Okrug". Adopted on 24, March 2004 and changed on 5 July 2005.
53 Milena Gligich-Zolotareva, "Novye tendentsii zakonotvorchestva v sovremennoi Rossii", *Kazanskii Federalist* 2, 10, Spring 2004. http:// www.kazanfed.ru/publications/kazanfederalist/n10/4/.

54 *Gorodskaya Gazeta*, 27 September 2005. http://www.berezniki.ru/topic/gorod/050927_4/print.
55 *Izvestiya*, 20 July 2005.
56 For legal analysis of temporary financial administrations, see, for example, Gligich-Zolotareva (Novye Tendentsii). http://www.kazanfed.ru/publications/kazanfederalist/n10/4/.
57 Chirkunov, "Mogu pozvolit", http://www.krai.perm.ru/ pressa. asp?id=666.
58 See, for example, interview with Oleg Chirkunov. http://www.finmarket.ru/z/nws/hnews.asp?id=311426&hot=420909.

3
Collaborative or Hegemonic? Tatarstan and Conflicting Visions of Federalism in Putin's Russia[1]

David Cashaback

In this chapter, I examine the developments in federalism in the context of Vladimir Putin's federal reforms. These represent a move away from the practice of asymmetrical negotiated federalism in favour of a centralizing interpretation of the 1993 Constitution. In other words, the objective was to settle many of the ambiguities and unsettled questions – for instance, asymmetries and contradictions between federal and regional laws and constitutions – and reassert the primacy of the Constitution and federal control. *A priori*, therefore, these reforms appear to target Tatarstan's differentiated status. Analysis of the nature of Putin's reforms and their implementation in Tatarstan provide a window on how Tatarstan's claims for recognition and jurisdiction have fared. Although republican elites continue to advocate a different model of federalism based less on federal control or hegemony and more on regional autonomy, they complied with many of Putin's reforms. Constitutional changes in Tatarstan acknowledge the republic's place within Russia, and, increasingly, its leaders argue that Russia needs more, not less, federalism. The shift is significant – although Tatarstan continues to advocate a different model of federalism, it does so within the context of Russia's changed presidential politics and how this impacts on federal design. That is not to say that Tatarstan has abandoned its claims for recognition and jurisdiction. The 1994 bilateral treaty, although stripped of many of its operative and power-sharing provisions, continues to perform important political functions. The importance which Tatarstan's elites continue to attach to the treaty and to the model of cooperative federalism it embodies is intact: the treaty serves as a reminder of what federalism was and could be in the Russian Federation.

The chapter is organized as follows. First, I examine Putin's institutional changes to Russia's federal design, the federal government's conception of the division of competences, and key Constitutional Court rulings on the status of republics. Second, I analyse the counterview of the division of powers and federal design proposed by Shaimiev and turn to the way in which Putin's reforms were implemented in Tatarstan. Finally, I assess the role of Tatarstan's bilateral treaty in the current context.

Putin's federal reforms[2]

Putin shows a keen awareness of the abuses of power that resulted from negotiated federalism and the lack of federal control over Russia's regions. For Kahn, Putin's reforms " ... were, more than anything else, a reaction to Yeltsin's federal legacy of weak institutions and lack of consensus on basic questions of sovereignty and inter-governmental relations in a federal state".[3] Upon acquiring power in 2000, Putin set out to re-establish a "power vertical" in the federal system, roll back the asymmetry which had come to characterize the system and restore federal–regional relations on the basis of the 1993 Constitution. Of particular concern was the legislative and constitutional dissonance which existed between federal and regional governments. In 2000, Russia's Prosecutor General reported that 70 per cent of regional legislative acts deviated from federal legislation, and 34 per cent contradicted the federal constitution.[4] According to the Russian Ministry of Justice, 18 of twenty-one republican constitutions, and a third of 16,000 laws it examined contradicted federal law.[5] The reforms Putin carried out were not new, but had been discussed since 1996. Whereas Yeltsin's attempts at federal reform had been ignored, Putin followed up on his promises for change and implemented concrete reforms from the very start of his term.[6] Putin's annual address to the Federal Assembly in July 2000 unveiled the strategic direction as well as the famous formula, "dictatorship of the law". Putin voiced much concern on the question of the effectiveness of the state: indecision and weakness of state structures reduced policy and governance capacity. The time had come to bridge the regional "islets of power" and reassert central power.[7] Regional autonomy was seen to have taken the upper hand and created situations in which "centrifugal forces had gained such momentum that they were threatening [to destroy] the state itself".[8] Putin criticized the lack of transparency of bilateral treaties, arguing that under Yeltsin they were concluded "behind the backs of constituent units of the Federation" and "without any preliminary discussion and the securing of a public consensus".[9] Putin does not condemn the principle of treaty-making, conceding it was a way of responding to the political exigencies of the 1990s, and could be a means to accommodate regional specificities.

But he stressed the need to "precisely determine where the powers of the federal bodies should be and where the powers of the subjects of the Federation [should be]".[10] In sum, Putin's objective was to consolidate the central government's power, strengthen its capacity to control the implementation of law and policy throughout the country and re-impose the authority of the federal constitution.

The most sustained push for reforms occurred between 2000 and 2002, a time when most of the institutional changes were implemented. Between 2002 and 2004, federal reform as a topic of discussion all but disappeared from the centre's rhetoric, which was increasingly focused on administrative reform.[11] A renewed interest in federal reforms was sparked in late 2004 when the president abolished direct elections for regional leaders and again in 2005 with an announcement of the government's intention to roll-back some of its earlier reforms and amend the division of competences.

Institutional changes to Russian federalism

Putin adopted a number of reforms to increase the federal government's monitoring and control capacity. The first reform aggregated the monitoring function, which already existed under Yeltsin. The previous system, under which a plenipotentiary representative (PR) was appointed in each federal subject to monitor political, social and economic conditions and represent federal interests, was seen as unwieldy because of the large number of representatives and their lack of resources: the federal envoy often depended on the regional government for resources, thus compromising his authority.[12] Putin's reform reorganized the federation into seven umbrella administrative regions (federal districts) headed by an appointed plenipotentiary representative subordinate to the head of the Presidential Administration.[13] In so doing, Putin sought to remove the influence of regional leaders on the activities of the representatives and explained that the territorial aggregation of this monitoring function was not a federal or a constitutional but a "managerial reform" designed to facilitate the implementation of a unified legal space.[14] In practice, an envoy's effectiveness has depended on his particular personality, interests, ability and relationships.[15] Reddaway and Orttung conclude that the reform has successfully depersonalized the relations between the president and most governors, except for relations with the leaders of Tatarstan, Bashkortostan and St Petersburg.[16] For instance, within the Volga Federal District Tatarstan continues to take political issues up directly with Moscow, circumventing the office of the PR.[17] As I will show below, inter-elite relations continue to be the norm in the management of the Russia–Tatarstan relationship.

In a further effort to remove regional leaders from direct access to the levers of power in Moscow, a July 2000 law modified the composition of the Federation Council.[18] Since 1995, leaders of regional executive and legislative branches sat in the upper chamber on an *ex officio* basis, providing regional leaders with significant presence and influence at the centre. The new law directs regional legislative and executive branches to select one representative each to sit in the Federation Council. Not surprisingly, regional leaders reacted strongly to the proposal and vetoed it. To secure passage of the bill, amendments were proposed to allow governors to keep their seats until their own terms expired, and ensure that the terms of incoming representatives were identical to the terms of the bodies which appointed them.[19] Federation Council reform is considered to have produced dubious results. According to Gel'man, in many cases regional governments appointed Moscow-based lobbyists and business elites who maintain informal relationships with the Kremlin and who can wield their influence behind the scenes. A significant proportion of regional representatives have little or no connection to the region they represent. In some cases, governors appoint potential rivals to the Federation Council to minimize their influence on decision-making within their region and to strengthen their own grip on the domestic political scenes.[20]

To compensate them for their removal from the Federation Council, Putin created the State Council, an intergovernmental forum where leaders of all 89 subjects meet on a quarterly basis. The body's presidium comprises the president and seven regional leaders, one per district, appointed for a six-month term.[21] Although the body is consultative, its aim is to promote the participation of regional leaders in the "preparation and passing of important national decisions."[22] In its first five years, the State Council convened 15 times, its presidium held forty-five meetings. Speaking on the occasion of the Council's fifth anniversary in Kazan, Putin concluded it evolved into "one of the most influential political institutions in the country" and constitutes an "extended government, able to find national solutions and approaches to complex problems."[23] At the same session, regional leaders echoed Putin's positive appraisal, even though the institution had been greeted with scepticism in 2000. For Shaimiev, it plays "a useful and productive role". Luzhkov suggests the Council is the perfect forum to give regional leaders a more substantial role in the consideration of the federal budget.[24] The Council has become a key institution for discussion of federal–regional concerns (sessions on topics as diverse as housing, federal design, education policy and national security have been held). Although it is only a consultative body, it nevertheless performs the function of intergovernmental representation of regional interests.

Following the terrorist attack in Beslan in September 2004, Putin acted quickly to abolish elections for leaders of regional governments. The rationale for the change was a need for stronger executive control: "The bodies of executive authority in the centre and in the subjects of the Russian Federation [...] must work as a single integrated organism with a clear structure of subordination. Until now, such a system has not been put in place".[25] Shaimiev backed the reform guardedly, conceding Putin's rationale: "In many regions the people who come to power do so as protégés of capital or on the basis of populism", which hinders the ability of "the people at the helm [to] actually steer".[26] Putin convened the State Council for closed-door sessions on the proposed reforms. Unsurprisingly, little dissent was voiced publicly by leaders for whom loyalty to the Russian president would become a job requirement. Thus, many approved the proposals, including Moscow mayor Luzhkov and St Petersburg mayor Valentina Matvienko and argued that the reform would provide the federal government with the ability to instil discipline at the regional level and provide regional leaders with levers with which to govern.[27] Amendments were brought to the 1999 law on the bodies of state power to give the president the power to appoint regional leaders,[28] and a decree was issued to refine the administrative procedure: presidential envoys select a candidate "in consultation" with regional leaders, civil society groups and public organizations for the president's approval.[29] Once nominated, the regional assembly must confirm the choice. If the nominee is refused twice, the president is empowered to dissolve the assembly.[30]

Although Tatarstan's State Council approved Putin's proposals by 57 votes to 19, at the United Russia party conference in November 2004 members from Tatarstan were outspoken in their criticism of Putin's proposals and suggested that the dissolution of regional assemblies be prohibited and a sunset clause be included in the law.[31] Shaimiev was supportive of the decision to appoint regional leaders, but strongly criticized the power Putin gained to dissolve regional assemblies that vetoed his choice: "Under no circumstances can we agree with [those provisions]. The people elect Parliament, thus it is the voice of the people."[32] In the meantime, many regional leaders, including Shaimiev, circumvented the procedures established by Putin's December 2004 decree by appealing directly to the Russian president to renominate them. Shaimiev reported that Putin asked him to accept a fourth term as president because the "price of stability in a republic like Tatarstan is too high."[33] Consequently, Shaimiev submitted his pre-term resignation, was nominated by Putin and confirmed by the Tatarstan State Council on 25 March 2005. Simultaneously, Tatarstan's constitution was amended to suspend (not annul) the clauses on the election of Tatarstan's president. Both Shaimiev and Farid Mukhametshin, speaker of Tatarstan's State Council, justified the move to suspend rather than rescind the clauses by saying they believed the suspension of elections is only temporary and the reinstatement of direct elections is "merely a question of time".[34] Many incumbent governors have been reappointed and so far no nominations have been blocked by regional assemblies. While it is too early to assess the consequences of this reform, analysts fear the anti-federal tendencies of the change and the potential for conflict it creates should regional assemblies start to reject presidential nominees.[35] By increasing Moscow's control over regional leadership, it will likely make it difficult to isolate the centre from future policy failures. Consequently, the reform could focus future discontent on the federal government, rather than diffusing it between it and the regions.

In addition to the changes affecting the place of regional leaders, Putin strengthened the federal government's ability to combat contradictions in legislation, dubbed "separatism in the legal sphere". The 1993 Constitution designates the president as guarantor of the federal Constitution (art.80§2) and grants him the right to suspend legislative acts which contradict federal law or the Constitution (art.85§2). The 1999 law on the bodies of state power was amended to give the president the power to dismiss regional leaders or parliaments who enact or fail to rescind contradictory legislation. However, this power is not discretionary as the courts have ruled that courts of three jurisdictions must concur that regional legislation is delinquent before the president can invoke the procedure. In 2000, a key tool was created in the struggle against legislative dissonance: the Federal Registry of Legal Normative Acts. All subjects of the federation are required to forward their normative legal acts to the federal Ministry of Justice for assessment.[36] The purpose of the Registry is further defined in a government resolution: it "controls the correspondence of normative legal acts of subjects of the federation with the constitution of Russia and federal laws" and creates the "means to obtain information about the normative legal acts of subjects of the federation".[37] Thus, in addition to fostering more transparency, the registry creates a material and institutional basis for the systematic analysis of the correspondence of regional and federal laws.[38]

Re-imposing federal supremacy in the division of powers

Following his 2001 Annual Address, Putin appointed a "Presidential Commission for the Demarcation of Powers Between the Federal, Regional and Municipal Levels of Government", naming a former colleague from the administration of St Petersburg and trusted deputy, Dmitrii Kozak (then the deputy head of the Presidential Administration, now the Presidential Representative to the Southern Federal District), to direct its work. Kozak's Commission would eventually regroup the State Council working group headed by Shaimiev and Luzhkov's working group on state system reforms. The Commission's report, *Concept of Federal Reforms*, was presented to the State Council and regional leaders in early 2002. The Concept calls for a better division of powers in areas of joint competences to ensure tasks are executed and financed properly, and an increase in the centre's capacity to assess and control regional policy implementation. Kozak's model makes the federal government responsible for setting national standards, while regional governments are held responsible for the execution of policy. In such a system, bilateral power-sharing would be used only in exceptional circumstances to take into account "geographic or other particularities."[39] In the wake of the report, two laws were enacted. Approved in July 2003, the law "Amendments to the Federal Law On General Principles of the Organization of Legislative and Executive Bodies of State Power of the Subjects of the Russian Federation" proposes a clear delimitation of federal–regional competences and circumscribes the use of treaties. "On General Principles of Local Self-Government in the Russian Federation" was adopted in October in order to promote the economic and policy capacities of municipal government. Although both laws were the subject of intense scrutiny by Duma committees, the fundamental principles of Kozak's vision emerged unscathed.

Whereas issues of jurisdiction and accountability were left unanswered in Putin's previous reform initiatives, these laws establish a balance of interests and powers between orders of government and resolve ambiguities and unfunded mandates so "power becomes accountable to its citizens."[40] A key element in both laws is the reassertion of the supremacy of federal law and the federal Constitution. In areas of joint jurisdiction, the laws enumerate the tasks which will be controlled by Moscow and those to be funded and executed by the subjects of the federation and by municipal governments. A higher-level government is empowered to set policy objectives and charge lower-level governments with their implementation. In an attempt to eliminate the problem of unfunded mandates, the law forbids the delegation of powers to another level of government without an accompanying budgetary envelope, and empowers the delegating body to sanction or suspend leaders who misuse funds earmarked for a specific purpose.[41]

Article 267 of the Law on the bodies of state power addresses bilateral intergovernmental agreements. Bilateral treaties can be pursued in exceptional circumstances, to accommodate the "economic, geographic or other peculiarities" of subjects of the federation. Ethnicity appears to have been downgraded as a reason to pursue bilateral power-sharing since the earlier (1999) version of the law listed ethnicity as a motive. In addition, the law adds several requirements, purportedly to increase the transparency of the process, the consequences of which would make concluding treaties increasingly difficult. First, all subjects of the federation have a right to consult and comment on draft treaties (art.267§5). Second, a treaty must be approved by both the federal and regional parliaments (art.267§4 and §8). Efforts to make the process more transparent and institutionalized may reduce its effectiveness. Since the law foresees treaties to be used to address regional particularities and entrench some degree of asymmetry, by requiring the approval of parliament, the law creates the potential for increased federal–regional conflict. The effectiveness of bilateral agreements is potentially reduced as a coping mechanism. Since all remaining treaties needed to be ratified by the Federal Assembly before July 2005, the law has effectively rendered them moot as operative documents.

Two years after the Kozak reforms effectively withdrew policy-making capacity in areas of joint jurisdiction, Putin announced during a State Council session in Kaliningrad on 2 July 2005 that powers would be handed back to regions. One hundred and fourteen competences will be handed back "to change the quality of the work of regional bodies and raise their role and accountability in the socio-economic sphere."[42] "The delegation of additional powers to regions [...] is not the result of some administrative itch (*zud*)" but designed to promote more effective economic policy.[43] The president did not specify which powers would be transferred to the regions at this meeting, although it has been reported they include forestry management, veterinary services, the protection of historical monuments, science, education, housing, etc.[44] When the State Council reconvened in Kazan on 26 August 2005, Putin confirmed a law was being drafted to ratify the changes announced in Kaliningrad.[45] One competence he immediately handed over to regional leaders was the power to select the directors of federal agencies (of the Ministry of Justice, civil affairs, internal affairs, etc.) in the regions.[46]

Rostislav Turovsky believes the announcements reflect a realization by Moscow that the strict power vertical does not sufficiently insulate it from unpopular decisions. For instance, the protests which occurred in many regions in response to changes in social benefits and housing policies demonstrated the centre's vulnerability.[47] Now that regional leaders are federal appointees, Moscow is more comfortable delegating power back to regions, knowing it possesses greater control over those exercising it. Moreover, although the law is forthcoming, Putin has made clear his conception of how the powers are to be exercised: " ... competence, in the first instance, means responsibility. The federal centre will carefully observe how it is used."[48] It is not a reform aimed at increasing regional policy autonomy, since it is not "competences" but "duties" or "obligations" (obyazannost') that are to be delegated. Indeed, these reforms appear to be more about presidential power than about federalism.

Court interpretations of republican status

At the same time as Putin adopted measures aimed at strengthening the centre's hand in its relations with regional governments, the Russian Constitutional Court (KSRF) handed down landmark rulings in June 2000 which asserted the supremacy of the federal Constitution and provided the impetus for bringing republics' constitutions in line with it. While the Court issued rulings in the 1990s which already confirmed the supremacy of federal legislation in matters of joint competence (especially its rulings on the fundamentals of the tax system (1997) and on the Forestry Code (1998)), the June 2000 rulings took aim at the most fundamental of republics' claims: that they constitute sovereign entities within Russia.

The 7 June 2000 ruling annulled provisions of Altai's constitution which defined the republic as sovereign, possessor of its natural resources and subject of international law. In addition, the Court rejected the republic's claims that its status was based on a bilateral treaty with Russia. Sovereignty, the Court ruled, is an attribute of the Russian people as a whole, and indivisible: "The Russian Constitution does not allow any other bearer of sovereignty or source of power besides the multinational people of Russia".[49] Moreover, the Court reasserted the equality of all subjects of the federation, and the supremacy of the federal Constitution and laws: neither the 1992 Federal Treaty nor any bilateral treaty trumps the provisions of the 1993 constitution.

On request from a group of State Duma deputies who challenged the constitutions of several republics, including Tatarstan's, the Court issued a Determination on 27 June 2000. Based on the 7 June ruling as well as its 1992 opinion on Tatarstan's referendum on state sovereignty, the Court concluded that "Sovereignty [...], the supremacy and independence of state power, the entirety of legislative, executive and judicial power on its territory and independence in international relations constitute essential characteristics of the Russian Federation as a state."[50] Sovereignty is indivisible: only Russia may sign international treaties and republics cannot claim to be subjects of international law or sovereign states. Tatarstan's claim to be "united" with Russia constitutes an "unconstitutional modification of its constitutional status."[51] Moreover, the republic cannot claim possession of natural resources or any other competences which contradict the division of competences established by the federal Constitution. In April 2001, Volga District presidential envoy Sergei Kirienko complained that republics had not amended their constitutions to reflect the Court's rulings. The Constitutional Court answered with a clarification, stating any constitutional provision deemed to be unconstitutional is inoperative and that its rulings apply to all federal subjects.[52]

The June 2000 rulings did not break new ground. The Court had already ruled, in its 1992 decision on Tatarstan's referendum, that republics could not make changes to their constitutional status.[53] The rulings did, however, remove any remaining ambiguities regarding republics' claims to be sovereign entities: only Russia can claim sovereignty. Moreover, claims that republics possess special status, or, in the case of Tatarstan, that it is "united with Russia" are unconstitutional. One major difference with the Court's previous rulings on the federal structure was the impetus they provided to bring regional legislation, and especially republics' laws and constitutions, in line with federal law. While previous rulings had been ignored, in the context of Putin's Russia, they signalled the beginning of campaigns by federal prosecutors to rid regional law books of contradictory provisions in their effort to establish legislative and constitutional coherence.

Visions of federalism in Putin's Russia

Putin's institutional reforms, taken with the Constitutional Court's rulings, provide an impression of the centre's vision of federal design and federalism. Foremost, federalism is about symmetry in the federal government's relations with the subjects of the federation, and between the subjects themselves. The Constitutional Court rejected an interpretation of the Constitution that allowed subjects of the federation to possess sovereignty, even in areas of exclusive regional competence. Effectiveness and political stability are conceived as emanating from a strong and unified system of executive governance and, I would add, dominance. Indeed, the Kozak reforms reflect a view of the division of competences as hegemonic, aiming less at protecting regional autonomy than providing measures for federal control over implementation of policy in Russia's regions. "The division of powers", Putin explained, "is not like a Chinese wall between centre and regions."[54] Similarly, Putin's federal reforms minimize the role of power-sharing or shared sovereignty because this "aggravates the problem of inequality" among subjects of the federation and between them and the federal government.[55] Reforms of federal design under Putin question the extent to which Russia still constitutes a federal political system. Presidential control over the appointment of regional leaders further cements Moscow's control and the view that regions are executors rather than initiators of policy. Federal reforms consolidate a model of hegemonic federalism – with tendencies toward centralized authoritarianism – which emphasizes central control over regional autonomy or self-rule.

To get a better idea of the way in which this vision of federalism has been implemented in Russia, I turn to examine how these reforms were received and acted upon in Tatarstan. Tatarstan's political elite, while complying with many of these reforms, continue to articulate a different vision of federalism. The areas of continued disagreement – Tatarstan's persistent claim to sovereignty and its call for jurisdictional autonomy – are a useful foil to grasp the extent to which consensus has been achieved over federal design.

Tatarstan's competing vision of federalism: collaborative versus hegemonic

The reaction in Tatarstan to Putin's various initiatives was a mixture of public opposition and agreement. It was clear that the balance of power shifted in favour of the centre once Putin gained power. Shaimiev welcomed Putin's efforts to create a single legal space in Russia and supported, if sometimes only tacitly, the Russian president's reform programme. For Shaimiev, legal dissonance and contradictions which emerged during the 1990s needed to be clarified, but in a different way than Kozak would eventually suggest:

> We adopted a lot of different laws to reach some definite political and economic goals in a short period. We've done a lot, now it's time to fix this mess. It's necessary to make a clear division of [competences], what belongs to the centre and what to the subjects of the federation, without interfering with each other's exclusive powers.[56]

In 2001, Putin appointed Shaimiev to direct a State Council working group on the division of powers, which was subsequently folded into Kozak's working group on federal reforms. Regional leaders and republics were not shut out of the reform process, even if the resulting laws did not please all participants. As Lankina notes, regional support for the law on the division of powers was secured by giving them a voice in the process. Moreover, in exchange for their support of the law on municipal government, governors obtained powers to select or remove municipal leaders and control over municipal spending.[57] Although Shaimiev criticized provisions of the Kozak report and of the laws which emerged from it, in the end he complied while underlining that Tatarstan possessed a different conception of federalism. This has become Tatarstan's principal reaction to Putin's federal reforms: they are criticized but endorsed with the leadership making it clear it remains committed to an alternate conception of federalism.

One of the main objectives of Shaimiev's working group was to correct the imbalance in the distribution of competences in the federal Constitution. For Tatarstan's president, the division of competences in the 1993 Constitution permits federal control by stealth: since federal law in areas of shared jurisdiction is supreme, subjects of the federation are reduced to the execution rather than elaboration of policy.[58] As I showed above, this is the view entrenched in Kozak's reform bills, and it is the way in which Russia's courts interpret regional laws which diverge from federal legislation on matters of joint jurisdiction.

What Putin called "separatism in the legal sphere", Shaimiev sees as a sign that the federal principle needs to be better implemented in Russia. The working group's report, the "Draft Concept of State Policy on the Division of Competences and Powers between Federal, Regional and Municipal Bodies" (hereafter Concept), proposes a model of federal design in which the centre would legislate to establish strategic orientations while giving regional government more latitude to implement the law according to local needs and particularities. The Concept outlines the lacunae in Russia's federalism: there are too many shared competences, each level of government's respective rights and obligations are not well demarcated, and Moscow interferes too much in regional and shared jurisdictions.[59] Furthermore, the Constitution does not define the terms it uses to denote each government's powers and obligations. The report objects to the wide interpretation which the centre has given of its right to establish "general principles" in areas of joint jurisdiction in order to shut out regional governments from legislating in these areas.[60] In their rulings on issues of joint competence, Russia's courts have tended to adopt similarly broad interpretations.

The Concept outlines a number of reforms to Russia's federal design. These fall into three categories: the need for a model of cooperative federalism; a clearer division of powers; and the use of treaty relations. First, it establishes a wholly different normative vision of federalism. It argues federalism must be viewed as both an institutional structure (*ustroistvo*) and a principle of political behaviour; as providing the means for self- and shared-rule.[61] In this sense, cooperative federalism is contrasted to the existing model and practice of hegemonic federalism in Russia. Under a model of cooperative federalism, shared sovereignty is possible, as is increased cooperation in fields of joint jurisdiction. The purpose of such a change of vision is to "promote better relations between the central and regional governments" and "increased respect for and support of the political, cultural and national diversities of Russian society."[62] Regional autonomy, therefore, is a key component of this vision.

Second, the implementation of a model of cooperative federalism must begin with a reform of the division of competences. Constitutional competence implies a right to make policy and obligation to carry it out. This is the same principle which guided the work of Kozak's working group and the State Council's sessions in July and August 2005 on the division of powers. However, the Kozak reforms did not reorganize the constitutional division of powers, but provided detailed lists of which level of government was responsible for financing and implementing given tasks. As I discussed above, these reforms emphasize compliance over autonomy. Mukhametshin indicates that 300 federal laws exist in areas of joint jurisdiction, and few provide clear direction on the rights and obligations of each level of government.[63] Tatarstan's leaders argued federal laws in areas of joint and regional jurisdiction should also be subject to review and that harmonization of conflicting legislation should not only be a top-down phenomenon. Shaimiev's Concept calls for federal law-makers to be more attuned to regional legislative and policy approaches and create more room for regional and municipal governments to tailor legislative initiatives to their specific needs and goals.[64] Three levels of competence are envisioned: strategic (federal), territorial (regional) and local (municipal). Russia would keep its power to set national objectives, but the other levels of government would gain more latitude to determine how these objectives should be implemented.[65] In this Concept, "subsidiarity", defined as giving competence to the level of government most suited to carry it out, should trump hierarchy and verticality.[66] It provides no detail on how such a system would be implemented or how it would operate. While subsidiarity is advanced as being more dynamic and cooperative, in a federation of 89 members one wonders how workable it would be. The report argues that Russia's Constitution already contains many of the mechanisms that could facilitate a transition to cooperative federalism, such as article 11 which foresees the use of bilateral agreements.[67]

Third, bilateral treaties are given an important role in this model of cooperative federalism. The Concept rejects the way in which treaties were used under Yeltsin. Treaties in the 1990s often contained unconstitutional provisions and delegated exclusive federal or joint powers to regional governments. Shaimiev's report makes it clear that treaties should not establish "treaty-constitutional" relations or contravene the Constitution. They should be used as tools to determine priorities in the regulation of joint competences, take regional concerns into account or help resolve conflicts between central and regional governments.[68]

Shaimiev's Concept was presented to the State Council Presidium on 26 December 2000. Although its contents were controversial, the Presidium approved and recommended it be brought to the attention of the full State Council.[69] But the report was never scheduled for consideration.[70] It received minimal coverage in the republican press, apart from *Zvezda Povolzh'ya* which published an excerpt and the journal *Kazanskii federalist* which published the report verbatim. Shaimiev defended his vision, arguing that "Russia's power and strength reside in the strength and independence of its regions" and that stability "can only be ensured by diversity and not blind unification."[71] For Dmitrii Kozak, the implementation of the report's provisions "would lead to the destruction of the unity of the country's legal system [...] and to separatism among Russia's well-off regions."[72] This assessment was echoed by State Duma members whom the Kremlin appointed to consider the report.[73] The Kremlin's dissatisfaction with Shaimiev's Concept prompted Putin to appoint Kozak to head a separate working group on the division of powers, into which Shaimiev's working group was incorporated.

Although little came of Shaimiev's report, I focus on it because of the alternate vision of federalism it articulates. Two features are remarkable. First, it does not call for outright constitutional reform. Although its implementation would significantly change the way federalism is practised in Russia, Shaimiev illustrates that on paper the 1993 Constitution already provides a basis for cooperative federalism. Second, the Concept does not challenge the federal government's role to legislate on matters of state importance or to set state-wide approaches. Instead it argues that in areas of joint jurisdiction, more attention needs to be paid to regional specificities. Thus, although the report itself reads like a series of idealistic proposals, its principles inform many of Tatarstan's arguments on the changes required to Russia's federal design. This belief in the value of a more cooperative federalism sheds light on the way in which Tatarstan implemented Putin's federal reforms, and on the nature of its persistent claims for recognition and jurisdiction.

Reacting to Putin's federalism: legislative harmonization

At the same time as Shaimiev's working group drafted its concept of federal design, Tatarstan's leadership began implementing Putin's federal reforms.

A Commission was created under the aegis of the Volga district presidential envoy, Sergei Kirienko, to bring Tatarstan's legislation in line with the Russian Constitution.[74] Kirienko sought to clarify that the law, not personalities, was to guide the process: "It is not the personal relations of Sergei Kirienko and Mintimer Shaimiev that count in this case, it is the necessity of the unification process ... Conciliation commissions must not rely on any other documents than the two constitutions."[75] The Commission's inaugural meeting classified 45 laws as constituting "political conflicts", linked to competences which Tatarstan claimed had been delegated by the 1994 treaty, including property and natural resource rights.[76] Mukhametshin argued that since Tatarstan had assented to neither the Federal Treaty nor the 1993 Constitution, the bilateral treaty was the only link between Moscow and Kazan and its provisions needed to be respected. Since the contradictions were "political, not juridical" they needed to be discussed by Putin and Shaimiev instead of the conciliation committees.[77] Shaimiev reported that he had taken up these "political conflicts" with Putin and that the Russian president agreed that the harmonization committees needed to take the treaty's provisions into account.[78] Thus, contrary to Kirienko's wishes, nontransparent executive negotiations appear to have informed the harmonization process. Notwithstanding Putin's attempts to depersonalize federal–regional relations, it is clear that inter-elite negotiation and mediation have retained their importance as mechanisms of accommodation.

Federal prosecutors, however, were indifferent to the nuance between political and juridical contradictions. Soon after the Constitutional Court's June 2000 rulings, Russian Deputy Prosecutor General Alexander Zvyagintsev challenged 20 republican laws including the constitution because they placed "[Tatarstan's] legal system outside the federal legal system."[79] On orders from Russia's Prosecutor General, Tatarstan's own prosecutor also issued challenges. The Tatarstan State Council's Permanent Commission on Legislation began considering prosecutors' protests in late 2000. Results were immediately apparent. Chief Federal Inspector in Tatarstan, Marsel Galimardanov, reported that as of January 2001, 89 of 115 documents challenged had been harmonized with federal law.[80] In his year-end summary of the State Council's activities, Mukhametshin calculated that the parliament spent a majority of its 2001 session dealing with harmonization.[81] In 2001, prosecutors challenged 73 laws, 31 of which were amended and 17 rescinded. Of 37 protests that went to court, Tatarstan won only three cases.[82] The Federal Registry of normative acts still lists Tatarstan as the biggest offender among Russia's federal subjects: as of 31 December 2004, 19 acts (or 20 per cent of total state-wide) were found to contradict federal law. Ninety-two laws contain provisions which violate federal law.[83] What explains the persistence of legal dissonance?

During the harmonization process, Tatarstan's Prosecutor, Kafil Amirov, reported that a number of republican laws were "more progressive" than Moscow's.[84] But the Federal Registry does not include federal laws and these are not subject to similar assessment by the Ministry of Justice. Consequently, State Council deputies protested the double-standard and claimed federal laws should be held to the same standard. In fact, deputies found at least twenty federal laws that violated the federal Constitution but were told federal prosecutors are not empowered to protest federal laws.[85] In a speech given in Kazan, Yurii Chaika, Russia's Minister of Justice, stated that "federal laws need to be respected since Russia is a federal state", but better regional legislation could be used to replace outdated federal laws.[86] This is a possibility Shaimiev also raised in his Concept. However, in the absence of a mechanism to implement such a procedure, prosecutors and judges have no basis to dismiss federal challenges. This has prompted Shaimiev to complain about the asymmetries of the harmonization process: "while Moscow needs efficient vertical power, it should be concerned about what might happen if central officials, including prosecutors, act too vigorously." "Federal ministries", he continued, have "begun to trespass on Tatarstan's power."[87]

Constitutional harmonization and Tatarstan's 2002 Constitution

Tatarstan's Constitution was also the subject of intense scrutiny: between 1999 and 2001, 103 complaints were filed.[88] In May 2000, a federal–regional expert group was created to harmonize Tatarstan's Constitution with the federal Constitution.[89] The group, which included jurists from Tatarstan and the federal Presidential Administration, undertook a detailed analysis of every article of Tatarstan's 1992 Constitution. In response, Tatarstan's State Council formed a Constitutional Committee in September 2000 to implement the expert group's findings. The main obstacle to harmonization was disagreements about Tatarstan's status: Moscow's negotiators pressed Tatarstan to drop provisions that it is "united with Russia" and clearly specify its place within Russia.[90] Tatarstan's leaders explained the persistence of constitutional contradictions by the fact that the republic had adopted its law before Russia and the treaty bridged the differences. Like the "political issues" which arose during the work on legislative harmonization, disagreements on Tatarstan's Constitution were reserved for further discussion by presidents Shaimiev and Putin. Bilateral, closed-door meetings between both presidents were held in the autumn of 2002, which Shaimiev qualified as "very detailed" on the issue of Tatarstan's state structures, and that consensus was reached between the heads of state on the changes that were required to Tatarstan's Constitution.[91] The secretive nature of these discussions and their outcomes makes it difficult to assess the basis of their agreement, or whether there was any consensus at all.

Nonetheless, the Tatarstan State Council's Constitutional Commission worked on amendments from 2000 to 2002. The drafting process received wide coverage in the republican press and media.[92] 1,242 amendment proposals were received, including 273 from State Council deputies, 319 from municipal bodies, 404 from public organizations and citizens (including 73 from the Tatarstan New Century movement, 32 from the Tatar Public Centre, eight from Ittifak), and 149 from media organizations. Of these proposals, the Commission considered 514 amendments, refused 286, passed 126 and 102 were withdrawn.[93] The draft constitution was approved in first reading on 28 February 2002 by a margin of 116 to 1 amid intense debate on the wording of the provisions on Tatarstan's sovereignty and citizenship.[94] Federal prosecutors indicated the draft constitution was unsatisfactory and did not resolve contradictions. Parliamentary committees deliberated another month before the State Council resumed debate on the second reading on 29 March 2002. On the eve of the debate, Mukhametshin stated that although federal authorities were urgently pushing for harmonization, contradictions would remain in the final document.[95] During the State Council's debates, Shaimiev argued that unless article 61 (on Tatarstan's status) was amended there was no point in amending the Constitution at all since it was the biggest point of friction with Moscow.[96] Perhaps the insistence on the need to review the expression of Tatarstan's status provides a clue on the agreement reported to have been reached by Shaimiev and Putin. The State Council approved the draft in second and third readings on 19 April and the Constitution was signed into law by Shaimiev a week later. Three-quarters of the Constitution's articles were reworked, and it was shortened to 124 articles (from 167 in the 1992 version). Conscious that the document still contained provisions which contradicted federal law, Shaimiev was stoic: "We should be able to formulate our principles and have enough courage to defend them for the benefit of the future federation."[97]

Whereas the 1992 Constitution placed Russia at arms' length, the 2002 version acknowledges Tatarstan as a subject of the federation and recognizes the constitutional division of powers.[98] Article 1 contains the most significant provisions, both in terms of recognition of Tatarstan's status in Russia and preservation of its ambiguities. The provision defining Tatarstan as "united with Russia on the basis of the Russian and Tatar constitutions and the bilateral treaty" was maintained (art.1§1). But no claim to sovereignty in areas of exclusive federal or joint jurisdiction is made: Tatarstan exercises its sovereignty only within the spheres of competence which belong to it exclusively. The constitution drops Tatarstan's claim to being a "subject of international law" but asserts its right to engage in international relations and trade on matters within its jurisdiction (art.1§4). The provision on the existence of republican citizenship is maintained, but contrary to the 1992 version, Tatarstan citizenship is automatically granted to Russian citizens living in the republic, and citizens of Tatarstan are simultaneously citizens of Russia (art.21). Compared to the 1992 Constitution, the latest version represents a remarkable change in Tatarstan's stance. Whereas the claim for recognition (its status as "united with Russia") is maintained, Tatarstan positions itself more as a federated unit of Russia than as a confederal partner.

The Constitution maintains provisions on the inviolability of Tatarstan's territory (art.5) and that its status cannot be changed without its consent (art.1§3). To further entrench its status and democratic legitimacy, article 1 of Tatarstan's Constitution can be changed or rescinded only by referendum (art.123). By evoking the 1992 referendum, the leadership seeks to insulate Tatarstan's status claims from further challenges and court rulings. Notwithstanding previous Constitutional Court rulings which found that Russia's federal subjects cannot unilaterally amend their status, this article places Tatarstan's citizens as the bearers of sovereignty and the source of authority (art.3). Consequently, the status of Tatarstan as "united" with Russia is framed as the expression of popular will and not the leadership's whim.

As Mukhametshin makes clear, the ambiguities which remain in the amended version are not accidental: "In many provisions of the new constitution there are contradictions. But we consciously maintained our course because Tatarstan has its own position, especially on the question of sovereignty over the competences which are determined [by the 1994 treaty]."[99] The Constitution maintains ambiguous provisions on republican competences, including citizenship, the place of the treaty and, most significantly, its claim to sovereignty. Although the document clearly circumscribes the norm of sovereignty to those powers over which Tatarstan has exclusive jurisdiction, its lawmakers deliberately ignored the Constitutional Court's June 2000 rulings by maintaining a claim to sovereignty. Compared to the 1992 version, the current Constitution does not advocate a confederal state structure. The centre's prerogatives are recognised, a big difference with the 1992 Constitution in which Russia is mentioned only twice. The underlying constitutional disagreement about status and the way in which republican jurisdiction should be protected in federal practice remains.

Indeed, federal challenges to these remaining ambiguities have not abated. Russian Deputy General Prosecutor Zvyagintsev issued protests against the 2002 Constitution, arguing the State Council ignored court rulings by maintaining provisions on republican sovereignty (articles 1, 11, 23, 121), citizenship and on the bilateral Tatar–Russian relationship.[100] Almost as soon as the State Council had passed the constitution, it created another commission to consider the latest challenges. Mukhametshin refused to concede that the norm of republican sovereignty in the new Constitution was unconstitutional, accusing prosecutors of interpreting the federal Constitution "in their own way."[101] For him, the new constitution addressed Russia's concerns and the rulings of the Constitutional Court: limited sovereignty, "expressed by the possession of full state power outside Russia's field of competence", is both lawful and adheres to article 73 of the federal Constitution.[102] The Tatarstan Supreme Court began hearings to consider the prosecutor's challenges in January 2003.[103]

However, the proceedings ground to a halt while the Russian Constitutional Court considered a case brought by Bashkortostan and Tatarstan disputing the prosecutors' power to challenge their constitutions in courts of general jurisdiction. The Constitutional Court ruled that even if the basic law of a subject of the federation was found to violate federal law, it was not sufficient grounds to declare the document unconstitutional. Before, a prosecutor would ask an administrative or civil court to ascertain the constitutionality of a regional constitution. The Constitutional Court ruled that constitutions of subjects of the federation are not "ordinary legal acts" and have a special relationship with the Constitution of the Russian Federation. Consequently, only the Constitutional Court is empowered to ascertain constitutionality.[104] This unexpected ruling added several hurdles to the centre's ability to challenge federal subjects' basic laws. Yet it does not appear the ruling signalled a more region-friendly attitude but was a way for the Constitutional Court to secure its own authority vis-à-vis the Russian Supreme Court and other courts which were usurping its competence in this area.

Following this ruling, in December 2003 the Tatarstan Supreme Court resumed Zvyagintsev's case against the Tatarstan constitution.[105] After years of procedural and legal wrangling, the Court ruled in March 2004 that provisions of Tatarstan's Constitution (on sovereignty, state status, republican citizenship) contradicted federal law (and not the federal

Constitution).[106] In June 2004, the Tatarstan Supreme Court invalidated Tatarstan's 1990 Declaration of state sovereignty and its claims to sovereignty and ownership of natural resources. Marat Galeev, who represented the State Council during the hearings, argued that the Court should not consider the declaration a legal act, but a political document endowed with symbolic importance.[107]

All the provisions adopted to express Tatarstan's differentiated status have been invalidated. The 1990 Declaration of sovereignty and constitutional provisions on its sovereignty and status are inoperative. But Tatarstan's leadership has refused to officially rescind the provisions. Galeev's argument about the symbolic value of the provisions is part of the explanation. Two additional reasons are used to justify their refusal to rewrite these articles of the republican Constitution. First, Tatarstan's leaders argue that sovereignty in a federal system is divisible. Shaimiev states this position clearly:

> [Article 1 of the Tatar Constitution expresses] our view regarding federalism [and] our principal position ... Can anyone show me any academic works proving that a state can exist without sovereignty? [In our Constitution], we speak of limited sovereignty within the framework of our powers ... This doesn't violate the Russian Constitution. Moreover, it seems to me that not everybody has read the Russian Constitution to the very end. In its last part, there is a section about sovereign republics within the Russian Federation.[108]

Second, the Tatarstan Constitutional Court (which is separate from the Russian Constitutional Court) issued a ruling which vindicates Tatarstan's position and is used to counter federal claims. Twenty-nine State Council deputies asked the Tatarstan Constitutional Court (KSRT) to provide an interpretation of the first article of Tatarstan's 2002 Constitution and its relationship to the federal Constitution. Since Article 5 of the federal Constitution defines republics as states, the appellants maintained Tatarstan's constitutional claim to sovereignty was not out of line since it only included "full command and independence in resolving questions emanating from its exclusive sphere of competences."[109] The KSRT agreed that sovereignty is an attribute of states, and that Tatarstan can claim sovereignty (*samostoyatel'nost'*) over the power which belongs exclusively to the republic.[110] In its determination, it provides a detailed analysis of the historical context of Tatarstan's political-legal status, from the 1978 Constitution to the 1990 Declaration of sovereignty and 1992 ruling by the Russian Constitutional Court. Tatarstan's Court found that the republic is entitled to claim the status of subject of international law (*pravosub'-ektnost'*) in areas where it has international and economic contacts, and reaffirms the republic's state-legal status as defined by both the Tatar and Russian constitutions *and* the 1994 treaty.[111]

The Tatarstan Constitutional Court has issued rulings which directly contradict prior rulings of Russia's Constitutional Court. How and why are such competing court rulings significant? First, the conflicting rulings point to a gap in Russia's Constitution on the place and competence of republican constitutional courts. The chairman of Tatarstan's Constitutional Court explains his court is independent from Russia's: each court has its own competences determined by the division of powers in the federal and republican constitutions, and their decisions are final and cannot be appealed.[112] Zheleznov points out that no mechanism is in place to determine which ruling must be enforced.[113] This is a novel situation which has not yet been addressed.[114] Second, in the absence of a conciliation procedure (and Zheleznov contends constitutional amendment may be required to rectify the situation), the colliding rulings become the object of political struggle. Each level of government can claim "its" court vindicates its position. Most of my interlocutors in Tatarstan were critical of Russia's Constitutional Court and the motives for its rulings.[115] They see federal judges as being politically biased in their rulings on sovereignty since in many of their academic publications, judges, including former Court chairman Marat Baglai, have admitted the existence of partial sovereignty for components of a federation. As a result, the Russian Constitutional Court continues to be seen as responding to political rather than only legal criteria in their rulings.[116] Conversely, it is hard to conceive that the Tatarstan Constitutional Court would rule against republican interests. Although Putin's federal reforms and court rulings have eliminated the legal basis of Tatarstan's claims to special status and jurisdiction, they remain politically sensitive and salient issues.

The fate of the 1994 Bilateral Treaty

Since it was signed in February 1994, the treaty is considered to be the cornerstone of Tatarstan's relationship with Russia: it recognized Tatarstan's differentiated status, its special relationship with Moscow with respect to the delegation of powers, and it provided a bridge between Russia's and Tatarstan's constitutions. But the treaty did not insulate the republic from Putin's federal reforms, even if it was invoked to justify the persistence of legal and constitutional contradictions. One of Putin's priorities in 2000 was to review the treaty practice. He charged the Kozak working group to revise all treaties and identify those which should be rescinded. As a result, 28 of forty-two treaties were abolished.

Seeking to pre-empt a challenge to Tatarstan's treaty, Shaimiev reiterated on the sixth anniversary of its signing in 2000 that the treaty had "become an ideology for Tatarstan" and its people would "not accept attempts to infringe in any way on the relations it establishes."[117] During a visit to Kazan, Putin emphasized that the relations between Russia and Tatarstan should be based on the Constitution. "Experience has shown that at the time, that treaty was the right solution, and maybe even the only viable one" but "the Constitution stipulates that all Federation members are equal" and "Tatarstan [...] understands that."[118] Kozak signalled his working group would not target Tatarstan's treaty, stating that disagreements between Tatarstan and Russia had been solved thanks to the "constructive and wise position of Mintimer Shaimiev, President Putin, and the federal government", in other words, nontransparent negotiations.[119]

It is unclear, however, how these disagreements were solved. The future of the treaty and uncertainties over whether it would be renewed were the subject of political discussions. Although it is difficult to track the outcome of these closed-door discussions, what is clear is that parties have been involved in negotiations over a new version of the agreement. A republican commission was formed on 3 June 2002 to begin drafting amendments to the 1994 treaty. Mukhametshin, who chaired the commission, stated "there would be no talk of renouncing the treaty", but that they would seek to amend the treaty so that the republic's interests, especially its "national-territorial" interests, were protected.[120] Mukhametshin subsequently announced the creation of a Russia–Tatarstan working group on the examination of the bilateral treaty, co-chaired by himself and Sergei Kirienko. Since 2002, announcements have been made regularly that the treaty is almost ready for presidential approval.[121] Khakimov indicated that the persistent stumbling blocks in the negotiations are Tatarstan's claim to be "united with Russia", and its powers in foreign economic relations.[122] Mukhametshin downplays expectations regarding the contents of a revised bilateral agreement: "I do not think we will be successful in obtaining additional financial preferences, but we will try and preserve some competences."[123] For Faroukshin the treaty is merely a shell. He is pessimistic about the ongoing negotiations estimating that a revised agreement will be "empty" since Tatarstan possesses little power to constrain Moscow to make significant concessions.[124]

The 2003 law on the bodies of state power set July 2005 as the deadline for bringing existing treaties in line with federal law. Consequently, to all intents and purposes, Tatarstan's treaty is invalid and irrelevant as a legal/constitutional document. Nevertheless, Tatarstan's leaders continued to profess their confidence in the model of federal–regional relations which the bilateral treaty represents. The treaty provides recognition of Tatarstan's place in Russia's federal order, which is of utmost symbolic importance. For Shaimiev, the treaty is important because it "gave Tatarstan a voice, something we really value."[125] Tatarstan's political elites have shifted their emphasis when speaking of the document's importance and role. In a 2004 roundtable about the treaty's significance, Khakimov – an architect of the original agreement – implied it was a transitory tool: "In the period of transition from a unitary to federal country, a concrete mechanism was needed to found the relations between subjects and centre on democratic principles. The 1994 treaty fulfilled that role, and constituted a guarantee of stability in that volatile period."[126] In the wake of constitutional rulings which have annulled republican sovereignty, Galeev believes that the "treaty is not operative but its constructive inertia continues to work."[127]

Conclusion

Putin's federal reforms sought to restore the federal Constitution as the basis of relations between Russia's federal and regional governments. "The aim", Sakwa writes, "was to achieve constitutional federalism rather than the ad hoc asymmetrical federalism that had emerged under Yeltsin".[128] In many respects, Putin has been successful in reasserting the central place of the constitution in Russia's federal design. His reforms have eliminated legal and constitutional dissonance. But the reforms to the division of powers and the appointment of regional leaders point to the implementation of a model of hegemonic federalism in Russia based less on regional autonomy than on control by and from Moscow. Recent announcements of plans to delegate powers back to regions are evidence, however, that a process of federal–regional accommodation still exists. Moscow is inclined to respond to regional demands for increased authority, especially if, as is the case, it is clearly in the centre's interests. However, in many respects, "personalism" still outweighs "proceduralism" in Russia's federative relations.[129] By controlling the appointment of regional governors, Putin has acquired even more power to influence regional politics.

Tatarstan's reactions to Putin's reforms and the extent to which they were implemented in the republic provide a window on whether the reformed system constitutes a basis for future stability, and for stable accommodation of Tatarstan's specificities and claims. Although the use of "sovereignty" by Tatarstan was always somewhat ambiguous, in the current context, claims for sovereignty can be interpreted as claims for autonomy. In the 2002 constitution, Tatarstan no longer defines itself at arms' length from Russia but as a subject of the Russian Federation. A degree of consensus on federal design has emerged. Yet the persistence of Russia's claims for recognition, and the continued importance – even if it is only symbolic – on concluding a new bilateral treaty demonstrates that Tatarstan's elite cling to a different model of federalism. Tatarstan's leadership emphasizes Russia's need for "real" federalism and the protection of federal subjects' autonomy. Shaimiev repeated his vision during a meeting of the State Council in Kazan:

> The division of competences between the subjects and federal centre in any state is one of the key questions. There must be an overall legal space, uniform rules of state policy, and an understanding of the general values of society. We cannot consider democracy as anarchy or the "power vertical" as a negation of federalism. Democracy is based on law, and federalism on a clear differentiation of powers, where each level of government knows its rights and responsibilities.[130]

Shaimiev, in essence, continues to argue that the constitutional disagreement must be addressed: he seeks a consensus on the place and autonomy of Russia's constituent units within Russia's federal design. Yet it appears that such a balance has not yet been achieved. For Marat Galeev, Putin's federal reforms have not reassured Tatarstan that its autonomy is something the centre considers worthy of protection: "Current legislation looks more and more like that of a unitary state ... While Tatarstan argues that having autonomy and regulatory [rather than only executory] power is important and should belong to the subjects of the federation, it does not have the administrative resources to remedy the situation within current conditions."[131]

In Tatarstan, there appears to be a sense that for the time being, the pendulum has shifted towards central control, and that the republic must bide its time. The processes of intergovernmental mediation, prominent during the 1990s, continue to function. Negotiations on a bilateral treaty are ongoing. Similarly, although the courts have struck out provisions on republican status from Tatarstan's constitution, federal authorities have not sought to force the republic to rescind the provisions altogether. While the federal government does not share Tatarstan's concerns, it has not sought to directly oppose them either. Constitutional ambiguities and intergovernmental negotiation continue to operate as coping mechanisms. However, it is clear that for the republican elite the balance of power has shifted towards the centre. Shaimiev, who sees in Putin's power to dissolve regional assemblies that refuse to ratify his choice of governor a violation of democratic principles, ultimately backed down, stating that "confrontation in the actual political situation would [lead to] crisis".[132] In many interviews and discussions I conducted in Tatarstan, the phrases "within current conditions, within the current situation" came up, reflecting ambivalence about the current state of federalism, but also a degree of hopefulness that "real" federalism is still possible. As Khakimov remarks, "Only Tatarstan continues to speak for federalism, and as long as democracy lives in Tatarstan, we will not veer from that."[133] Even in the context of Putin's centralizing reforms, the persistence of political discussions and legal interpretations of the extent to which Russia's Constitution can and should foster a truly federal separation of powers and is a way to exercise power in Russia is evidence of the value of the federal idea in Tatarstan, and the Russian Federation.

Notes

1   I wish to thank James Hughes, Gwendolyn Sasse, Kim Meier and Natalia Leshchenko for their comments on earlier versions of this paper. The research for this paper was assisted by financial support from the Social Sciences and Humanities Council of Canada and Commonwealth Scholarship Commission.
2   For a more detailed analysis of the federal reforms undertaken during Putin's first term see D. Cashaback, "Risky Strategies? Putin's Federal Reforms and the Accommodation of Difference in Russia", *Journal on Ethnopolitics and Minority Issues in Europe 3*, 2003, as well as D. Cashaback, *Accommodating Multinationalism in Russia and Canada: A Comparative study of Federal Design and Language Policy in Tatarstan and Quebec*, PhD Thesis, University of London, 2005.
3   Jeffrey Kahn, *Federalism, Democratization, and the Rule of Law in Russia* (Oxford: Oxford University Press, 2002), p. 277.
4   Matthew Hyde, "Putin's Federal Reforms and their Implications for Presidential Power in Russia", *Europe–Asia Studies*, 53, 5, 2001, p. 731.
5   Kahn, *Federalism* p. 173.
6   A 1996 presidential decree and 1998 government resolution were issued in an attempt to circumscribe the use of bilateral treaties, so that they were used only to regulate issues of joint control, or accommodate a federal subject's "geographical, economic, social, national or other specificity". See Presidential Decree no. 370, 12 March 1996; and Government Resolution no. 129, 2 February 1998. In addition, the federal government enacted a law on the bodies of state power of the subjects of the federation which re-established the supremacy of the federal Constitution and of its articles 71 and 72, on the division of competences: "Ob obshchikh printsipakh organizatsii zakonodatel'nykh (predstavitel'nykh) i ispolnitel'nykh organov gosudarstvennoi vlasti sub'ektov

Rossiiskoi Federatsii", no. 95-F3, 6 October 1999. Under Yeltsin, these initiatives were never fully implemented.

7 Vladimir Putin, "Annual Address to the Federal Assembly of the Russian Federation", 8 July 2000, www.kremlin.ru.

8 *RFE/RL Newsline*, 8 October 2002.

9 Vladimir Putin, "Annual Address to Federal Assembly of the Russian Federation", 18 April 2002, www.kremlin.ru.

10 Vladimir Putin, "Annual Address to Federal Assembly of the Russian Federation", 3 April 2001, www.kremlin.ru.

11 M. Faroukshin, Professor of Political Science, Kazan State University. Interview with Author. Kazan: Kazan State University, 23 April 2004.

12 Decree no. 696, 9 July 1997; William A. Clark, "Presidential Prefects in the Russian Provinces: Yeltsin's Regional Cadres Policy", in Graeme Gill (ed), *Elites and Leadership in Russian Politics*. (Basingstoke: Macmillan, 1998) p. 37.

13 Decrees no. 849 (2000) and 97 (2001).

14 *ITAR/TASS*, 22 May 2000; *Nezavisimaya Gazeta*, 24 April 2003.

15 *Russian Regional Report*, 27 September 2002; S. Mikheev, "Ispolnyaetsya dva goda prezidentskim namestnikam", *Izvestiya* 12 May 2002.

16 Peter Reddaway and Robert W. Orttung (eds), *Dynamics of Russian Politics: Putin's Federal–Regional Reforms Volume I* (London: Rowman & Littlefield Publishers Inc., 2004).

17 G. Sharafutdinova and A. Magomedov, "Volga Federal Okrug", in Reddaway and Orttung, *Dynamics*.

18 "O poryadke formirovaniya Soveta Federatsii Federal'nogo Sobraniya Rossiiskoi Federatsii", 113-F3, 5 August 2000.

19 Eugene Huskey, "Political Leadership and the Center–Periphery Struggle: Putin's Administrative Reforms", in Archie Brown and Lilia Shevtsova (eds), *Gorbachev, Yeltsin, and Putin: Political Leadership in Russia's Transition* (Washington: Carnegie Endowment for International Peace, 2001) p. 114; Hyde (Putin's), p. 729.

20 V. Gel'man, "The Rise and Fall of Federal Reform in Russia", PONARS Policy Memo 238, 2001, p. 2.

21 "Ukaz Prezidenta Rossiiskoi Federatsii O Gosudarstvennom Sovete Rossiiskoi Federatsii", no. 602, 1 September 2000.

22 Putin, Annual Address 2000.

23 Intertat, 26 August 2005.

24 Ibid.

25 *Rossiiskaya Gazeta*, 13 September 2004.

26 *ITAR/TASS*, 14 September 2004.

27 *ITAR/TASS*, 18 October 2004.

28 "Ob obshchikh printsipakh organizatsii zakonodatel'nykh (predstavitel'nykh) i ispolnitel'nykh organov gosudarstvennoi vlasti sub'ektov Rossiiskoi Federatsii", no. 95-F3, 6 October 1999, art.5§3a.

29 "Ukaz Prezidenta Rossiiskoi Federatsii O poryadke rassmotreniya kandidatur na dolzhnost' vyshego dolzhnostnogo litsa (rukovoditelya vyshego ispolnitel'nogo organa gosudarstvennoi vlasti) sub'ekta Rossiiskoi Federatsii", no. 1603, 27 December 2004. The original decree called on the presidential envoy to establish a short-list of two candidates, to be submitted to the Head of the Presidential Administration. Putin's changes to the procedure, made

in June 2005, increased envoys' powers: no longer needing to coordinate their choice with the presidential administration, they are free to nominate only one candidate for approval. "Ukaz Prezidenta Rossiiskoi Federatsii O vnesenii izmenenii v Polozhenie o poryadke rassmotreniya kandidatur na dolzhnost' vyshego dolzhnostnogo litsa (rukovoditelya vyshego ispolnitel'nogo organa gosudarstvennoi vlasti) sub'ekta Rossiiskoi Federatsii, utverzhdennoe Ukazom Prezidenta Rossiiskoi Federatsii ot 27 dekabrya 2004 g.", no. 756, 29 June 2005.

30   "Ob obshchikh printsipakh organizatsii zakonodatel'nykh (predstavitel'nykh) i ispolnitel'nykh organov gosudarstvennoi vlasti sub"ektov Rossiiskoi Federatsii", art. 9.

31   *Nezavisimaya Gazeta*, 27 October 2004 and 11 November 2004.

32   *Respublika Tatarstan*, 26 October 2004.

33   *Respublika Tatarstan*, 12 March 2005.

34   *Tatar-Bashkir Daily Report*, 31 March 2005.

35   *Nezavisimaya Gazeta*, 14 September 2001 and 5 November 2004.

36   "Ukaz Prezidenta RF O dopolnitel'nykh merakh po obespecheniyu edinogo pravogo prostranstva Rossiiskoi Federatsii", no. 1486, 10 August 2000, art. 2.

37   "Polozhenie o poryadke vedenii federal'nogo registra normativnykh pravovykh aktov sub'ektov Rossiiskoi Federatsii", no. 904, 29 November 2000, art. 2.

38   The Registry is a fascinating resource that lists normative acts of Russia's federal subjects, challenges made (by federal or regional prosecutors, or courts) and what action was taken by the regional government (whether the protest was acknowledged or challenged). It is available online: http://www.registr.bcpi.ru.

39   Komissiya pri Prezidenta Rossiiskoi Federatsii po podgotovke predlozhenii o razgranicheniya predmetov vedeniya i polnomochii mezhdu federal'nymi organami rosudarstvennoi vlasti, organami rosudarstvennoi vlasti sub'ektov Rossiiskoi Federatsii i organami mestnogo samoupravleniya, "Kontseptsiya razgranicheniya polnomochii mezhdu organami gosudarstvennoi vlasti, organami gosudarstvennoi vlasti sub'ektov Rossiiskoi Federatsii i organami mestnogo samoupravleniya po obshchim voprosam organizatsii organov gosudarstvennoi vlasti i mestnogo samoupravleniya", *Izvestiya*, 25 July 2002.

40   Kozak quoted in *Gazeta.ru*, 21 February 2003.

41   *Russian Regional Report*, 27 September 2002.

42   Vladimir Putin, "Opening Address to State Council", 2 July 2005, www.kremlin.ru.

43   Ibid.

44   *Rossiiskaya Gazeta*, 24 August 2005.

45   *Respublika Tatarstan*, 27 August 2005.

46   "Ukaz Prezidenta Rossiiskoi Federatsii O vnesenii izmenenii v Polozhenie o poryadke rassmotreniya kandidatur na dolzhnost' vyshego dolzhnostnogo litsa (rukovoditelya vyshego ispolnitel'nogo organa gosudarstvennoi vlasti) sub"ekta Rossiiskoi Federatsii, utverzhdennoe Ukazom Prezidenta Rossiiskoi Federatsii ot 27 dekabrya 2004 g.", no. 756, 29 June 2005.

47   *Novaya Gazeta*, 7 July 2005.

48   Putin, "Opening Address".

49   "Postanovlenie Konstitutsionnogo Suda Rossiiskoi Federatsii po delu o proverke konstitutsionnosti otdel'nykh polozhenii Konstitutsii Respubliki Altai i

Federal'nogo zakona 'Ob obshchikh printsipakh organizatsii zakonodatel'nykh (predstavitel'nykh) i ispolnitel'nykh organov gosudarstvennoi vlasti sub'ektov Rossiiskoi Federatsii'", no.10-P, 7 June 2000, par. 2.1.

50 "Opredelenie Konstitutsionnogo Suda Rossiiskoi Federatsii po zaprosu gruppy deputatov Gosudarstvennoi Dumy o proverke sootvetstviya Konstitutsii Rossiiskoi Federatsii otdel'nykh polozheniy konstitutsiy Respubliki Adygeya, Respubliki Bashkortostan, Respubliki Ingushetiya, Respubliki Komi, Respubliki Ossetiya-Alaniya i Respubliki Tatarstan", no.92-O, 27 June 2000, par. 2.1.

51 Ibid., par. 3.2.

52 "Opredelenie Konstitutsionnogo Suda Rossiiskoi Federatsii po khodataistvu polnomochnogo predstavitelya Prezidenta Rossiiskoi Federatsii v Privolzhskom federal'nom okruge ob ofitsial'nom raz'yasnenii opredeleniya KSRF ot 27 iyunya 2000 goda", no.65-O, 19 April 2001, par.3.

53 "Postanovlenie Konstitutsionnogo Suda Rossiiskoi Federatsii po delu o proverke konstitutsionnosti Deklaratsii o gosudarstvennom suverenitete Tatarskoi SSR ot 30 avgusta 1990 goda, Zakona Tatarskoi SSR ot 18 aprelya 1991 goda 'Ob izmeneniyakh i dopolneniyakh Konstitutsii (Osnovnogo Zakona) Tatarskoi SSR', postanovleniya Verkhovnogo Soveta Respubliki Tatarstan ot 21 fevralya 1992 goda 'O provedenii referenduma Respubliki Tatarstana po voprosu o gosudarstvennom statuse Respubliki Tatarstan'", no.3-P, 13 March 1992.

54 *Izvestiya*, 19 July 2001.

55 Ibid.

56 *Tatar-Bashkir Daily Report*, 16 October 2000.

57 Tomila Lankina, "Federal, Regional Interests Shape Local Reforms", *Russian Regional Report*. no. 8, 29 September 2003.

58 Paul Goble, "Shaimiev Urges Division of Powers", RFE/RL Russian Federation Report, 30 August 2000.

59 "Proekt Kontseptsii gosudartvennoi politiki po razgranicheniyu predmetov vedeniya i polnomochii mezhdu federal'nym, regional'nym i munitsipal'nym urovnyami vlasti", *Kazanskii Federalist*, no. 1, 2002, pp. 101–3.

60 Ibid., p. 105.

61 Ibid., pp. 103–4.

62 Ibid., p. 104.

63 *Tatar-Bashkir Daily Report*, 1 July 2002.

64 "Proekt", p. 114.

65 Ibid., p. 104.

66 Ibid., p. 116.

67 Ibid., pp. 108–9.

68 Ibid., pp. 120–2.

69 "Protokol zasedanii Prezidiuma Gosudarstvennogo Soveta no. 6", Moscow, 20 February 2001.

70 "Proekt", p. 106 n1.

71 *Izvestiya*, 19 February 2001.

72 *East European Constitutional Review*, 10, 4, Fall 2001, p. 34.

73 *Tatar-Bashkir Daily Report*, 19 February 2001.

74 Several bodies were established to work on legislative and constitutional harmonization in addition to the Kirienko commission: a joint Tatar–Russian commission on the Constitution, committees of the Tatarstan State Council and a republican Constitutional Committee.

75 Quoted in *Tatar-Bashkir Daily Report*, 30 October 2000.
76 *Zvezda Povolzh'ya*, 14–20 September 2000.
77 *Vostochnyi Ekspress*, 28 September 2001; Sharafutdinova and Magomedov (Volga Federal Okrug), p. 160.
78 *Respublika Tatarstan*, 14 November 2000.
79 *Interfax*, 26 June 2000.
80 *Tatar-Bashkir Daily Report*, 11 January 2001.
81 *Respublika Tatarstan*, 28 December 2001.
82 *Respublika Tatarstan*, 28 December 2001.
83 Summary posted on http://www.bcpi.ru/svodka/svodka.html.
84 *Tatar-Bashkir Daily Report*, 30 January 2001. Some of the laws listed include: on a tax to eliminate housing slums; on private detectives and security activities; on illegal drug trade and usage; on violations to the land code; on the minimum wage; on land resources; on farms; on the restoration of the Latin script; as well as Tatarstan's water, land, and forestry codes, *Tatar-Bashkir Daily Report*, 6 September 2000.
85 *Respublika Tatarstan*, 28 December 2001.
86 *Respublika Tatarstan*, 14 November 2000.
87 *Gazeta.ru*, 7 March 2001.
88 *Respublika Tatarstan*, 28 December 2001.
89 The Expert group on harmonization of the Russian and Tatarstan constitutions: Gruppa ekspertov po soglasovaniyu KRT s KRF i federal'nymi zakonami.
90 *Vostochnyi Ekspress*, 28 September 2001.
91 *Tatar-Bashkir Daily Report*, 24 October 2001; *Tatar-Inform*, 12 November 2001.
92 Particularly in *Respublika Tatarstan*, *Zvezda Povolzh'ya* and *Vechernyaya Kazan* in January–April 2002.
93 *Respublika Tatarstan*, 2 April 2002.
94 *Tatar-Bashkir Daily Report*, 28 February 2002.
95 *Tatar-Bashkir Daily Report*, 28 March 2002.
96 *Tatar-Bashkir Daily Report*, 1 April 2002.
97 *Tatar-Bashkir Daily Report*, 29 April 2002.
98 All references to *Konstitutsiya Respubliki Tatarstan*, 2002.
99 *Respublika Tatarstan*, 30 April 2002.
100 *Tatar-Bashkir Daily Report*, 15 March 2002.
101 *Tatar-Bashkir Daily Report*, 9 September 2002.
102 *Respublika Tatarstan*, 6 February 2003.
103 *Tatar-Bashkir Daily Report*, 27 January 2003.
104 "Postanovlenie Konstitutsionnogo Suda Rossiiskogo Federatsii po delu o proverke konstitutsionnosti polozhenii statei 115 i 231 GPK RSFSR, statei 26, 251 i 253 GPK Rossiiskoi Federatsii, statei 1, 21 i 22 federal'nogo zakona 'O Prokuratore Rossiiskoi Federatsii' v svyazi s zaprosami gosudarstvennogo sobraniya – kurultaya Respubliki Bashkortostan, Gosudarstvennogo Soveta Respubliki Tatarstan i Verkhovnogo Suda Respubliki Tatarstan, no.13-P'", 18 July 2003, par. 4.3.
105 *Tatar-Bashkir Daily Report*, 24 March 2004.
106 *Tatar-Inform*, 31 March 2004.
107 *Tatar-Inform*, 17 June 2004.

108   *Respublika Tatarstan*, 24 April 2002.
109   "Postanovlenie Konstitutsionnogo suda Respubliki Tatarstan po delu o tolkovanii polozheniya chasti pervoi stati 1 Konstitutsii Respubliki Tatarstan, no. 8-P". 7 February 2003, par.2.
110   Ibid., par. 7.
111   In a separate ruling, Tatarstan's Constitutional Court provided an interpretation of the constitutional provisions on republican citizenship (articles 5 and 21). The Court upheld the powers delegated to the republic in the 1994 treaty (art.3§13), namely Tatarstan's competence to establish its own citizenship, but adds that Russian citizenship is primary: one must be a citizen of Russia to become a citizen of Tatarstan. "Postanovlenie Konstitutsionnogo suda Respubliki Tatarstan po delu o tolkovanii otdel'nykh polozhenii statei 5, 21, 91 Konstitutsii Respubliki Tatarstan, no.9-P", 30 May 2003.
112   S.X. Nafiev, "Nasha zadacha – obespechit' verkhvenstvo prava", *Vestnik Konstitutsionnogo Suda Respubliki Tatarstan* no. 1, 2001, p. 94.
113   B. Zheleznov, Professor, Department of Law. Author's notes. Nauchno-prakticheskaya konferentsiya: Federalizm v Rossii, Kanade i Bel'gii: opyt sravnitel'nogo issledovaniya, Kazan, 2004.
114   B. Zheleznov, Conversation with author. Kazan: During Conference "Nauchno-prakticheskaya konferentsiya: Federalizm v Rossii, Kanade i Bel'gii: opyt sravnitel'nogo issledovaniya", 18 May 2004.
115   Author's interviews with Midkhat Faroukshin, Marat Galeev, Rafael Khakimov, Razil' Valeev, 2004.
116   S.X. Nafiev, Author's notes of conference paper. Nauchno-prakticheskaya konferentsiya: Federalizm v Rossii, Kanade i Bel'gii: opyt sravnitel'nogo issledovaniya, Kazan; *Tatar-Bashkir Daily Report*, 12 November 2002.
117   *Russian Regional Report*, 1 March 2000.
118   *Russian Regional Report*, 19 April 2000; *Izvestiya*, 19 July 2001.
119   Interview quoted in *Tatar-Bashkir Daily Report*, 23 April 2002.
120   *Respublika Tatarstan*, 8 June 2002.
121   For instance, the working group announced in late 2004 that a treaty would be ready in June 2005, in time for the celebrations of Kazan's millennium. Meanwhile, the deadline has come and gone.
122   R.S. Khakimov, State Advisor to President on Political Affairs. Interview with Author. Kazan: Presidential residence, Kremlin, 12 April 2004.
123   *Respublika Tatarstan*, 23 November 2004.
124   M. Faroukshin, Interview with Author.
125   *Tatar-Bashkir Daily Report*, 17 July 2001.
126   *Respublika Tatarstan*, 14 February 2004.
127   Ibid.
128   Richard Sakwa, *Putin: Russia's Choice* (London: Routledge, 2004), p. 137.
129   Peter Reddaway, "Is Putin's Power More Formal than Real?", *Post-Soviet Affairs*, 18, 1, 2002: pp. 31–40.
130   Intertat, 26 August 2005.
131   M.G. Galeev, Chairman, State Council Committee on Economy, Investment and Property. Interview with Author. Kazan: Tatarstan State Council, 8 June 2004.
132   *Respublika Tatarstan*, 26 February 2005.
133   R.S. Khakimov, Interview with Author.

4
Not So Different After All? Centre–Region Relations: a Ukrainian Comparison

Kerstin Zimmer

Introduction

Questions of centre–periphery relations in modern states and related institutional arrangements have been among the key questions of political science.[1] Most advocates of democratization in Central and Eastern Europe have emphasized that decentralization is a key issue.[2] Centre–periphery relations have been central in many studies of both post-Soviet Russia and Ukraine, albeit with somewhat different foci.[3] So far, however, there has been surprisingly little comparative scholarly work on the systems of regional governance in Russia and Ukraine.[4] This seems logical only if one pays attention to the formal regulations: Russia is a federation while Ukraine is a unitary state. For that reason, one might assume that there is little to compare. However there are several underlying similarities that make the two systems remarkably well suited for comparative analysis. Once one includes the dominant political culture and the informal logic of political action that exists in both countries, the case for comparison is clear: an authoritarian and pragmatic political culture and specific forms of clientelism dominate both polities and manifest themselves in electoral and budget politics regulating the relationship between the centre and the regions.

Since 1991, both Russia and Ukraine have faced the dual transition to the market and to democracy, however flawed and beset by setbacks. The two countries have been threatened with the loss of territorial integrity, both in real terms and in the form of political threats and blackmail. In reaction, the respective ruling elites chose divergent ways of dealing with heterogeneity and of pursuing the aim of state survival. Both approaches, federal and unitary, were functional with regard to the interests of the power preservation of the ruling elites, especially the president, and both were adjusted

108

constantly. Both were also imposed on and interacted with informal relationships, various forms of clientelism, and an inherited political culture.

This chapter is a first attempt to compare the two post-Soviet states with a focus on the informal logic of centre–region relations. It proceeds as follows. First, I outline some conceptual assumptions, drawing mainly upon the concept of the path dependence of institution-building and its usefulness and limitations when applied to the post-Soviet context. Then, I briefly summarize the preconditions for the newly evolving centre–periphery relations in Ukraine and Russia, referring both to the Soviet and to the pre-Soviet past, explaining the (shared) origin of political culture and informal relations. Next, I detail the logic of recent centre–periphery relations, with a more exhaustive treatment of Ukraine; I refer principally to budgetary relations and machine politics as a specific form of clientelism, showing its function in a neo-patrimonial setting, which I illustrate with a case study of Donetsk oblast. Finally, I summarize the findings, emphasizing the role of Soviet legacies.

Path dependence: continuity in change and change in continuity

Many early approaches to the transformation of state socialist societies assumed that one could build democratic and market institutions, including those related to governance, from scratch.[5] Other scholars, however, disagreed with this legal constructivist approach and the teleological assumptions of the concomitant theoretical concepts. They argued that the process of "transformation" should not be measured by the deviation from its anticipated outcome, i.e. democratic capitalism, but in terms of the given historical setting.[6] Along these lines, Stark[7] conceptualized transformation as a recombination of components of the previous social order. The underlying assumption was that only the formal façades and some of the previous regime's mechanisms had collapsed, while actors' constellations, networks, routines and informal practices continued to function. In this sense, political elites were not perceived as disembedded, impartial agents of transformation, but as individuals, groups, and networks having their own agenda. Accordingly, transformation was framed as a path-dependent[8] process of institutional change,[9] and attention was paid to political and economic elites' manifest strategies in the specific context. The process of institutional change was conceived of in terms of successive changes in the institutional opportunity structure. These changes resulted from elites' interests, but they also modified these interests and thus spurred further institutional change.[10] While structures of long duration[11] obviously play a role, path dependence does not imply that change is "unfeasible". Rather, we are confronted with continuities in change and change in continuity,[12] generated by the interplay of actors and structure.

The historical legacy in Russia and Ukraine

If one accepts the assumption that historical legacies do play a role in state- and institution-building, it is indispensable to briefly consider the Soviet and even the pre-Soviet past. As both countries were part of the Soviet Union, Ukraine and Russia seem to share a common starting point from which the devolution of power developed and which provided the basis for the present divergent economic and political power of regional entities.[13]

Throughout its history, the Russian state always dominated over society. The lack of an institutionally and legally based constraint on power was the crucial basis of the Russian political system,[14] which had distinct patrimo- nial traits. Political rule was regarded as an extension of property rights over territory and people. Yet the Tsarist Empire remained "under-administered" outside the political centre in Moscow. Although single individuals from the nobility were integrated into decision-making in the nineteenth and early twentieth centuries, this did not fundamentally change the system because their integration always occurred on an informal basis, reflect- ing patron–client relationships but not universalist rules. These patterns were extended to new territories which came under Tsarist rule.

The Ukrainian case is slightly different. Crudely reducing historical complexity, one might argue that the territories of present-day Ukraine have belonged to two different development regions. Until 1917, the east of the country, i.e. the left bank of the Dnepr, formed a part of Tsarist Russia and then became part of the Soviet Union. The west of the coun- try (the right bank) was never part of the Tsarist Empire. From 1569 until 1772 it belonged to the dominion of the Polish Commonwealth. Among these territories Galicia was part of the Habsburg Empire between 1772 and 1918.[15] During the interwar period, the very western part of Ukraine belonged to Poland, Czechoslovakia, Hungary or Romania, while the east was already part of the Soviet Union. After the Second World War, the whole of present-day Ukraine came under Soviet rule.

In terms of central control over the periphery, the Soviet Union was both a continuation and an abrogation of the Tsarist past. But without doubt, segmented centralism was a factor of continuity, now under the control of the Communist Party. The relationship between the political centre and the regional units was not regulated by a constitution or laws in a prac- tical sense. Instead, the interplay of formal hierarchies as represented by the Communist Party (CPSU), informal practices and bargaining as well as patron–client relations determined this relationship.[16] Clientelism served as a substitute – not a functional equivalent as Eisenstadt and Roniger[17] argued – for universalistic mechanisms such as the market or the rule of law.[18] In order to implement central–state policies and to keep the country under control, the centre was dependent on regional bosses and their personal networks.[19] Although regional cliques and clientelist networks were constantly fought by central bureaucratic units, they were constituent parts of the Soviet patrimonial system[20] in which political power was fragmented and personalized.[21] The nomenklatura system made local party functionaries important actors[22] and guaranteed the CPSU's monopoly of power. After 1953, the reforms initiated by Khrushchev (1953–1964) decentralized the nomenklatura system and induced the proliferation of regional cliques and the strengthening of regional party-bosses.[23] Even though re-centralization followed, it could not reverse the existence of regional principalities, which later, under General Secretary Leonid Brezhnev, were further strengthened.[24] On the whole, the task of plan fulfillment required a dense network of informal relations which ran across enterprises, planning agencies and local administrative and party organizations. All these informal practices compensated for the weaknesses of the economic system,[25] and although they were officially criticized, they were unofficially accepted. The weak professionalization of the state apparatus offered opportunities for clientelism,[26] although during the Soviet period the power of the party apparatus limited the opportunistic behaviour of the subordinate actors.[27]

With the beginning of perestroika and the introduction of quasi-market mechanisms, the central, vertically organized control system started to crumble[28] and individual networks were strengthened. The conditions of perestroika provided advantageous possibilities for those who had good connections to state-owned companies and public officials on all levels,[29] and thus by applying strategies based on what Staniszkis called political capitalism,[30] reaped great economic advantages. Consequently, the dissolution of the Soviet Union and the Communist Party led to the actual autonomy of enterprise directors, regional bureaucrats and party functionaries in both Russia and Ukraine. The systemic change, however, did not release them as atomized actors, but as networks of actors which changed their nature over the years.[31] After the banning of the Communist Party in both Russia and Ukraine, the "new" political elite mainly gathered around the executive structures and formed party-like associations or non-institutionalized political groupings – the so-called party of power – which in turn continued to control the executive structures and the interfaces between the various domains.[32] Immediately after independence there was little central control over the regions and regional economic assets in either state, especially as many powerful regions had maintained tight relationships with the Soviet power centre in Moscow, but not with the national ones in Kyiv or Moscow; the regions were to some extent "free-floating".

The above-mentioned networks were especially strong in particular regional contexts. According to Richard Sakwa,[33] "(a)lthough the regional institutions of the USSR created powerful patronage and political networks, their persistence was determined by specific regional coalitions able to exploit the new political and economic conditions." This applied especially to regions with a strong industrial base such as Donetsk and Dnipropetrovsk in Ukraine and to Tatarstan in Russia.[34] Here, political elites had abundant experience of lobbying various levels of government (in the Soviet Union), which was an advantageous precondition for successfully establishing new clientelist relations. While this does not necessarily imply personnel continuity, the interplay of actors and structure led to the continuation of certain behavioural patterns, as we will see below.

Electoral clientelism in centre–region relations

As shown above, the preconditions for the establishment of a functioning, transparent relationship between the centre and the regions were poor. The tradition of informalizing and personalizing formal administrative relations for both private gain and political survival proved to be a heavy burden for effective regional governance, no matter whether in a federal or unitary system. Consequently formal political reforms, such as the introduction of multi-party elections, did not lead to the institutionalization of formal rules but to modified forms of clientelism. This has prompted several scholars to apply the concept of "machine politics" to parties and other political organizations in the former Soviet Union, drawing parallels with phenomena prevalent in urban America in the late nineteenth and early twentieth centuries. In this context, the terms "political machines" and "machine politics" refer to the informal functioning of elections: "A political machine is a business organization in a particular field of business – getting votes and winning elections."[35] In this interpretation, a political machine is an organization headed by a single boss or a small autocratic group that has at its formal or informal command a sufficient number of votes to sustain political and administrative control over a city, county, or state, irrespective of the strategies used. According to a narrower definition,[36] machine politics refers to individualized clientelist strategies only. In the post-Soviet context, clientelist strategies are regularly combined with coercion (application of administrative resources) and fraud, albeit in a creative mixture.[37] This form of clientelism is embedded in an institutional setting determined by formal administrative regulations and budgetary processes, and is therefore to some extent a reflection of the actual degree of autonomy of the regional entities. But parties are not the only form of political (electoral) machine. Rather, the concrete organizational forms of electoral clientelism vary. According to Hale,[38] party weakness in both Russia and Ukraine can be explained by the competition of party substitutes. Hale identifies two possible competitors: provincial political machines and politicized financial-industrial groups that provide incentives and services for candidates. These different organizational forms, however, are not mutually exclusive, and in many cases we come across a mixture or fusion. Parties are important as ordered structures that guarantee continuity between elections by nursing voters through public works, charity, jobs, festivals etc.,[39] and they create a solid basis of support. Informal political machines controlled by governors have access to administrative resources and politicized financial-industrial groups provide financial assistance to candidates.

There are two explanatory models for the emergence and success of machine politics and the application of administrative resources in the post-Soviet states. The first model suggests that these practices are immediate relics from the Soviet period. By pointing to the existence of "regional fiefdoms" and regional "bosses", Matsuzato[40] claims that despite the absence of free elections, these patterns already existed in the Soviet Union. A closer look at the successful political machines in contemporary Russia and Ukraine, however, reveals that their leaders are more often than not former nomenklatura members, but they are individuals and networks who were able to adjust quickly to the new volatile conditions, from which they made substantial political and economic profit.[41] The introduction of formal democratic elections and the valorized role of parties led to the surfacing of new actors and new techniques. Hence, supporters of the second model claim that political machines are in part the consequence of power and resource concentrations originating from the Soviet period. At that time pliable sections of the population greatly depended on the state and many continue to do so in the new era, so that they can easily be manipulated by regional and local bosses. This accumulation of power is a structural legacy of the Soviet past, which facilitates the successful implementation of machine politics and administrative resources in the new era.[42] Therefore, Hale argues, machine politics in Russia's regions is as much a product of the political transition and leadership as of direct legacies from the Soviet past. He maintains that "the (informal) continuities in practice were greatest where the formal continuities were greatest".[43] This applies especially to company towns or regions composed of several company towns. On the one hand, specific behavioural patterns established during the Soviet phase continue to function irrespective of concrete actors. On the other hand, these patterns are modified by the new institutional framework and incentives, representing a tangible example of the interplay between institutions and actors mentioned above. But machine politics, and to a certain degree the application of administrative resources, seems to depend on a specific sociopolitical setting. It develops in regions where political competition is weakly institutionalized, where political processes enjoy a low degree of autonomy, and where political culture is pragmatic. The latter refers to the inclination of individuals or groups to remain or participate in ruling factions by any means, while people remain indifferent to the political or moral reliability of their rulers as long as they are good managers.[44]

Regional governance in the Russian Federation: the role of machine politics

Under both Boris Yeltsin and Vladimir Putin, the development of Russian federalism was shaped by political calculations rather than a strict political design.[45] Under President Yeltsin (1991–1999) the relationship with the 89 subnational units was strongly shaped by the president's determination to preserve his power and to keep the country from disintegrating. The first stage (1991–96) mainly consisted of crisis management,[46] whereas during the second stage (1996–99), the central administration attempted to gain control over the regions by legal means. Yeltsin's dependence on regional power wielders became apparent on several occasions: at the end of the Soviet era, during the constitutional crisis in 1993[47] and again in 1996 during his presidential re-election campaign.[48] These developments went hand in glove with a weakening of central control over the regions, which was partly manifested in legal changes such as the introduction of elections for regional officials, and the parcellization of legal space. A complex and unstable balance was drawn between the claimed prerogatives of the centre and the de facto powers of the regions.[49]

Although the 1993 Constitution took the first steps toward establishing federalism, it left many boundaries between central and regional prerogatives indistinct. Starting from 1994, single federal subjects concluded so-called power-sharing treaties with the national centre, clarifying some of the boundaries of shared powers. By 1997 about half of the federal sub-units had concluded power-sharing agreements with the centre. These bilateral treaties stabilized Russian statehood by preventing the state from falling apart by tying the regions, or rather their leaders, formally (and informally) to the centre. The informality and the high degree of personalization of these relationships were demonstrated by the fact that the power-sharing treaties were not signed by the legal representatives of the federal subjects, but personally by the leaders of single regions and the federal authorities.[50] The relationship was also determined by the different nature of regional bargaining power, which was mostly related to economic clout and electoral performance. Therefore, asymmetries arose not only because of Yeltsin's dealings with the governors, but because of the actual differences between the regions with regard to history, economic and political resources, and political culture.[51] The asymmetry in federal relations was exposed blatantly in budgetary questions. The centre redistributed a large part of the budget and thus made regions dependent. But tax transfers to the centre were also uneven. Regions with more political bargaining power were able to negotiate special tax breaks, additional subsidies or soft credits.[52]

The increasing informalization and personalization of centre–region relations was accompanied by a strengthening of the governors in their respective regions, where they often coalesced with strong business actors. The regional leaders were free to rule in their territories provided they did not pursue secession. In practice, this was an exchange of privileges against loyalty.[53] The free hand extended to the manipulation of local and regional elections aimed at preserving the power of incumbents. In return, the centre demanded the manipulation of national and presidential elections to favour the incumbent and his allies. But in 1997, the Russian leadership started to curb the governors' independence. The federal government succeeded in cutting back some of the regional control of fiscal levers[54] and some of the laws passed at the regional level.

Yeltsin's bilateral treaties were effectively a tool to preserve unity in times of crisis,[55] although this "live-and-let-live policy"[56] was only a temporary solution. It resulted in an ambiguous and volatile situation, which provided a crucial challenge for Yeltsin's successor as president. After having been publicly elected in 2000, President Vladimir Putin initiated a campaign to strengthen central state power. With a presidential decree of 13 May 2000, he divided Russia's 89 federal subjects into seven bigger administrative districts, establishing an administrative layer between the federal centre and the regions headed by envoys appointed by the president. Several legal and administrative changes curtailed the political ambitions of the governors to play a decisive role at the national level and deprived them of their control over federal agencies in the regions.[57] Putin also attempted to terminate most of the bilateral treaties concluded between 1994 and 1999. Moreover, Putin had several laws adopted by the Duma allowing for the legal removal of governors and parliaments once it was proven in the courts that they had consciously passed legislation contradicting the Russian Constitution, a power confirmed by the Constitutional Court in 2002. Eventually, the Kremlin and the Duma allowed most of the governors to run for a third or even a fourth term. But in December 2004, the president was given the power to appoint new regional leaders. However, even given this apparent power shift in a central direction, president and regional leaders have remained mutually dependent. Governors who can secure their own election have the power to help the president win re-election and place his allies in the Duma. Consequently, the president depends on them to some degree for electoral assistance, granting them some freedom to run their fiefdoms as they consider appropriate to win their electoral support for themselves and for their national patrons.[58] Thus Putin limited the governors' power at the national level, both formally and informally, by re-centralizing decision-making power, but the governors' power in the regions has not been completely broken as they can still rely on vested power networks.[59] Even under somewhat modified formal regulations, mutual dependence continues to operate.

Within this changing institutional framework, machine politics has been a persistent leitmotif. Machine politics began to develop during Yeltsin's presidency in the context of his management of centre–regional relations by way of negotiated bilateral treaties. Despite the Putin administration's public disapproval of such an approach, it has adopted a general disposition towards the regional elites which has tacitly encouraged the kind of machine politics which developed at a time when regional elites enjoyed much freedom as long as they remained loyal to the centre in Moscow. The key form this loyalty took was the reliable supply of votes in presidential and parliamentary elections. Marsh et.al. maintain that Putin and especially the leaders of the ethnic republics developed a firm and lasting condominium with regard to mutual support between Moscow and the ethnic republics on this basis.[60] Tatarstan and Bashkorstan are leading examples of this, with Tatarstan discussed elsewhere in this volume.

Ukraine: segmented unitarism

As in Russia, inter-regional disparities in Ukraine have been noted repeatedly in scholarly research, but they have mostly been analysed with a focus on the ethnic dimension.[61] The fact that the country did not simply follow one path of transformation but rather many distinct, regional ones, has hardly ever been considered. Those paths in the different functional and regional subsystems do not necessarily lead in the same direction, and they differ not only in degree but also in substance. These disparities are not of an ethnic, national or linguistic nature, but a matter of profound regional cleavages resulting from historically based sociocultural diversity[62] and the different, often contradictory, experiences with centre–region relations. In addition to sociocultural factors, economic structure and the degree of elite (dis-)continuity, the administrative composition of the state determines the political life of the single administrative units. The divergent transformation paths after 1991 have added to the disparities and made them more visible. Within Ukrainian political reform discourse, the regional cleavages have repeatedly served as an argument for the reinvigoration of the central executive forces as a means of preventing the country from falling apart,[63] although there have never been any serious, and publicly supported, separatist challenges, with the exception of the Crimean Peninsula.

Institution-building

After independence Ukraine built up its own administrative structures, but they were essentially a Soviet inheritance. However, under Kuchma, Ukraine finally developed into a neo-patrimonial state[64] with the president formally and informally controlling many aspects of political and economic life by applying neo-patrimonial strategies and using the formal legal and administrative framework for the preservation of his own power. A neo-patrimonial state is characterized by the formal, but not the actual separation of private and public spheres.[65] Neo-patrimonialism refers to the coexistence and mutual penetration of patrimonial and legal-rational bureaucratic elements in a densely intertwined structure. Neo-patrimonial rule is exercised within the structure of and with the claim to rational-procedural bureaucracy and "modern" statehood,[66] so that there are two logics of action, with the patrimonial system permeating the legal-rational one without gaining full control.[67]

Administratively, Ukraine is divided into 24 oblasts, the Autonomous Republic of Crimea and the cities of Kyiv and Sevastopol'.[68] Each oblast is divided into raions. Bigger cities enjoy the same status as raions; rural raions are subdivided into towns and villages. So, there are four tiers of government: national, oblast, raion/city, and municipal. Politically in the first half of the 1990s, Ukraine seemed to be in limbo between a unitary state and varying degrees of decentralization,[69] accompanied by constant legal changes attempting to regulate the relationship between the centre and the regions. These legislative changes were a reflection of power struggles between the centre and the regions on the one hand, and the president and the parliament (Verkhovna Rada) on the other. All reform projects, as well as actual legal changes, were about the relationship between vertical autonomy and dependency as well as about the relationship between the formal separation of powers and the fusion of executive and legislative powers at the regional and local levels.[70]

From 1991 until 1994, the oblast enjoyed considerable freedom from central control. This was reflected in legislation, even providing for the election of top regional officials in 1994. But recentralization started with the beginning of Leonid Kuchma's presidency in 1994.[71] In June 1995 the president and the Verkhovna Rada signed the "Constitutional Treaty", which gave Kuchma the right to appoint all chairmen of raion and oblast parliaments (radas) as heads of the oblast and raion state administrations. Oblast and raion radas lost their executive bodies and the oblast and raion state administrations were formed, leading to a fusion of oblast radas (as self-governing bodies) and bodies of state power, a place where elected bodies of self-government and the authorities of the central state collide, and collude, directly. As the oblast and raion radas no longer have executive bodies, they "delegate" many tasks to the oblast and raion state administrations,[72] thereby losing their ability to act autonomously. The vertical and horizontal hybridity of state power and local self-government on nearly all administrative levels furthered informal agreements and coalitions between superordinate and subordinate bodies and the emergence of vertical networks. Subsequently, recentralization was translated into more formal terms. The 1996 Constitution, going beyond the 1995 Constitutional Treaty, formally established a unitary state. But as Konitzer-Smirnov[73] correctly observes, the Constitution did not fully institutionalize unitary state structures. Instead, the diffusion of political power to the oblasts started again, although even more informally than before, behind, and taking advantage of, the formal unitary structures. While in principle the oblasts are centrally controlled, significant variations among the regions are accepted.[74] This reflects the neo-patrimonial logic, in which centre–region relations are crucial and where the heads of the oblast state administrations are subject to elite competition.

The oblast state administrations are bodies of executive power run by officials who are formally nominated by the prime minister and confirmed by the president, and they can be dismissed by the president.[75] These officials are hybrid forms of "governor" – a representative of the oblast in the centre – and a prefect – a representative of the centre in the oblast. This is made clear by the fact that, in spite of the appointment system, they are normally appointed from among local politicians, following the logic of informal relations: in order to fulfill their tasks, public officials cannot count on formal competencies only, but unquestionably need to rely on informal practices and contacts they have established prior to their appointment. Heads of the raion administrations are nominated by the cabinet of ministers and must be confirmed by the higher regional administrations. This generates a direct dependence of the raion administration on the oblast administration and extends the president's "power vertical" further down. Moreover, the fact that bodies of self-government do not have the right to appeal to the Constitutional Court but can only address the higher level authorities,[76] adds to the vertical dependency and furthers clientelist behaviour. These examples show how legal regulations and informal practices are not independent of each other. Formal rules are often purposefully designed to ensure that informal patron–client relations must be used in order to act successfully and that all actors are potentially vulnerable. The legal framework thereby creates uncertainty and can simultaneously be used as an instrument to exercise control and power.[77]

Due to the informalization of centre–region relations, the formally uniform power vertical did not therefore lead to any sort of homogenization, but to further fragmentation. The fact that Ukraine has become informally segmented is reflected in budgetary relations and in appointment and dismissal policies at the oblast and raion levels.

Financial dependence

The relationship of vertical dependence is not confined to the formal power vertical which is itself maintained and controlled through appointment policy, intimidation and blackmail,[78] but it is reinforced by the way the oblast and local budgets are formed. Lower level budgets are dependent on higher level budgets, a system often referred to as "budgetary matryoshka".[79] Moreover, budget formation is characterized by instability and a lack of transparency, so that the formal political autonomy of municipal authorities becomes a farce.[80]

The most significant element of budget formation is the extensive, centralized and rather whimsical redistribution of funds. Substantial exclusive sources for the municipal authorities do not exist. Their revenues mainly consist of a share of national taxes collected on the territory of the respective body.[81] As a rule, a superordinate parliament decides on the size of this share. For villages and towns subordinate to the raions, it is the raion rada, while the raions and cities which are subordinate to the

120

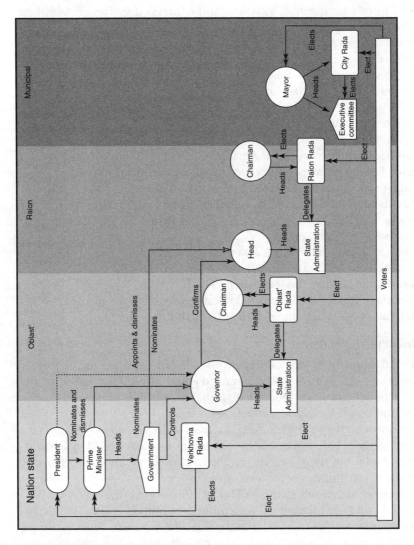

Figure 4.1 Structure of political power in Ukraine

oblast, are apportioned their budget by the oblast rada. As the radas no longer have their own executive bodies, the local bodies have to negotiate with the respective state administration, which drafts the budget. This puts the heads of the oblast administrations in a controlling position in relation to the mayors. Despite legislation to the contrary, interactions between state administrations and elected local radas leave the latter fiscally dependent on the central state.[82] Local politicians thus become part of the power vertical as they have to involve themselves in the clientelist struggles for redistribution, whether they like it or not. Moreover, the exclusive revenues of the local bodies decreased from 50 percent in 1992 to less than 10 percent in 1998, thereby making planned and ad hoc transfers from the national budget significant.[83]

This type of vertical dependence was reinforced by the frequent, often sudden and arbitrary changes in the basis of allocation, both ad hoc and negotiated with single regions, causing a lack of security and transparency.[84] In 1998, the increasing budget deficit at the national level led to the reduction of equalization transfers to the regions by more than 50 per cent. As the transfers continued to be based on ad hoc measures, the central government permitted some, more influential and powerful, regions to receive all the transfers, while others experienced cuts of up to 80 per cent.[85] As a consequence, regional disparities steadily increased. The budget law thus allowed for nontransparent and arbitrary decisions. As it did not delineate between the fiscal powers of central and local authorities, it created scope for bargaining between levels of government, or put differently, it consciously produced insecurity and forced the local actors into clientelist dependencies. Over the years, these practices became institutionalized.[86]

Rewards and punishment: the role of electoral clientelism

For a more profound understanding of the relationship between the centre and the regions, it is not sufficient to look at the regulations and practices, both formal and informal, inside the administrative realm. Nor is it enough to view budget formation and appointment policies as tools of control and reward. Instead, one has to clarify who is rewarded (with budget resources and career possibilities) for what services, and what determines the bargaining power of single actors in this arrangement. I would argue that the fusion of different spheres goes beyond the administrative realm and comprises electoral processes as well. Elections are used to maintain control over the country, including the oblast level. Regional actors who are formally and informally integrated into the power vertical control the oblasts via clientelist practices and power politics, at times leading to the fusion of political parties, informal networks and regional state administrations.

Punishment and reward depend strongly on the course and the results of elections, which establish the formal balance of power at the national level. Since the enactment of the Constitution in 1996, Ukraine has formally been a semi-presidential regime.[87] The president is directly elected by the population for a five-year term. The same person can be elected president for no more than two consecutive terms. The Verkhovna Rada is a unicameral parliament. Elections take place every four years. The law "On Elections of People's Deputies of Ukraine" adopted in 1993, accords every citizen aged 18 years of age and over the right to vote in a free, equal, direct and secret ballot. In 1994, the 450 deputies to the Verkhovna Rada were elected in single mandate districts on a pure majority formula. But in 1997 the Verkhovna Rada enacted a new law, which provided that half of the members of parliament would be elected from party lists, the other half in single mandate constituencies.[88]

In the first half of the 1990s, electoral clientelism was not very effective, but it became so after the adoption of the Constitution and the ensuing creeping authoritarian tendencies under Kuchma. It proved to be a crucial pattern during the presidential elections in 1999 and 2004 and the parliamentary elections in 2002. The governors played a central role in this process. In spite of the appointment system, elections are relevant for the governors and the heads of the raion administrations. Matsuzato[89] perceived an "extremely politicized exploitation of the appointment system of governors". Kuchma dismissed governors who failed to mobilize enough votes for him personally in the 1999 presidential election or for his allied parties or electoral alliances in the 2002 general election.[90] Despite the personalization and the informality of these machines, political parties have come to play an important and growing role.[91] Parties have become part of the structure of machine politics and administrative resources; in 2002 most governors could be attributed to specific parties or had created their own parties.[92] In this way, some of the informal political machines of the governors were formalized, and two of the "competing" forms identified by Hale[93] merged.

Case Study, Donetsk: elections in a captured region

"Electoral ability" is unevenly distributed in Ukraine, with the effectiveness of machine politics limited in both time and space. While one might argue that the old industrial region of Donetsk oblast is not characteristic of all Ukraine, it represents an intensified version of the general Ukrainian transformation regime, especially its neo-patrimonial features. For that reason the conclusions drawn from this case are valid for the rest of Ukraine, provided that one takes into account the region's peculiarities. In 1994 and 1998, elections in Donetsk oblast were deemed reasonably fair and free, just as in the whole of Ukraine. But the oblast became renowned as a result of the parliamentary elections in 2002 and the presidential elections in 1999 and 2004; the election in 2004 even gained international attention. To understand this, it is imperative to focus on the regional elite, its links with the local population on the one hand, and its embeddedness in and power over economic and political networks at the regional and national levels on the other. In the second half of the 1990s, Donetsk oblast was practically captured by its economic and administrative power elite,[94] a fact that prompted some observers to label it the "Belarus" of Ukraine. The elite, formally represented by the oblast state administration then headed by Viktor Yanukovych, gained control over the distribution of practically all patronage and financial resources. It exercised effective control over subordinates and "starved out" the opposition. How was this achieved?

Until 1998 different regional elite groups were at odds with one another, with the Communists, which were strong in the region, able to take advantage of this. Violent conflict arose over the redistribution of state property, and intensified with the acceleration of the privatization process after 1995. Clashes also occurred over the control of strategic assets and the flows of energy and finances. After the appointment of Viktor Yanukovych as Donetsk governor, the regional elite consolidated politically and elaborated its electoral control over the region.[95] Before the 1999 presidential election when Kuchma ran for a second term, he faced similar problems to those of his predecessor Kravchuk during the 1994 election. He lacked support, especially in the southeastern regions, including Donetsk, and thus relied on the governors and their formal and informal subordinates to mobilize votes for him by using administrative resources and clientelism. In this emerging "electoral meritocracy",[96] the governors were given additional access to important economic assets in their regions, while licenses for gas trading in the regions[97] were given to regionally-based financial industrial groups which were normally linked to the governors. In Donetsk, these "rewards" were supplemented by the promised creation of a Free Economic Zone, which was actually established in 1999 and provided favourable incentives and tax breaks for the regional economic elite. During the 1999 presidential election, then Governor Viktor Yanukovych and most of the political and economic actors in Donetsk supported Leonid Kuchma. As Matsuzato noted, the strong and self confident Donetsk elites formed effective electoral machines that worked for Kuchma as long as the latter's politics vis-à-vis the region were considered to be to their advantage. In the second round, in Donetsk, Kuchma unexpectedly defeated his communist challenger Petro Symonenko, despite the fact that the latter is from Donetsk oblast and even though the Donetsk electorate traditionally favoured leftist candidates. In 2000, President Kuchma initiated a referendum by presidential decree aiming at the enhancement of presidential power and taking a further step in an authoritarian direction. In Donetsk oblast, there was an extremely high voter turnout and the propositions of the referendum were endorsed by more than 90 per cent of the voters.[98] During the presidential election of 2002, the voters from the traditionally "red" Donbas predominantly voted for the bloc "For a United Ukraine", which was close to President Kuchma. And most of the single-member districts were won by representatives of "For a United Ukraine", often local bosses or influential entrepreneurs.[99] All "centrist" parties at the regional level supported the election campaign and their regional leaders were co-opted.[100] In the run-up to the election, Yanukovych had stated, that he was interested in getting as many as possible similarly thinking deputies (komanda edinomyshchlennikov) into the Verkhovna Rada.[101]

After they had demonstrated their electoral ability in 1999, the Donetsk elite did not act merely as henchmen for Kuchma in the 2002 parliamentary election, but pursued their own interests, cashed in on their electoral success, and to a growing extent had their own way in struggling with the centre. They were aware of their power and increasing indispensability to Kuchma,[102] and demanded more representation in political bodies at the national level that would match their economic and political strength. This was even more marked after the 2002 election, when Donetsk was the only oblast where the pro-presidential bloc was victorious. The centre could no longer refuse to include Donetsk actors in national politics. After Viktor Yanukovych became prime minister in 2002, Ukrainian analysts expressed fears for the "integration of Ukraine into the Donbass", i.e., the extension of the regional rules of the game to the entire country.[103]

Organized clientelism and administrative resources

In explaining why these results were achieved, we have to differentiate between the methods and strategies applied on the one hand and structural factors that allowed these strategies to function so successfully on the other.

In order to achieve these electoral victories, several strategies were applied: in 1999 and 2002, there was a focus on clientelism and administrative resources, but for the 2004 presidential election in which Yanukovich was nominated by the "party of power", the composition of the recipe was changed. While clientelism declined, administrative resources were applied unabated, and fraud became even more widespread, especially during the run-off on 21 November 2004. What exactly were these strategies?

Until the end of the 1990s, clientelist and coercive practices in Donetsk oblast were exercised via the informal political following and the administration of the governor, who from 1997 was Viktor Yanukovych. In 2002, the regional party of power was formalized through the foundation and consolidation of the Party of Regions that comprises all relevant actors from the region. During the 2002 parliamentary election, the Party of Regions joined the pro-presidential electoral bloc "For a United Ukraine". In the run-up to the election, their most noteworthy clientelist strategy was the conclusion of so-called "social contracts" between candidates of "For a United Ukraine" and individual voters or social groups. In these contracts, the voters were promised an improvement of their social situation.[104] Similar contracts were concluded with regional organizations such as the Afghanistan veterans or the Victims of Chornobyl.[105] In this way, these organizations declared their symbolic, or even active, support for the electoral bloc. The post-Soviet trade unions at the regional level also supported the bloc "For a United Ukraine", and this was documented in a separate agreement on partnership.[106] This agreement was the most important of the agreements as it allowed for heightened influence on workers in many firms. Prior to the day of the election, roughly 200,000 of these contracts had been signed, but the plan for one million contracts was not achieved.[107] It remains questionable whether all contracts were concluded on a voluntary basis.

Although the oblast state administration was not a contracting party, it described this strategy as follows:

> Today, the project of the "social contract" between representatives of the bloc and the voters is a real "reserve" for the rating of the electoral bloc ["For a United Ukraine"]. The conclusion of the social contracts does not only enhance the actual success of the bloc, but also adds hundreds of thousands of new voters to its supporters.[108]

This statement reflects the fact that the administrative actors were not impartial and that a complete fusion of the party and the administrative apparatus had taken place. This interaction with the electorate was typical of large parts of the Ukrainian party system. The Committee of Voters of Ukraine observed in November 2001, that 34 per cent of all violations of the electoral law consisted of the distribution of goods or services to voters.[109] Yet in the case of the Party of Regions, the relationship with the voters was formalized to an exceptional degree. This strategy was again applied in 2004, but was less successful.[110]

The second strategy for achieving the desired election results involved the application of so-called administrative resources, regularly in combination with the clientelist strategies noted above. The application of administrative resources involves the misuse of state resources for political gain. This may refer to the use of administrative levers to influence the composition of election committees or, via control of local courts, to curb the possibilities for election campaigning of rival candidates. These do not appear to be "suspicious" because, although laws are applied selectively, the actors maintain the appearance of the rule of law. It may also refer to attempts to influence the political decisions of voters by coercive means, stemming from the exploitation of administrative levers. Workers in public administration and other public institutions could be intimidated by people taking advantage of their dependence as employees. For example, in 1999 university lecturers were pressurized to influence their students in their voting decisions,[111] while during the 2002 parliamentary elections, in the city of Artemovsk, Donetsk oblast, students were forced to put up "For a United Ukraine" campaign posters during an official visit by President Kuchma.[112]

Although the oblast authorities attempted to influence the voters directly, normally they could not verify who actually voted for the desired candidate or party. But there were ways of direct and indirect control. In 2004, some voters were made to believe that their ballots could be traced back to their registration.[113] In other cases control was much easier; for example, in company towns where voters' affiliation to electoral precincts and companies coincided the directors of these companies were able to pressure their employees. In other cases, control was purposefully created or prolonged, such as in precincts with voters under "special circumstances"; for example, the prison population comprises one per cent of the oblast population and they voted unanimously for "For a United Ukraine". Similar election results were recorded on ships and in hospitals. In 2004, the inmates at one prison were told that they had to deliver a 90 per cent vote for Yanukovych to retain the possibility of early release, family visits, and privileges.[114]

These strategies were supplemented by direct fraud, or the manipulation of vote-counting and violations of the electoral law in the narrower sense. These violations were quite textbook-like, but also inventive. In Donetsk, the 2004 elections were manipulated very openly. This reflects two factors: it demonstrates that the competition was tight and that the cost of winning had increased, so the authorities were more willing to take the risk, and more importantly, it shows how self-assured the local and regional authorities were of getting away with stealing the election. They were successful in this in Donetsk oblast, but not at the national level.

We now turn to the second question: what renders substantial parts of the regional population susceptible to both the abuse of administrative resources and machine politics? The particularities of Donetsk oblast relate not only to its elite. If one abandons the actor-centred view and takes structural factors into account, the situation becomes more plain. The oblast hosts much of Ukraine's industrial potential and is the home of about 10 per cent of the Ukrainian electorate, making it attractive for elite capture. In addition, the social legacies of the Soviet era prove to be strong and relevant for successful machine politics and the application of administrative resources: dependency and a specific political culture. Here, the admiration of a *"khoroshii khozyain"* (good master) is widespread.[115] Moreover, a large part of the population depends on mass patronage by the state or, even more often, the personalized support provided at their workplaces. Therefore the dependence of miners and industrial workers on their bosses continues to be strong. And their independent interest articulation is continuously impeded by the strategic moves of the regional elite, which either co-opts or marginalizes the opposition.[116] In addition, the regional elite could appeal to institutionalized electorates.[117] An institutionalized electorate is a group of people possessing a strong group self-consciousness due to past state policies and institutions that defined important sets of opportunities and treated people differently on the basis of these categories. This applies to miners in Donetsk or the entire industrial workforce, and it was and continues to be extrapolated to the whole population via "constructivist" identity-politics from above,[118] which referred to many Soviet patterns and self-images and which produced feelings of difference from and superiority toward the rest of Ukraine.

As we have seen, a remarkable feature of the Ukrainian case is the mixing of several types of abuses for political aims. The governors misuse the power given to them by the formal legal framework in order to safeguard their power in the regions. They have networks of clients below or next to them, which mobilize votes for them and are rewarded with advantages taken from the resources provided by the legal framework. They may also receive other kinds of support from the governor, who can use the resources of his network reaching to Kyiv. At the same time, all of these incentives can be reversed and serve as a threat. Subordinate actors, such as mayors or heads of raion administrations, are exposed to the pressure of superordinate authorities, as the oblast administration in fact decides on the distribution of budget resources and on how much the subordinate authorities can distribute in a clientelistic manner. In addition, the governor indirectly influences the career paths of heads of raion administrations by his right to withhold his approval to their appointment. In case of non-compliance, protection and resources are withdrawn. The most decisive services in return "from below" are the delivery of desired election results.

Conclusion

The description of the systems of regional governance in Russia and Ukraine reveals that electoral clientelism works independently from the formal administrative makeup of the state. The unitary structure in Ukraine and the federal structure in Russia produced similar results. In addressing the reasons for these striking similarities, theories of neo-institutionalism are useful. John Meyer and his colleagues[119] have pointed out that since the end of the Second World War, national states have adopted remarkably similar constitutional frames and institutional structures, which reflect internationally accepted norms that aim at common progress and individual rights and equality. Thus, the diffusion of these norms produces institutional isomorphism, i.e. homogeneous forms of states, with all the "essential" attributes. Most importantly, states and governments win international legitimacy through the adoption of universalistic standards. The phenomenon of isomorphism is facilitated by the possibilities of considerable "decoupling" of structure and content, i.e. nation-states may adopt forms without closely linking them to practice. In this context, Russia and Ukraine are remarkable cases, somehow turning Meyer's paradigm upside down. Even though the two states have adopted divergent formal structures with regard to regional governance, their practices are surprisingly similar; in other words, the forms are different, while the decoupled practices are alike.

One form of decoupling typically encountered in the post-Soviet environment is associated with the diagnosis of "partial reforms"[120] in the political and economic spheres, leading to a new systemic "equilibrium". In the administrative sphere, one might argue, the term "partial reforms" refers to the fact that either unitary or federal forms have been adopted but implementation and practice partially adhere to different (informal) rules, informed by Soviet legacies and immediate power interests. Due to the decoupling of structure and practice, Soviet legacies become effective in both Russia and Ukraine. The informalization and personalization of power continue to guide political behaviour. Moreover, in both countries, the ruling elite adheres to a political culture which is extremely state-centred and feeds itself from a particular understanding of political power. The strength of the state is not measured in its effectiveness to deliver public goods. Rather, the central question is whether the state, understood as the ruling group, manages to push through its own interests, to maintain and to boost them. Actors on all levels try to exercise full authority on their territories, not willing to share power.[121] This does not mean that power is formalized and regulated by legal means, but is "hedged" in personalized and informalized networks characterized by both cooperation and fierce competition. The actors make use of familiar and rewarding forms of behaviour while retaining the formal elements of a democratic state. Elections as an accepted and valued attribute of democratic states rather serve to stabilize the system due to the kinds of manipulation referred to above. The position of the power wielders is not endangered, but legitimized by their victories in formally competitive elections.

However such institutional decoupling can never be complete. Machine politics is a product of Soviet legacies and post-Soviet institutional reforms. Legacies interact with the "institutional factor", understood as local and regional actors' opportunities defined by the macro-political context of the transformation regime and by the legal framework for regional governance. Yet the formal administrative systems with their rules and democratic principles such as elections and their legal bases are not mere façades, because they do structure the behaviour of the actors involved. In addition, the formal adoption of "Western" institutions can develop a self-binding power. This is exemplified by the Ukrainian case, where opposition groups insisted on the realization of their political rights. In this context, the indistinctness of the institutional framework created scope for action and eventually brought about the end of the Kuchma regime.

Notes

1 For a discussion of various western states, see Yves Mény and Vincent Wright, *Centre–Periphery Relations in Western Europe* (London: Allen & Unwin, 1985); Michael Keating, *State and Regional Nationalism: Territorial Politics and the European State* (New York: Harvester Wheatsheaf, 1988); and Robert J. Bennett (ed.), *Territory and Administration in Europe* (London: Pinter,1989). For a more general discussion, especially on federalism. see Alfred Stepan, "Federalism and Democracy: Beyond the U.S. Model", *Journal of Democracy* 10, 4, 1999, pp. 19–34.
2 Melanie Tatur, "Introduction: Conceptualising the Analysis of 'Making Regions' in Post-Socialist Europe", Melanie Tatur (ed.), *The Making of Regions in*

*Post-Socialist Europe – the Impact of History, Economic Structure and Institutions. Case Studies from Poland, Hungary, Romania and Ukraine (Wiesbaden: Verlag für Sozialwissenschaften, 2004), pp. 317–18.

3   The Russian case has mainly been analyzed from the angle of the political system. There are many case studies and some abstract analyses. In contrast, the Ukrainian case has mostly been analyzed with reference to ethno-linguistic differences and identities. On ethnolinguistic differences, see Dominique Arel, "Language Politics in Independent Ukraine: Towards One or Two State Languages?", *Nationalities Papers*, 23, 3, 1995, pp. 597–622; Andrew Wilson and Valeri Khmelko, "Regionalism and Ethnic and Linguistic Cleavages in Ukraine", in Taras Kuzio (ed.), *Contemporary Ukraine: Dynamics of Post-Soviet Transformation* (Armonk: M. E. Sharpe, 1998), pp. 60–80; and Andrew Wilson, "Elements of a Theory of Ukrainian Ethno-National Identities", *Nations and Nationalism* 8, 1, 2002, pp. 31–54. On identities, see Stephen Shulman, "Competing Versus Complementary Identities: Ukrainian–Russian Relations and the Loyalties of Russians in Ukraine", *Nationalities Papers*, 26, 4, 1998, pp. 615–32; Stephen Shulman, "Asymmetrical International Integration and Ukrainian National Disunity", *Political Geography* 18, 8, 1999, pp. 913–39; and Stephen Shulman, "The Contours of Civic and Ethnic National Identification in Ukraine", *Europe-Asia Studies* 56, 1, 2004, pp. 35–56. Administrative and political differences have played a minor role and there are fewer case studies.

4   Since intra-state comparisons prevail, both countries remain by and large remarkably underutilized in comparative political studies. A notable exception is Andrew Konitzer-Smirnov who compares the logic of incumbents remaining in their positions. Andrew Konitzer-Smirnov, "Serving Different Masters: Regional Executives and Accountability in Ukraine and Russia", *Europe–Asia Studies*, 57, 1, 2005, pp. 3–34. Kimitaka Matsuzato's work implicitly compares Russia and Ukraine applying the concept of machine politics. Kimitaka Matsuzato, "From Communist Boss Politics to Post-Communist Caciquismo – the Meso-Elite and Meso-Governments in Post-Communist Countries", *Communist and Post-Communist Studies*, 34, 2, 2001, pp. 175–201 and Kimitaka Matsuzato, "From Ethno-Bonapartism to Centralized Caciquismo: Characteristics and Origins of the Tatarstan Political Regime, 1990–2000", *Journal of Communist Studies and Transition Politics*, 17, 4, 2001, pp. 43–77.

5   Jeffrey Sachs, "My Plan for Poland", *The International Economy*, 3, 6, 1989, pp. 24–29.

6   For a discussion of the usefulness of the "transition paradigm", see Thomas Carothers, "The End of the Transition Paradigm", *Journal of Democracy*, 13, 1, 2002, pp. 5–21.

7   David Stark, "Nicht nach Design: Rekombiniertes Eigentum im osteuropäischen Kapitalismus", *Prokla* 24, 1, 1994, pp. 127–42.

8   For the concept of path dependence in economic history, see Douglass C. North, *Institutions, Institutional Change, and Economic Performance* (Cambridge: Cambridge University Press, 1990).

9   Jadwiga Staniszkis, Chester A. Kisiel and Ivan Szelenyi, *The Dynamics of the Breakthrough in Eastern Europe: The Polish Experience* (Berkeley: University of California Press, 1991), and David Stark, "Path Dependence and Privatization

Strategies in East Central Europe", *East European Politics and Societies*, 6, 1, 1992, pp. 17–54.

10 Jadwiga Staniszkis, "Postkommunismus – Versuch einer soziologischen Analyse", *Prokla*, 112, 3, 1998, pp. 375–94, and Tatur, "Introduction".

11 Fernand Braudel, "Geschichte und Sozialwissenschaft. Die Lange Dauer", in Fernand Braudel (ed.), *Schriften zur Geschichte 1. Gesellschaften und Zeit* (Stuttgart: Klett-Cotta, 1992), pp. 49–87.

12 Tatur, "Introduction".

13 Mikhail Filippov and Olga Shvetsova, "Asymmetric Bilateral Bargaining in the New Russian Federation. A Path-Dependence Explanation", *Communist and Post-Communist Studies*, 32, 1, 1999, pp. 61–76.

14 Andreas Kappeler, *Russische Geschichte* (München: Beck, 2002),pp. 47–8.

15 Habsburg rule introduced civil rights and minority rights. The region gained some experience in self-government and inherited specific legal traditions such as the Magdeburg Code. Claudia Šabić, "The Ukrainian Piedmont: The L'viv Region", Tatur, *The Making of Regions*, pp. 135–229. It is not clear, how powerful the mentioned traditions are and whether they are presently translated into political action. Martin Aberg, "Putnam's Social Capital Theory Goes East: A Case Study of Western Ukraine and L'viv", *Europe–Asia Studies* 52, 2, 2000, pp. 295–317; and Šabić (The Ukrainian Piedmont).

16 Matsuzato, "From Communist Boss".

17 S. N. Eisenstadt and Luis Roniger, *Patrons, Clients, and Friends: Interpersonal Relations and the Structure of Trust in Society* (Cambridge: Cambridge University Press, 1984).

18 Tatur, "Introduction", p. 26.

19 Gerald Easter, "Networks, Bureaucracies and the Russian State", Klaus Segbers (ed.), *Explaining Post-Soviet Patchworks, vol. 2: Pathways from the Past to the Global* (Aldershot: Ashgate, 2001), p. 47.

20 T.H. Rigby, "Early Provincial Cliques and the Rise of Stalin", *Soviet Studies*, 33, 1, 1981, pp.3–28; Günther Roth, *Politische Herrschaft und persönliche Freiheit* (Frankfurt: Suhrkamp, 1987); and James Hughes, "Patrimonialism and the Stalinist System. The Case of S. I. Syrtsov", *Europe–Asia Studies* 48, 4, 1996, pp. 551–68.

21 Easter, "Networks" and Matsuzato, "From Communist Boss", p. 180.

22 They were responsible for the political and economic control of the region and for the performance of regional enterprises. Therefore, they acted as coordinators and made sure that the regional companies were adequately provided with inputs and workforce. See Jerry F. Hough, *The Soviet Prefects: The Local Party Organs in Industrial Decision-Making* (Cambridge, MA: Harvard University Press, 1969).

23 Hough, *The Soviet Prefects*.

24 Peter Rutland argues that the economic role of regional party functionaries decreased after the abandonment of Khrushchev's reforms, because from then on the industrial ministries in Moscow and their local agencies assumed controlling and guiding functions. Thus, for the enterprise directors, their relationships with the central ministries regained importance, while involving informal aspects as well. Peter Rutland, *The Politics of Economic Stagnation in the Soviet Union: The Role of Local Party Organs in Economic Management* (Cambridge: Cambridge University Press, 1993).

25 Melanie Tatur, "Interessen und Norm. Politischer Kapitalismus und die Transformation des Staates in Polen und Rußland", Hellmut Wollmann, Helmut Wiesenthal and Frank Bönker (eds), *Transformation sozialistischer Gesellschaften. Am Ende des Anfangs. Leviathan Sonderheft 15* (Opladen: Westdeutscher Verlag, 1995), pp. 93–116.

26 Herbert Kitschelt and Regina Smyth, "Programmatic Party Cohesion in Emerging Postcommunist Democracies: Russia in Comparative Context", *Comparative Political Studies* 35, 10, 2002, p. 1234.

27 Steven L. Solnick, *Stealing the State: Control and Collapse in Soviet Institutions* (Cambridge, MA: Harvard University Press, 1998), pp. 26–9.

28 Donald A. Filtzer, "The Contradictions of the Marketless Market: Self-Financing in the Soviet Industrial Enterprise, 1986–90", *Soviet Studies* 43, 6, 1991, pp. 989–1009.

29 Lev Freinkman, "Financial–Industrial Groups in Russia: Emergence of Large Diversified Private Companies", *Communist Economies and Economic Transformation* 7, 1, 1995, p. 53.

30 Jadwiga Staniszkis, "'Political Capitalism' in Poland", *East European Politics and Societies*, 5, 1, 1991, pp. 127–41.

31 Tatur, "Introduction".

32 Andrei Ryabov, "'Partiya vlasti' v politicheskoi sisteme sovremennoi Rossii", in Michael McFaul, Sergei Markarov and Andrei Ryabov (eds), *Formirovanie Partiino-Politicheskoi Sistemy v Rossii* (Moscow: Carnegie Centre, 1998), pp. 80–96.

33 Richard Sakwa, *Putin: Russia's Choice* (London: Routledge, 2004), p. 132.

34 Matsuzato, "From Ethno-Bonapartism", p. 49.

35 Edward C. Banfield and James Q. Wilson, *City Politics* (Cambridge, MA: Harvard University Press, 1963), p. 115.

36 James C. Scott, *Comparative Political Corruption* (Englewood Cliffs: Prentice-Hall, 1972).

37 Kerstin Zimmer, "The Comparative Failure of Machine Politics, Administrative Resources and Fraud", *Canadian Slavonic Papers* 47, 1–2, 2005, pp. 361–84.

38 Henry E. Hale, "Why Not Parties? Electoral Markets, Party Substitutes, and Stalled Democratization in Russia", *Comparative Politics* 37, 2, 2005, pp. 147–66.

39 Scott, *Comparative Political Corruption*, p. 100.

40 Matsuzato, "From Communist Boss".

41 Henry E Hale, "Explaining Machine Politics in Russia's Regions: Economy, Ethnicity, and Legacy", *Post-Soviet Affairs* 19, 3, 2003, pp. 228–63.

42 Ibid.

43 Ibid. p. 258.

44 Matsuzato "From Communist Boss".

45 Jeronim Perovic, *Die Regionen Russlands als neue politische Kraft. Chancen und Gefahren des Regionalismus für Russland* (Bern: Lang, 2001), p. 116.

46 Peter Kirkow, "Im Labyrinth russischer Regionalpolitik: Ausgehandelter Föderalismus und institutionelle Veränderungen", *Osteuropa* 47, 1, 1997, pp. 38–51.

47 Peter Reddaway, "Historical and Political Context", Peter Reddaway and Robert W. Orttung (eds), *Dynamics of Russian Politics: Putin's Federal-Regional Reforms* (Lanham: Rowman & Littlefield Publishers Inc, 2003), pp. 1–18.

48 Robert Orttung, "Key Issues in the Evolution of the Federal Okrugs and Centre–Region Relations under Putin", Reddaway and Orttung, *Dynamics of Russian Politics*, pp. 19–52.

49 Richard Sakwa, "Federalism, Sovereignty and Democracy", in Cameron Ross (ed.): *Regional Politics in Russia* (Manchester: Manchester University Press, 2002), p. 1. Some observers termed this development the "medievalization" of politics to depict the fragmented administrative and legal space. Vladimir Shlapentokh, "Early Feudalism – the Best Parallel for Contemporary Russia", *Europe–Asia Studies*, 48, 3, 1996, pp. 393–411, and Sakwa, "Federalism, Sovereignty and Democracy", p. 2.

50 Sakwa, "Federalism, Sovereignty and Democracy", p. 9.

51 Ibid. p. 6.

52 Kirkow, "Im Labyrinth", p. 45, and Elizabeth Teague, "Putin Reforms the Federal System", in Ross, *Regional Politics*, p. 208.

53 Sakwa, "Federalism, Sovereignty and Democracy", p. 131.

54 Orttung, "Key Issues", p. 20.

55 Perovic, *Die Regionen Russlands*, p. 130.

56 Teague, "Putin Reforms", p. 209.

57 Sakwa, *Putin*, pp. 141 and 145.

58 Orttung, "Key Issues", p. 26.

59 Jeronim Perovic, "Regionalisierung unter Putin. Alte Muster und neue Trends", *Osteuropa* 52, 4, 2002, pp. 427–42.

60 Christopher Marsh, Helen Albert and James W. Warhola, "The Political Geography of Russia's 2004 Presidential Election", *Eurasian Geography and Economics*, 45, 4, 2004, p. 199.

61 For studies of this type, which often focus upon the political attitudes of the population, see Paul Kubicek, "Regional Polarisation in Ukraine: Public Opinion, Voting and Legislative Behaviour", *Europe–Asia Studies* 52, 2, 2000, pp. 273–294; Taras Kuzio, "National Identity in Independent Ukraine: An Identity in Transition", *Nationalism and Ethnic Politics*, 2, 4, 1996, pp. 582–608; Taras Kuzio, *Ukraine: State and Nation Building* (London: Routledge, 1998); John O'Loughlin and James Bell, "The Political Geography of Civic Engagement in Ukraine", *Post-Soviet Geography and Economics*, 40, 4, 1999, pp. 233–66; Stephen Shulman, "The Cultural Foundations of Ukrainian National Identity", *Ethnic and Racial Studies*, 22, 6, 1999, pp. 1011–36; and William Zimmermann, "Is Ukraine a Political Community?", *Communist and Post-Communist Studies*, 31, 1, 1998, pp. 43–55.

62 Lowell W. Barrington, "Examining Rival Theories of Demographic Influences on Political Support: The Power of Regional, Ethnic, and Linguistic Divisions in Ukraine", *European Journal of Political Research*, 41, 4, 2002, pp. 455–91; and Lowell W. Barrington, "Region, Language and Nationality: Rethinking Support in Ukraine for Maintaining Distance from Russia", in Paul D'Anieri and Taras Kuzio (eds), *Dilemmas of State-Led Nation Building in Ukraine* (Westport, CT: Praeger, 2002), pp. 131–46. In this approach, Ukraine can be subdivided into some four to nine distinctive regions.

63 Oleg Varfolomeyev, "Ukrainian Party Politics Gets a Boost", *Transition* 1998, p. 81.

64 Hans van Zon, "Neo-Patrimonialism as an Impediment to Economic Development: The Case of Ukraine", *Journal of Communist Studies and*

Transition Politics 17, 3, 2001, pp. 71–95. Claudia Šabić and Kerstin Zimmer, "Ukraine: The Genesis of a Captured State", in Tatur, *The Making of Regions*, pp. 107–30.

65 This notion has its roots in Max Weber who discussed patrimonialism. For an analysis of neo-patrimonialism see Eisenstadt. Engel and Erdmann applied the concept to African states while Roth (1987) used it to analyze the Soviet Union. Max Weber, *Wirtschaft und Gesellschaft: Grundriß der verstehenden Soziologie* (Tübingen: Mohr, 1980); S. N. Eisenstadt, *Traditional Patrimonialism and Modern Neopatrimonialism* (Beverley Hills: Sage, 1973); Ulf Engel and Gero Erdmann, "Neopatrimonialism Reconsidered – Critical Review and Elaboration of an Elusive Concept", Conference Paper 45th Annual Meeting of the African Studies Association, Washington DC, 4–8, December 2002.

66 Engel and Erdmann, "Neopatrimonialism Reconsidered".

67 For a general discussion of the neo-patrimonial character of the Ukrainian political regime and the institutionalization of informality, see Kerstin Zimmer, "Informal Institutions and Informal Politics in Ukraine", in Gerd Meyer (ed.), *Formal Institutions and Informal Politics in Central and Eastern Europe: Hungary, Poland, Russia and Ukraine* (forthcoming).

68 For more details see Šabić & Zimmer, "Ukraine" and Konitzer-Smirnov, "Serving Different Masters".

69 Konitzer-Smirnov, "Serving Different Masters", p. 6.

70 For more details see Šabić and Zimmer, "Ukraine" and Konitzer-Smirnov "Serving Different Masters".

71 Konitzer-Smirnov, "Serving Different Masters", p. 7.

72 UNDP/Institute of Politics, *Ukraine – 1998: Summary of the Year* (Kyiv, 1999).

73 Konitzer-Smirnov, "Serving Different Masters", p. 7.

74 Nancy Popson, "Conclusion: Regionalism and Nation-Building in a Divided Society", in D'Anieri and Kuzio *Dilemmas*, p. 198.

75 Parallel to this structure, there are central government agencies at the regional level: ministries and other central organs with nationwide authority operate with different territorial organs subordinated to them. In fact, there is dual subordination.

76 Irina S. Shchebetun, "Legal Guarantees of Protection of Local Self-Government", *Donetsk University Law Journal*, 3, 1999.

77 Zimmer, "Informal Institutions".

78 Keith A. Darden, "Blackmail as a Tool of State Domination: Ukraine under Kuchma", *East European Constitutional Review*, 10, 2–3, 2001.

79 Sergei Slukhai, "Some Recent Trends in Ukrainian Local Government's Fiscal Performance", Kansas City, ABFM Conference, 2000, http://www.ukans.edu/~kupa/ABFM2000/slukhai.abfm2000. pdf.

80 The fiscal relationships between the different levels of administration were reformed in 2001 when a new law on budget and local taxes was passed. However, it has never been entirely implemented because the administrative regulations have not been passed or are not adhered to.

81 The local budgets are regulated by the law "On local government in Ukraine", "On the budget system in Ukraine" and the annual state budget. In addition, the different tax laws influence the formation of the budget, especially the law "On local taxes and fees".

82 Era-Dabla Norris, Jorge Martinez-Vazquez and John Norregaard, "Making Decentralization Work. The Case of Russia, Ukraine, and Kazakhstan", Conference Paper: Conference on Fiscal Decentralization, Washington, DC, 20–21, November 2000, p. 5.

83 USAID, "Democratic Local Governance"; Nina Bubnova and Lucan Way, *Trends in Financing Regional Expenditures in Transition Economies: The Case of Ukraine* (Washington, DC: World Bank, 1998); Aleksandr Lyakh, "The Economic, Social and Political Situation in the Donbas Region and the Aims of National Policy", in Aleksandr Lyakh and Wlodzimierz Pankow (eds), *The Future of Old Industrial Regions in Europe. The Case of Donetsk Region in Ukraine* (Warsaw: Foundation for Economic Education, 1998), pp. 13–21; Aleksandr Lyakh and Yekaterina Tkachenko, "Local Government Financial Security During Economic and Social Restructuring", Lyakh and Pankow, *The Future*, pp. 23–34; and UNDP/Institute of Politics, *Ukraine*, p. 49.

84 Inna Lunina, "The Relations between Central and Local Budgets in Ukraine", *Ukrainian Economic Trends* September–October 1997, pp. 4–9 and Norris, Martinez-Vazquez and Norregaard, *Making Decentralization Work*, p. 8.

85 Norris, Martinez-Vazquez and Norregaard, *Making Decentralization Work*, p. 12.

86 Zimmer, *Informal Institutions*.

87 Ellen Bos, "Das politische System der Ukraine", in Wolfgang Ismayr (ed.), *Die politischen Systeme Osteuropas* (Opladen: Leske + Budrich, 2004), pp. 469–514.

88 The 2006 parliamentary elections took place according to a pure proportional formula.

89 Kimitaka Matsuzato, "All Kuchma's Men: The Reshuffling of Ukrainian Governors and the Presidential Election of 1999", *Post-Soviet Geography and Economics*, 42, 6, 2001, p. 427.

90 Oleksiy Haran', "Ukraine", Adrian Karatnycky, Alexander Motyl and Amanda Schnetzer (eds), *Nations in Transit: Civil Society, Democracy, and Markets in East Central Europe and the Newly Independent States* (Washington, DC: Freedom House, 2001), pp. 392–404, and Matsuzato, "All Kuchma's Men". Konitzer-Smirnov, "Serving Different Masters" confirms this through regression analysis, showing that electoral performance is more important than economic success or failure in decisions about the dismissal of officials.

91 This can be explained by the change of the electoral law in 1997, which enhanced the role of parties.

92 Matsuzato analyzes the interesting case of Zakarpattya oblast, which the Social Democratic Party of Ukraine (United) had selected as its electoral principality. Directed from Kyiv, the region actually became a bastion of the party and its central leaders. This was a rare case of creating a machine from above, while most other political machines emerged from an informal interplay of central and regional forces. Kimitaka Matsuzato, "Elites and the Party System of Zakarpattya Oblast: Relations among Levels of Party System in Ukraine", *Europe-Asia Studies* 54, 8, 2002, pp. 1267–99.

93 Hale, "Why Not Parties?".

94 Kerstin Zimmer, "The Captured Region. Actors and Institutions in the Ukrainian Donbass", Tatur (The Making of Regions), pp. 231–348.

95 Zimmer, "The Captured Region", pp. 312–14.

96 Matsuzato, "From Ethno-Bonapartism", p. 43.

97   Konitzer-Smirnov, "Serving Different Masters", p. 7.
98   Central Election Commission, *Elections 2002*, 2002. http://195.230.
      157.53/pls/vd2002/webproc0e.
99   Most of them belonged to the Party of Regions, the local party of power,
      which joined the bloc "For a United Ukraine". In Donetsk, "For a United
      Ukraine" achieved 36.83 per cent of the votes, the Communists 29.78 per
      cent, and Our Ukraine 4.46 per cent. Central Election Commission,
      "Elections 2002". Donetsk oblast was the only region where the pro-presi-
      dential bloc achieved a majority of votes.
100   Serhii Harmash, "Legal Farce". *Zerkalo Nedeli* 6, 16–22 February 2002.
101   *ForUm*, 5 February 2002, *http://www.for-ua.com*
102   Kuchma had by this time been weakened by the Gongadze affair and inter-
      national isolation.
103   During the 2004 presidential election, this was actually attempted. Some of
      the rules that had a determining influence on the election campaigns and
      results in 1999 and 2002 were applied at the national level, but ultimately
      failed to achieve the desired victory for Viktor Yanukovych. Zimmer, "The
      Comparative Failure".
104   Evidently, the legal status of these contracts was questionable. Allegedly, the
      members of parliament would resign if they did not keep their electoral
      promises. Yet, it remained unclear who was to enforce this, and a time frame
      for the implementation was not given. *Ukrainian Regional Report* 6/2002.
105   *Ukrainian Regional Report*, 6/2002.
106   *ForUm* 28 February 2002, http://www.for-ua.com. The Ukrainian trade
      union movement is split into the successor organizations of the Soviet-era
      unions, and new independent unions, some of which have emerged from the
      strikes at the end of the Soviet era. The post- Soviet unions have more members,
      and their leaders have often been co-opted by the power elite. Zimmer, "The
      Captured Region", pp. 317–19.
107   *ForUm*, 28 March 2002; *ForUm*, 26 February 2002, http://www.for-ua.com
108   *Gazeta v gazete* 155, 14 March 2002. Right after the election, Viktor
      Yanukovych and the chairman of the regional parliament, Boris Kolesnikov,
      confirmed the significance of these contracts *Gazeta v gazete* 158, 4 April 2002.
109   Committee of Voters of Ukraine, Summary of Long Term Observation Report
      on 2002 Parliamentary Elections (Kyiv, 2001).
110   Zimmer, "The Comparative Failure".
111   Interview with a lecturer at the University, Donetsk, 2 November 1999.
112   Ukrainian Regional Report, 7/2002.
113   Eberhard Schneider, *Das politische System der Ukraine. Eine Einführung*
      (Wiesbaden: Verlag für Sozialwissenschaften, 2005), pp. 76–7.
114   Office for Democratic Institutions and Human Rights, Preliminary
      Statement on the Second Round of the Presidential Election in Ukraine, 21
      November 2004 (Warsaw: ODIHR, 2004).
115   This became obvious during interviews with company directors, trade
      union officials, and politicians in 1999 and 2000.
116   Zimmer, "The Captured Region", pp. 317–18.
117   Henry E. Hale, "Machine Politics and Institutionalized Electorates: A
      Comparative Analysis of Six Duma Elections in Bashkortostan", *Journal of
      Communist Studies and Transition Politics*, 15, 4, 1999, pp. 70–110.

118 Kerstin Zimmer, "The Donetsk Factor", *Transitions Online*, 17 December 2004.
119 John W. Meyer, John Boli, George M Thomas and Franciso O. Ramirez, "World Society and the Nation-State", *American Journal of Sociology*, 103, 1, 1997, pp. 144–81.
120 Joel Hellman, "Winners Take All: The Politics of Partial Reform in Postcommunist Nations", *World Politics*, 50, 2, 1998, pp. 203–34.
121 Perovic, "Regionalisierung".

5
The Influence of Russian Big Business on Regional Power: Models and Political Consequences

Rostislav Turovsky

Introduction

In the wake of the Russian transition to a market economy, the interaction of new post-Soviet business and regional/local government has become one of the most important issues on the political agenda. "Business–power" relations has also become one of the most important and popular themes in scholarly study. But there remains a need for a more scientific background to the study of this question.

One approach to this question has been the elitist approach, which tackles the theme in terms of elite transformation. Business elites are seen as an active part of society and of the national elite. Their economic interests encourage them to take part in power struggles and they often seek to become politicians. This leads to a horizontal circulation between political and economic groups. This phenomenon is well known from the history of many western democracies, including the USA and France. As a result, representatives of the business elite gain office in regional administrations and legislatures. The contrary process, politicians entering business, is also possible.

Another approach is instrumental. This discusses the issue in terms of interest (or pressure) groups, lobbies and patron–client relations. The interest groups have their origin in economic relations, but in order to pursue their economic interests, they need political support. Patron–client relations arise, for example, when business groups try to achieve their economic goals with the help of friendly state and municipal authorities. In the process of integration, business groups and politicians form political-economic clans.[1] This sort of development usually occurs in cases of less transparent political regimes with an underdeveloped public policy sphere.

The latter approach is also close to the theory of rational choice. In terms of "business–power" relations, rational choice theory points out that business groups use friendly political power in order to expand their business. They thoroughly calculate profit coming as a result of political bodies' decisions and look at how expenditures on political campaigns and lobbyism pay off.

These approaches seem relevant to studies of "business–power" relations in Russia. The processes of both regime and elite transformation in Russia made the strengthening of ties between ruling elites and a rising business inevitable. The transformation of Russian regional elites is closely tied with the gradual loss of the Soviet nomenklatura's influence. There are several reasons why the business elite began to come to power in the Russian regions.

1. The Soviet nomenklatura is losing its positions in the regions due to generational change.
2. Post-Soviet business is the only source of the new elite that originated in the course of the reforms. And it represents the socially active part of modern Russian society.
3. The reforms made possible the change of the dominating regional leaders' type from ex-Soviet to "capitalist" manager.

But elite rotation in the Russian regions is very gradual. Our studies show that the share of former Soviet nomenklatura representatives among the Russian governors became less than 50 per cent only in the last few years. When the governors were appointed by the president in 1991–1995, Yeltsin chose them from the politically loyal nomenklatura. Few appointees were directors of industrial and agrarian enterprises. In the beginning of the 1990s Russia had neither oligarchy nor lobbyism.

The development of capitalism in Russia and the regional authorities: from colonialism to clientelism

In post-Soviet Russia, the formation of capitalist relations was the principal factor determining "business–power" relations. At the beginning of the economic reforms, the ruling elites at all levels set and led the privatization process. They could define the results of privatization deals and auctions; they could also screw competitors. Russian capitalism is commonly portrayed as state-bureaucratic and crony in nature. The ruling elite was a mixture of the old nomenklatura, new economists and brand-new businessmen.

Under such circumstances the formation of clienteles including state officials and businessmen began:

- State officials became patrons for these clienteles, as a rule in regions with more stable and powerful ruling elites holding their positions from the Soviet times.
- Recently businessmen have taken the lead as they started to play the role of patrons and control regional bureaucracy in their own interests.

The business elite considered state and municipal offices as an opportunity to expand its business with the help of administrative powers and through the establishment of informal patron–client relations with their holders. A jocular interpretation of the Marxist formula became relevant: "Money – power – more money." The introduction of gubernatorial and mayoral elections in the mid-1990s strongly influenced the process of direct and personal involvement of businessmen in political activities, like elections and the holding of state and municipal offices.

In elections, businessmen had some advantages – a sufficient amount of money and sometimes an attractive image. The good image came from the impression of businessmen's personal activities and successes, sometimes even charisma, and the absence of negative associations with nomenklatura. The very new (though rare to find) type of Russian governor in the beginning and middle of the 1990s was the Moscow businessman of regional origin or authentic regional self-made man. The first important example was Kirsan Ilyumzhinov, a young Moscow businessman of Kalmyk origin, elected president of small and poor Kalmykiya in 1993.[2] The best examples of regional self-made men were Valentin Tsvetkov in Magadan oblast and Vladimir Butov in Nenets autonomous okrug, both elected governors in 1996.

The interaction between regional authorities and business elites has followed a particular pattern. In the beginning, regional-level businessmen came to hold regional power. Privatization in the regions was in the first stage conducted in the interests of regional players, both Soviet and post-Soviet by nature; federal business groups were virtually non-existent. In the 1990s, medium-sized regional business became more active in regional elections. Its political activity entailed elite rotation on regional and municipal levels.

The mayoral office was often seen as a starting point for regional businessman. The most interesting case was that of local businessman Yurii Trutnev who was elected mayor of Perm in 1996 and governor of Perm oblast in 2000. From the beginning, regional business seemed to be more active in municipal elections because it was easier to win such elections compared with the resource-exhausting gubernatorial elections. But regional business demonstrated rising interest in gubernatorial elections, though real success came in only a small number of cases. The best examples of such success were the victories of Sergei Dar'kin in Primorskii krai in 2001 and Mikhail Kuznetsov in Pskov oblast in 2004.

The direct influence of big Russian business on regional power followed the rise of integrated business groups.[3] This happened in the middle and second half of the 1990s. Big business in Russia is of Moscow origin, but it exploits regional resources. It started to look closely at the regions, and therefore at the regional authorities, as it formed its regional networks. Such networks came into being in the first Yeltsin term (1991–96). Initially integrated business groups paid little attention to their relations with the regional authorities. They followed the "colonial model", regarding the regions as conquered prey. Territory was understood as an object of exploitation, with its own interests and the interests of its inhabitants being neglected in favour of those of the exploiters.

In the second Yeltsin term (1996–99), big companies started to appreciate the importance of good and stable relations with regional elites. There were several reasons for this:

1. The process of privatization led to the victory of the core over the periphery. The economic-geographical core companies went to the regions and paid generously for the property formerly privatized by regional businessmen.
2. The political influence of oligarchy increased along with the coming of oligarchic capitalism in Russia in place of state-bureaucratic capitalism.[4]
3. Strong competition on the federal level for the status of Yeltsin's successor led to a very unstable political situation. Centres of decision-making moved to the regions. And the influence of regional elites rose because of the introduction of gubernatorial elections in 1996.
4. Leading companies started to think about gaining strong positions in strategically important regions. Sometimes this took place in the context of conflicts with local elites resulting from the operation of the colonial model. Big business started to perceive territory as a value and strategic resource that should be kept under control.

As a result, big business began to reject the initial colonial model in favour of the model of strategic partnership with the governors,[5] also called the clientelistic model. The colonial model meant very little interaction between exploiters of Moscow origin and regional elites. The clientelistic model proved to be more effective for business groups because it meant friendly relations of a patron–client type between profit-seeking business groups and politically influential regional authorities. It helped to overcome administrative barriers and to reduce political risks. However, after a short while, some companies started to implement a more radical model of power seizure by their representatives in the regions. This meant that the company became not a partner of regional authority, but the regional authority itself. This often happened after conflicts with local elites, reflecting the impossibility of implementing the model of strategic partnership. Both models led to the formation of vertically integrated clienteles, including federal business groups and the regional bureaucracy. The business groups of Potanin, Khodorkovsky, Alekperov, Fridman and Vekselberg were the most active in the regions, introducing the model of strategic partnership and, in some cases, the power seizure model.

The model of strategic partnership under regional mono-centrism

The ideal typical model of close and strategic relations between big business and regional authorities came into being around the turn of the millennium. These were the final years of Yeltsin's term and the beginning of Putin's term. This model was shaped by the mono-polar model of the regional political regime, with the governor as the key political and decision-making centre. Under such circumstances, relations with the governor in a majority of regions could solve almost all problems. This model of the regional political regime had appeared by 1995–96, following the dissolution of the soviets in 1993, which meant the abolition of a political counterbalance to regional executive power.[6] The mono-polar model lasted through the period 1997–2000, after the introduction of gubernatorial elections.[7]

Central to the mono-polar model, which has also been called regional mono-centrism and is a replica of federal-level political mono-centrism,[8] was the fact that regional leaders had enormous influence in their regions and felt rather independent in relations with the centre. The system of regional mono-centrism included a huge network of informal relations with the governor at its core. What was important for business was that a strong governor could informally influence federal-dependent structures in the regions, such as law enforcement and tax collection, and thereby gain privileges for business.

As a rule, the governor either subjected regional business to his authority or simply created his own network of loyal business. Only federal business groups, with their huge financial resources and sometimes their federal political support, could challenge such a system. In the 1990s, regional mono-centrism stimulated a stereotype according to which a dominating company "must" control regional executive power. But such companies and their candidates did not succeed everywhere because of the negative public reaction influenced by regional patriotism and anti-oligarchic feelings; a good instance is the political failures of Lukoil in Nenets autonomous okrug.

The strategy of a big company under regional mono-centrism was to make a governor its client or, in cases of desperate need, to make its person a governor. In the company's strategy, the governor was considered to be the key player. The relationship with him opened access to regional resources and eased the processes of formation, strengthening and expansion of business. Companies also took into consideration the fact that the Russian bureaucracy had many formal and informal opportunities to affect business. There followed the coalescence effect, with big business coalescing with the regional authorities; this may also be described as the creation of symbiotic relations. Such an effect characterized regions rich in resources, especially in oil and metals.

In analyzing the influence of big and middle business, it is very important to define the real meaning of this influence and the motives of businessmen. Two points are relevant. First, such analysis may be based on an understanding of the psychology of the business elite. Personal ambition often motivates a businessman to become a politician (governor, mayor, deputy, etc.). In this case, involvement in political activity is an appropriate response. According to the studies of Russian scholars, there are several explanations as to why businessmen enter political life:

1. Personal problems in business, the sale of property and change of job.
2. Political career becomes just a new step in personal career.
3. Pragmatic goal to enlarge business by acquiring political status which is seen as an opportunity for lobbying in favour of personal business interests.

Second, the political involvement of the business elite should be studied in terms of the effectiveness of political investments. This means that it should be clearly understood what is really useful for business when it gets or controls regional power. Principally this means that big business tries to manage its regional political risks through the control of regional power. The effectiveness of political investments is closely connected with the sharing of regional and municipal powers. The details of these powers in Russia have been constantly changing. Being a federation, Russia shares powers between federal and regional levels. There is also a sphere of municipal powers. As for the regional authorities, they have their own organizational structure comprising executive and legislative branches, each with their own powers. Finally, the governor's informal influence is very important. The scope and character of informal influence is unique for each region. The effectiveness of political investments will be shaped by these sorts of power configurations.

The rise of oligarchs-turned-governors

Oligarchs-turned-governors were one of the most interesting political phenomena in the early years (2000–2002) of Putin's first term.[9] The change of president in 2000 was a strong stimulus for Yeltsin's oligarchy to search for alternative or supplementary spheres of political influence. The oligarchies controlling the individual regions tried to stabilize their positions, foreseeing that the new president would bring to power new interest groups. The main and very symbolic event in regional political life under "early Putin" was the election of the former "purse" of Yeltsin's family, Roman Abramovich, to the office of the governor of Chukotka.

The number of direct representatives of Russian big business elected as governors was very small. It was more usual for Russian companies to move their top managers into gubernatorial offices, seeing the particular region as a sort of branch of the company. But such cases were rare and symbolic of the tendency to see the region as part of the company's bailiwick. The most common practice was staff interaction, or horizontal circulation, between the regional administration and the company. Managers of certain companies became deputy-governors and state officials obtained jobs in companies.

The best example of this was the policy of Interros, which helped Norilsk Nickel CEO Aleksandr Khloponin to be elected initially governor of Taimyr autonomous okrug (which is in Krasnoyarsk krai) and then governor of the whole of Krasnoyarsk krai. After Khloponin's election in Krasnoyarsk, another former representative of Norilsk Nickel management, Norilsk mayor Oleg Budargin, became Taimyr governor. Taimyr and Krasnoyarsk krai are actually two principal regions of Interros business interests. Norilsk Nickel could not control the power in both regions because their ruling elites were formed before Interros came to the regions. And Norilsk itself is a distant and isolated town. Geographically speaking, Interros was ill-placed. Failing to cooperate with the ruling elites of both regions, Interros used the model of power seizure with the help of its enormous financial resources, and succeeded.

Following the same pattern, Yukos oil company decided to move its manager, Boris Zolotarev, to the office of governor of Evenkiya autonomous okrug. Evenkiya was considered by Yukos as an important region of future oil exploitation. For its key oil regions, Yukos used a strategy of staff interaction. In Samara oblast, the most evident example was the appointment of Yukos top manager Viktor Kazakov to the vice-governor's office, the second-ranking person in the regional executive power. An example of staff interaction in another direction is in Tomsk oblast, where the former first deputy-governor Vladimir Ponomarenko, having become a client of Yukos, left the regional administration to head the Yukos office in Tomsk.

Towards a new model: tactical partnership in times of limited regional mono-centrism

A change in the dominating model of regional power started in approximately 2002. By this time regional political regimes had undergone serious changes, in particular the replacement of absolute by limited regional mono-centrism. The main reason for this was the new policy of the federal centre which, for the first time and in a tough way, strengthened federal control over the regional level. New state leaders implemented strong bureaucratic control over the regional level in order to strengthen new influential groups from St Petersburg and preserve the country's unity; or at least that was the ideology of the new leaders. As a result, federal-dependent offices (presidential envoys, law-enforcement, tax collection, etc.) were taken out of informal gubernatorial control, where they had been for a long time. The new typical conflict of Putin's time was the conflict between governor and the regional branches of federal offices. All this started in 2000 when Putin came to power, and by 2002 the new situation in relations between big business and the regional authorities had appeared. At the same time the central authorities redistributed powers in favour of the federation. In Russia this could be done within the sphere of concurrent powers partly regulated by federal laws, which in their turn have force over the whole country.

The new model of regional political regime comprises mono-centrism limited by rather strong federal authorities, and the centralization of powers. The gradual dismantling of regional mono-centrism under Putin combined the growing dependence of governors on the federal centre with the minimization of governors' informal influence upon federal structures in the regions. Under such circumstances, "business-power" relations in the regions should be studied with careful attention to the differences between regional political regimes and the economic interest of business elites in the regional and local government. The list of regional and local powers became very important for each businessman planning his regional expansion. Not all the companies were really interested in patron–client relations with regional and local governments. In the new situation big business cannot rely on its partnership with the governors.

Nevertheless big business retained a number of interests for which gubernatorial powers were relevant in the era of limited regional mono-centrism:

1. Interest in buying regional state property, which in some regions still remains large and attractive, e.g. shares of the biggest enterprises and prospective projects.
2. Interest in regional finances, budget and non-budget funds and regional development programmes. Many companies strive for orders from the regional or municipal account. The choice of partners by the regional authorities often remains non-public and corrupt.
3. Interest in tax breaks and other financial opportunities provided by the regional governments.

Analyzing "business–power" relations, one should pay attention to the fact that, according to the Russian Constitution, the ownership, use and disposal of land, forests, waters and other natural resources are part of the concurrent powers shared by the federal and regional authorities. Regional governments have their own powers in this important sphere. Their decisions can influence companies extracting raw materials. Russian big business has a raw materials bias, and this explains many companies' interest in controlling regional power.

One should also not forget about power sharing among branches and levels of government in the region. A new stage in defining relations between business and local government is tied up with current municipal reform in which a new federal law lists the powers of different local communities – municipal districts, settlements, and urban districts. The configuration of power in the regions (executive power, legislative power, territorial branches of federal executive power, and municipal power of one or two levels) forces companies to decide which regional power-holder and at what level will be really useful in terms of economic interests, i.e. where political investments will really pay. Recently, a need to reduce political risks caused by judicial power, law-enforcement and tax authorities made companies search for direct and informal relations with them. Companies moved their activity to the federal level because territorial branches of federal power strongly depend on their bosses in the centre.

In the time of limited regional mono-centrism, a new model of "business-power" relations in the regions has appeared: that is the model of tactical *ad hoc* partnership. Such a partnership appears and disappears while companies solve their specific problems with the regional and municipal powers. But companies that are interested in constant influence on the regional authorities still think in terms of strategic partnership.

Big business interests in tactical partnership

Under limited mono-centrism and centralization, big companies need to revise their interests in the regional authorities. A number of interests are relevant in this regard.

The company is interested if the regional government owns valuable property subject to sale

Big business has been looking closely at those regions characterized by state-bureaucratic capitalism where privatization was actually frozen. Such regions are often national republics. They have been characterized by a struggle between local groups close to the regional power on the one hand and Russian big business on the other. Furthermore local clans still hold the power while the federal authorities are not powerful enough to start privatization in the interests of the federal-level groups. There is at least one political reason for this: the Kremlin appreciates the so called "administrative resource" of republican leaders who bring a lot of votes to Putin and United Russia at the national elections. The Kremlin still does not risk undermining mono-centric political regimes in certain republics.

An important example of this is Bashkortostan, with its "tug-of-war" between the regional authorities and federal business groups. The republican president's son, Ural Rakhimov, has become one of the local oligarchs, controlling large parts of the oil industry. Among federal groups, it has been Gazprom[10] that has tried to include Bashkortostan in its sphere of influence. Gazprom manages a huge petrochemical plant, Salavatnefteorgsintez, that is owned by Bashkortostan's government. But it has still failed to incorporate other chemical plants in Bashkortostan into its own holding. Nevertheless "core" business is stronger than the local oligarchs. In 2005, shares of Bashneft oil company and oil refineries (about 20–30 per cent of different enterprises) were sold to AFK Sistema, one of the well-known Moscow groups specializing in telecoms.

The situation in neighbouring Tatarstan, another economically developed republic, is also very interesting. The regional political regime here appears to be the most stable in the whole of Russia, and it has even managed to neutralize the pressure from the federal authorities. The main enterprises are in the hands of the republican authorities or groups close to them. Federal business groups have little chance to seize this property. Moreover groups of republican origin are strong enough to acquire federal status and buy property in other regions. So the biggest regional groups (like Tatneft, the republican-owned oil company) turn into federal groups. And the regional economy in Tatarstan remains closed to big business of Moscow or St Petersburg origin.

But most regions in 2005 had little state property and it was not attractive to big business. A good example is Irkutsk oblast where the regional authorities try to sell their small shares in the huge and prospective gas field of Kovykta to Gazprom. But Gazprom refused to buy these shares because it wants full control, and regional shares do not mean a thing from its point of view.

The company uses regional powers in its commercial interests

A more flexible regional tax regime could be introduced in the interests of certain companies or to make the region appear more attractive to potential investors. One form of this was the development of the region as an internal offshore zone. Some big companies have used regions to minimize their tax payments. This helped to create relations between big business and a number of underdeveloped regions where the regional authorities wanted badly any sort of cooperation with leading Russian business groups. Big business was particularly interested in regional power to reduce or waive regional rates of profit tax (in Russia, the regional rate of this tax is much higher than the federal one).

In some cases companies formed political alliances with long-acting regional leaders. The best example was relations between Yukos and the small republic of Mordoviya (the republican leader Nikolai Merkushkin represents the former Soviet nomenklatura). Regional authorities gave Yukos' trading companies extensive tax breaks. Yukos also began to use tax breaks in Evenkiya where, as shown above, the company helped its own manager Zolotarev to be elected to the governor's office. Another example is Kalmykiya, another poor national republic. The difference is that the nomenklatura in Mordoviya stayed in power while the leader of Kalmykiya was a rather young businessman. And Mordoviya became a client of one business group while Kalmykiya worked with many of them. There is one unique case when a company's owner and the governor is the same person, that of Chukotka. It was the use of the region as an off-shore zone that was the main reason why Abramovich became its governor.

But this practice of becoming an internal offshore zone provoked a tough reaction by federal authorities in the 2000s. The reaction was even tougher because the federal budget had to subsidize these offshore regions. Such regions had shadow "business–power" relations while the regional budget was empty because of the tax breaks; for example in Kalmykiya in 2003, 85 per cent of collected taxes went to the federal budget.

Another means of making the region more attractive to outside investors was to have flexible tax policies. This was a less notorious practice aimed at reviving the industrial sector, and is commonly described as an improvement of the attractiveness of regional investments.[11] Such regions combined some tax breaks with measures aimed at fighting red tape. The classic example was Novgorod oblast, which was poor in terms of natural resources. Such regions had fewer shadow relations with business groups; their approach seemed to be more transparent, but the number of investors was rather large. But such regions attracted small and medium-sized businesses rather than the oligarchs.[12]

Another way of increasing a region's attractiveness is through the creation of special economic zones. This was introduced by federal laws in Kaliningrad oblast in 1996 and in the city of Magadan in 1999. But again these laws did not attract big business because it was interested either in raw materials producing regions or underdeveloped internal off-shores. Special economic zones, which favoured cheap imports because of easier customs rules, benefited local trading business and led to its symbiosis with the authorities.

After the transitional years of 2000–2002, the pendulum swung back to the opposite side. The federal authorities do not let their regional counterparts pursue their own, more flexible economic policies. The unification of regional political and economic regimes became a part of the ideology officially aimed at strengthening the country's unity. This ideology had its interpretation in fiscal policy seeking to fill the budget by all means and increasing tax revenues; at the same time financial stimuli for the new projects are underestimated. From 1 January 2004, internal offshore zones became impossible, with the regional rate of profit tax able to be reduced by no more than 4 per cent with the whole regional rate now at 17.5 per cent. As a whole, attractive regions started losing their attractiveness. Flexible economic policies could be qualified by the federal authorities as exceeding or even misusing regional powers. Federal tax authorities do not care about tax breaks given by governors. The very interesting example was a criminal investigation against Yaroslavl governor Anatolii Lisitsyn. This investigation examined the governor's decisions, which had previously been understood in terms of investments' attractiveness. And Yaroslavl oblast was considered to be one of the most attractive regions (see, for example, the well-regarded regional ratings of the journal *Ekspert*). The Lisitsyn case looked much the same as the Yukos case because one of the best-ruled regions became a victim, and that made the rest more confident. Consequentially regional economic policies became very much the same.

A simpler scenario resulted from this situation. Companies are interested in regions which have needed economic resources, on the condition that political risks in these regions are not extreme, as they are in the North Caucasus for example. There are a few cases of serious tax breaks. Amounts of saved money are not as big as compared with former internal offshores. For example, Moscow oblast attracts huge investments without any special tax breaks. The reason is simple: this region has a very good location and cheaper land (in comparison with Moscow city). Moscow oblast does have business groups close to the regional authorities, but they are rather small and do not dominate in the region. The regional authorities prefer good relations with all investors. Promises to provide tax breaks are made only in cases of really strong interregional competition; for example, Moscow oblast is ready to give tax breaks to automobile plants because it wants to attract Volkswagen.

But in 2005 a new story began; the pendulum moved slightly back towards more decentralization. Some powers again went to the regions according to a new law, with federally approved opportunities for regional tax breaks becoming a bit more apparent. Economically strong Perm krai has been reducing its profit tax rate by the maximum four per cent possible for all its taxpayers, including branches of Lukoil. For the first time in history, the Russian parliament adopted a law on special economic zones (SEZ). But these zones cannot coincide with regions and localities. And big business in Russia is not very interested in the sort of innovative industrial production the SEZs are meant to attract. Probably only Kaliningrad oblast, as the one and only region-made-SEZ, will become a good example of "business-power" partnership after the new federal law on this region has been adopted.

In conclusion, one can say that the main story during this period has been the coalescence of big business and ruling elites of underdeveloped regions which have used their powers to help companies to minimize tax payments. Now this story is almost over. But the pendulum in centre–region relations is ever moving, and new developments continue to occur.

Licensing the extraction of raw materials

It is common knowledge that the Russian economy depends on raw materials. This gives increased importance to bureaucratic procedures such as the licensing of mining operations. Up to 2005 Russia used the so-called "rule of two keys". According to this rule, a licence came into force after being approved by both the federal government and the regional administration. Under Yeltsin, many decisions were actually made at the regional level and were only approved by the federal authorities. Towards the middle and the end of the 1990s, the regional authorities actively handed out small deposits of oil and gas both to friendly big companies and to new small companies where regional government officials had their shares. Such practices were common in the Yamalo-Nenets and Nenets autonomous okrugs, and in Komi Republic.

On the one hand, this resulted in establishing new oil and gas companies controlled by the regional authorities or their business allies. A good example is the gas company Novatek, which is the second-ranking company in Russia in terms of specializing in natural gas exploration. This company appeared in Yamalo-Nenets autonomous okrug under the auspices of vice-governor Iosif Levinzon, former head of Purneftegazgeologiya, a company specializing in geological surveys and holding licences for the survey and pilot extraction of mineral deposits. But on the other hand, close relations between regional authorities and big companies took place in the prospective oil regions where big companies with the help of the regional authorities got licences for the new oilfields. Evenkiya autonomous okrug was a good example of this; Yukos was going to make Evenkiya a new oil region and started with an electoral victory. However, if agreements failed, the regional authorities and big company could become involved in a serious conflict. In Nenets autonomous okrug, governor Vladimir Butov opposed Lukoil expansion and distributed oil deposits among other companies, including Nenets Oil Company established by the regional authorities. Lukoil tried twice (in 2001 and 2005) to have its candidate Shmakov elected governor, but failed. The conflict between Butov and Lukoil was an important reason for the federal campaign for the abolition of the "rule of two keys".

Amendments to the federal law adopted in 2005 drastically changed this situation. Regional authorities now held powers only for so-called widespread minerals, like sand, road-metal, gravel etc. In the case of valuable minerals, the decision-making power moved to Moscow. Accordingly, this big business interest in the regional powers has decreased, while regions fight hard to regain their previous powers.

Other opportunities

The new stage of land reform that started with the implementation of the new Land Code gave rise to business interest in the regional powers selling or leasing of land. Municipal authorities also have powers in this field. Business groups could investigate agreements with both regional and municipal authorities, but only after they have established the real distribution of power in this regard in the particular region in which they have an interest.

But a strategic partnership is likely to develop on the municipal level when even a small enterprise can be of key importance for the local budget. As for the regional level, it is a more routine process, and political alliance or conflict can come in case of a really big deal. The new and important process is the development of relations between agro-holdings (now on the rise in Russia) and the regional authorities in Southern regions. One example is the close relations between Belgorod oblast administration and the agro-holding Stoylenskaya Niva created under its auspices, but which in turn is also a part of a federal business group. And there is a strong conflict between Belgorod governor and an unwanted newcomer – the Moscow group Inteko owned by mayor Luzhkov's wife. Similar processes will start after the adoption of a new Forest Code.

Companies revise their regional strategies

Contemporary trends in "business–power" relations are evidence of a change in the dominating model. The former model of regional mono-centrism and intensive patron–client relations changed in a number of ways under Putin. First, mono-centrism became much more relative because the system of informal gubernatorial patronage over federal structures in the regions has been partly dismantled. And it is such federal structures that create the most serious risks for companies. However mono-centrism is still real for regional and local government. Financially weak local government still remains under the informal control of the governor, and regional legislative power is still subject to gubernatorial pressure. Close relations with the governor are now useful but not sufficient for doing successful business in the regions.

Secondly, the governors' independence in their economic decisions has been restricted while federal control has been strengthened. The new, rigid, financial policy of the federal government has limited the governors' powers to give tax breaks and other privileges, while the federal centre has changed the law on natural resources so as to redistribute administrative powers to its benefit.

As a result of such changes, big business has been revising its regional strategies, including relations with regional government; the interest in having direct influence is decreasing. Of course, there are still many specific issues requiring agreement between regional government and business structures, but these are issues of strategic importance for regional business. Big federal business can achieve its strategic goals by way of interacting with federal authorities and then agreeing with regional governments on certain details. In the new situation, big business cannot rely entirely on its partnership with the governors, so it has redistributed its attention in favour of the federal authorities who again have become a more important source of political risks and economic opportunities.

The recent abolition of gubernatorial elections also affected companies' strategies. Now they can not make their people governors through elections, and their ability to change governors has become more limited. In the past, companies could "buy" elections, sometimes either not even asking for Kremlin support or "buying" this support. Now they need to persuade the Kremlin, but the president and his administration want to rule business and not to be ruled by the oligarchs, as used to be the case under Yeltsin. State-bureaucratic tendencies have again become more explicit under Putin in contrast to oligarchic tendencies. As a result, companies prefer to work with the existing regional rulers and not to waste time making the Kremlin appoint their people.

At present, a typical Russian business group uses a revised strategy of regional political risks management based on the following:

1. The use of administrative powers held by the regional or municipal authorities in the company's interests in those cases when the company considers such powers to be really useful.
2. Expectations of new changes in the permanently unstable relations between centre and regions in Russia. Such changes may lead to a new redistribution of powers in the regions' favour. Despite the centralization processes in recent years, Russia has not abandoned the federal model. In 2005, an opposite, small-scale redistribution of power to the regions began.
3. The persistence of the previous mono-centric model, especially in cases when some governors still retain absolute power in their regions (e.g. the republics, Kemerovo oblast etc).
4. Some (but not all) companies consider a favourable social and political environment in the regions of their economic activity to be important. They implement social and charity programs and work on their public image.
5. The basic pattern of Russian politics is patron–client relations. This means that it is better for governors and companies alike to have such relations than not to have them. But too great a dependence on such relations is considered to be risky in the unstable political situation. And such relations do not necessarily have economic benefits for the company.

The rise of oligarchs-turned-governors, which reached its climax in 2002 with Khloponin's election, was followed by their fall. In the beginning of the 2000s, oligarchs considered the governor's status as a useful supplement to their original status. But when its usefulness decreased, the desire to become governors almost disappeared. The reason is that the governor's status and powers were reconsidered and found to be too small for a real oligarch. This is clearly reflected in 2002 in Lipetsk oblast. The owner of Novolipetsk iron-and-steel plant (NLMK), one of the biggest in Russia, Vladimir Lisin, after long hesitation, refused to take part in the gubernatorial elections. Following his refusal to participate, Lisin's business developed extremely well. If Lisin became a governor, he may not have been able to go on turning NLMK into one of the leading business groups in Russia acting in several important regions. Furthermore the complicated relations between Lisin and governor Oleg Korolev did not affect Lisin's business at all. The governor understood that, at least, cold peace with the main enterprise in his oblast was much better than senseless war.

The intensity of big business' fight for control over regional authorities is also decreasing. Economic motives for such a fight still remain, but they are weaker. For example contradictions between Gazprom and Yamalo-Nenets governor Yurii Neyelov did not lead to a change of governor when Neyelov's term was over in 2005. At first, the media said that the main competitor was Aleksandr Ananenkov, Gazprom's deputy CEO and former head of one of the biggest of Gazprom's branches in Yamalo-Nenets AO. Then Pavel Zavalnii, the CEO of Gazprom's transport branch Tyumentransgaz, was identified. But Zavalnii had no influence in Yamalo-Nenets AO. Finally neither Ananenkov nor Zavalnii were included in the official list of candidates. Neyelov's only competitor, the deputy governor of Tyumen oblast Vladimir Yakushev, was purely formal and had no direct relations with Gazprom. Neyelov was appointed. Big business more often now thinks that it is big enough and the regional authorities are not so big, so they see no reason to waste resources in an attempt to subject the regional authorities. This passive strategy is the direct opposite to the former strategy of power seizure.

But the interest of medium-sized business in the regional and municipal authorities remains. In this case, decisions by friendly authorities can lead to the company's rapid development while conflict may cause its destruction. As a rule, the construction and food industries and the retail sector are the business sectors most affected by this. Such businesses usually succeed due to good relations with the authorities, and not necessarily regional ones. On the municipal level retail business and the authorities work in close contact because many shops and markets are still in municipal property or because municipal authorities control the distribution of realty and land.

As for the regional level, small-scale economic decisions can have great significance for them, and this is where symbiotic relations often develop. A most interesting example is the owner of a fishing company in the Russian Far East, Oleg Kozhemyako. In 2004 he took part in the gubernatorial elections in Kamchatka oblast and came third. In 2005 he was appointed governor in Koryak AO, formally a part of Kamchatka oblast. Gubernatorial powers, such as the distribution of fishing quotas, could help him to expand his business. But after the abolition of gubernatorial elections, regional businessmen have preferred to take part in mayoral elections. It is almost impossible for them to win the gubernatorial nomination unless they are among the leading politicians in their regions or in Moscow. In 2005, businessmen became mayors of several important cities, including Chelyabinsk (Mikhail Yurevich, food industry) and Arkhangelsk (Aleksandr Donskoi, retail business).

The revision of regional strategies means that the vertical of power is characterized by the following in "business-power" relations:

1. Big business gives priority to its relations with the central authorities. Regional interaction is to specify details and to form a more favourable business environment.
2. Medium-sized business solves its problems mainly on regional and municipal levels and has a real economic interest in controlling power at the municipal level.
3. The specific process is the political legalization of the regional business associated with the criminal world. Its political legalization follows economic legalization, which is the moving of business from shadow to legal activities. It is crucially important for criminal-based business to reduce political risks. It is most evident at the municipal level because such business is often present in spheres dependent on the municipal authorities, such as trading.

Analysis of the direct influence of big business on regional power enables us to propose a typology of contemporary situations:[13]

1. A real oligarch continues to work as a governor in only one region, Abramovich in Chukotka. But his interest in the governorship has become minimal.
2. In three cases, the top managers of leading Russian companies hold governors' offices, and all of these cases are found in Krasnoyarsk region: Khloponin in Krasnoyarsk krai, Budargin in Taimyr AO, and Zolotarev in Evenkiya AO. But with the abolition of autonomous okrugs in 2007, Krasnoyarsk krai will become one region.

3. The rest are mainly cases of more or less tense connections between the regional authorities and business structures. Governors usually represent either the former nomenklatura adapted to reforms or a new class of regional bureaucracy formed in post-Soviet governments (so-called "post-Soviet clerks"). A good example of this is Vologda oblast where governor Vyacheslav Pozgalev is closely connected with the iron-and-steel group Severstal.
4. Finally, there is a specific model in regions where very strong and long-serving governors have created strong and self-sufficient systems of loyal business (Moscow, Tatarstan, Bashkortostan).

The model of relations when the governor is an explicit lobbyist for a particular business group is very rare. When such governors were elected, this situation could lead to support of the opposition candidate by other businesses. If such a governor is appointed, there is the possibility of a struggle between unsatisfied business groups in structures influencing the nomination. In any case, the federal centre tends to appoint governors who are loyal to the Kremlin rather than to some oligarch. This is why an obvious connection exists between a governor and a certain company only in the simplest regions where one group or one businessman controls almost the whole economy. In other cases, governors prefer manoeuvring by making coalitions with business groups of different origins and territorial levels.

Finally it is important to define the main political consequences caused by the change of "business-power" relations under Putin. The vertical of power means that big business coordinates its regional activities at the federal level. This model characterizes both business activities (privatization, distribution of raw materials deposits etc) and political decision-making. As for politics, earlier the federal centre wanted companies to coordinate their decisions to support candidates for governors. Following the abolition of gubernatorial elections, the Kremlin must choose between two strategies – co-ordination of the candidacy with the company dominating in the region, or appointment of a neutral governor loyal to the centre only.

The interests of regional political elites

Governors originating from the big companies now prefer to demonstrate flexible policies with regard to business relations. Since the Yukos case, they have been afraid of losing office if their business group falls victim to a political campaign. Their patrons in the business group agree with these policies for the same reason. The Kremlin does not want to appoint the candidates of big companies for three reasons: first, because the Russian president wants to avoid any issue of double loyalty; second, the president does not want the appointment procedure to be associated with the selling of regional offices; and third, the president tries to avoid possible political instability if the appointment of some company's man provokes a strong negative reaction by competing companies.

From this point of view it is important to analyze the changing behaviour of Zolotarev and Khloponin. Zolotarev faced harsh reality when his patrons lost their political game. After that, Zolotarev became fully loyal to the federal authorities and agreed to unite Evenkiya AO with Krasnoyarsk krai. As for the economy, he openly supported proposed change of the owner of VSNK, the local oil company owned by Yukos.

Khloponin came to power in 2002 when "business-power" relations started to change. He has always been a flexible governor, loyal to the Kremlin. Immediately after Putin abolished gubernatorial elections, Khloponin started the unification of Krasnoyarsk krai with its autonomous okrugs, an evident sign of political loyalty praised by the Kremlin. In his business relations, Khloponin signed agreements with all business groups represented in the krai, including even that of Oleg Deripaska who fought against Khloponin at the time of elections. This improves his chances of being appointed in 2007. And Interros has no intentions to change Khloponin despite his tactical double-dealing.

Governors usually prefer to avoid relations that are too close with the one and only company in the region. The federal authorities left them little room to manoeuvre, but governors seek to enlarge it by means of business relations. But they do not want to be somebody's puppet. They prefer more serious roles, including:

- A broker dealing with the regional resources.
- A mediator between different business groups or between business and different power structures in the region.
- A referee who sometimes stimulates the competition in his region to make his role more important.

Complete political loyalty is the only possible strategy left for governors if they are to prevent the federal authorities from taking part in regional affairs; this is the way to minimize federal pressure. It helps to save assets and to get larger manoeuvre space in relations with business groups. The very experienced governor and politician Aman Tuleyev in Kemerovo oblast supports Putin whole heartedly. In his region he is the extremely influential leader and all the business groups prefer to start their activity in this rich industrial region by reaching agreement with its governor. And

Kemerovo oblast is also a case of a region where the governor still possesses informal ways to pressurize disloyal companies, even making them increase workers' salaries.

The interests of the federal ruling elites

With the appointment of governors, the Kremlin has chosen a new strategic relationship with the regional elites. Incumbent governors get the desired appointments on condition that they are loyal to Putin. The political game has become more important than the struggle for property. The Kremlin wants to be the one and only patron for governor. In appointing governors, the president has usually supported incumbents regardless of their different origins and business relations. Putin has accepted the situation when a governor closely associated with one or another business group demonstrates full loyalty to the president, as though saying that Putin is the only patron and there is no sign of double loyalty. And Putin is not going to change governors just because a particular company wants it. The most important thing for the Kremlin is the governors' ability to organize federal elections in its interest and not to play the double loyalty game. That is why Neyelov was appointed in Yamalo-Nenets autonomous okrug. He has ruled his region for more than ten years; and soon after his appointment, United Russia got more than 60 per cent of votes at the regional elections. Neyelov's latent conflict with Gazprom was not sufficient reason to change him.

The Kremlin sometimes seeks to play an active role in the regions. One form of this has been to reformulate the coalescence of business and power in terms of the notion of social responsibility as the federal authorities seek to get businessmen to invest in some remote and backward regions. A good example of this occurred in Chukotka in 2005 where the governor Abramovich and his firms pay their taxes; these constitute a main staple of the regional economy. Abramovich did not need to be a governor anymore, but the Kremlin convinced him to stay. Another form of involvement is to act as a mediator in relations between the regional authorities and investors. It organizes their dialogue in order to help the most loyal governors. Presidential envoys in federal districts are prominent in this process. For example the presidential envoy Georgii Poltavchenko helped backward Tambov oblast to become the host of an annual investment forum.

But if the president decides to change a governor, the new regional leader often comes from the business elite. Among such appointees, Kozhemyako (Koryak AO) and Valerii Kokov (Kabardino-Balkariya) can really gain economically from their new status. But appointments in Saratov

(Pavel Ipatov, CEO of the nuclear power station), Tula (Vyacheslav Dudka, deputy CEO of the defence industrial plant) and Irkutsk (Aleksandr Tishanin, CEO of the state railway company's branch) do not seem to be profitable for the governors' enterprises because these enterprises are federal and cannot gain due to their governors' actions. The reasons for their appointments were political: appointees were considered to be politically neutral in the context of a power struggle. But their appointments may also be seen in terms of elite analysis. We can take businessmen not as clients and agents, but as skillful managers just moving to a new job. Despite the ever-changing relations between big business and the authorities at all levels, the business elites have become a very important source of the regional ruling elite. Many of them are elected mayors or appointed governors and deputy-governors. And this fact marks the elite transformation going on in Russia.

Conclusion

Relations between the regional authorities and business elites in Russia depend on several variables. These relations change along with the changes in the existing rules of election or nomination of regional or municipal heads. The gubernatorial elections, for example, gave the big business tycoons more opportunities to move their people to the highest regional offices. When governors became appointed by president big business started lobby games but did not have much success. So the relations between region-bound business groups and the federal authorities become very important. The ideal situation for a business group is to agree with the Kremlin on the candidate. But the real influence of business groups in the Kremlin has been proved to look very different. In the meantime the powers of the regional or municipal head, both formal and informal (the latter being very different from region to region) define the "rational choice" of certain business groups to fight or not to fight for the control over certain offices in the region. One more "rational" impulse for business elites to fight is the regional property (or another state-controlled economic resource) subject to privatization or leasing. The joint business interests of regional state or municipal officials and business groups' owners or managers is an incentive for the clientele to retain power by all means. And finally the overall development of the national political process in terms of "business-power" relations defines in what form and at what distance the authorities and the business groups interact on political issues.

Notes

1   A.V. Makarkin, *Politiko-ekonomicheskie klany sovremennoi Rossii* (Moscow: Centre for political technologies, 2003).

2   A.K. Magomedov, "Korporatsiya Kalmykiya – vyrazhenie ideologii pravyaschei elity", *Mirovaya ekonomika i mezhdunarodnye otnosheniya* 12, 1995, pp. 106–13.

3   This term was introduced by Pappe. Y.S. Pappe, *Oligarkhi: ekonomicheskaya khronika 1992–2000* (Moscow: State University – Higher School for Economics, 2000).

4   Pappe, *Oligarkhi*.

5   B.I. Makarenko and R.F. Turovsky (eds), *Politika v regionakh: gubernatory i gruppy vliyaniya* (Moscow: Centre for Political Technologies, 2002).

6   V.A. Gel'man, "Regional'nie rezhimy: zaversheniye transformatsii", *Svobodnaya mysl'* 9, 1996, pp. 13–21.

7   R.F. Turovsky, "Gubernatory i oligarkhi: istoriya vzaimootnoshenii", *Politiya*, 5, 2001, pp. 120–39.

8   A.Y. Zudin, "Rezhim V. Putina: kontury novoi politicheskoi sistemy", *Obshchestvennyie nauki i sovremennost'*, 2, 2003, pp. 67–83.

9   Turovsky, "Gubernatory".

10 Although a state company, Gazprom is controlled by one of the influence groups close to Putin.

11 A.M. Lavrov and V.Y. Shuvalov *et al.* (eds), *Predprinimatel'skii klimat regionov Rossii* (Moscow: Nachala-Press, 1997).

12 V.A. Mau and O.V. Kuznetsova (eds), *Investitsionnaya privlekatel'nost' regionov: prichiny razlichii i ekonomicheskaya politika gosudarstva* (Moscow: The Institute for the Economy in Transition, 2002).

13 Turovsky, "Gubernatory"; and N.V. Zubarevich, "Prishel, uvidel, pobedil? (krupnii biznes i regional'naya vlast'", *Pro et contra*, 7, 1, 2002, pp. 107–19.

6
Economic Actors in Russian Regional Politics: The Example of the Oil Industry[1]

Julia Kusznir

In his analysis of the hindrances to reform of the economic policy of post-Soviet countries, Joel Hellman[2] begins with the assertion that resistance to further economic reforms did not come from those who stood to lose from such reforms, for example the unemployed or pensioners, but rather from those who first profited from reform, such as financial speculators. They benefited above all from the distortion of competition which characterized the early period of economic reform. During the process of privatization they could win preferential control of enterprises. Banks made considerable profits through speculative deals in unregulated financial markets. Local bureaucracies protected firms from competition in order to receive a share of the earnings from these monopolies. Therefore, according to Hellman, after the first phase of economic reform, the decisive conflict of interests with regards to the continuation of reform did not take place between political decision-makers and the classical losers from reforms, but rather between political decision-makers and those who had benefited from the initial period of reform. In Hellman's opinion the result of this conflict largely determines further economic development.

In Russia one group of beneficiaries from this distorted and unfinished reform is made up of the so-called "oligarchs": large-scale entrepreneurs who through financial speculation and successful participation in privatization auctions created industrial holding companies – the so-called FIGs (Financial-Industrial Groups). The small group of successful oligarchs cultivated close relations with President Boris Yeltsin and with the Russian government. In this way, they achieved considerable influence on Russian politics in the mid-1990s.[3] When he took over the office of president in the year 2000, Vladimir Putin set out with the declared aim of reducing the political influence of the oligarchs. In the following years, entrepreneurs who represented a political threat to Putin were systematically placed under pressure by the tax authorities and organs of criminal investigation. As a result, in 2000 and 2001 the financial magnate Boris Berezovsky and the media tycoon Vladimir Gusinsky lost control of their Russian businesses; in 2003 and 2004 the owner of the oil firm Yukos, Mikhail Khodorkovsky, suffered the same fate. Berezovsky and Gusinsky were forced to flee abroad and Khodorkovsky was placed under arrest.[4] Even those economic leaders who came to an arrangement with the Putin administration only had very limited access to political decision-making processes. In response to this they increased their efforts to influence politics at the regional level.

The retreat of the oligarchs into the regions

In the early 1990s the process of regionalization began. As part of this, regional political elites used the weakness of the federal system under Yeltsin in order to extend their own power. They began to use the Federation Council, that is the second chamber of the national parliament, as a means of protecting their regional interests.[5] But the most important role in the regional political process fell to the governors. A number of factors enabled them to strengthen their position in both the federal and regional political system during the 1990s. On the one hand, this was possible due to the system of regional representation on the federal level in the form of the Federation Council. Their double legitimacy, as elected executive and as senators in the Federation Council, in effect made the governors irreplaceable. On the other hand, the position of the governors was reinforced through the signing of bilateral treaties. These treaties defined the powers and the mutual delegation of authority between the federal centre and the regions. In each treaty the Constitution, the federal constitutional laws and the regional constitutions and laws were recognized. Moreover, such agreements regulated mutual economic relations, the establishment of economic contacts abroad and the relationship between the federal and regional budgets. The regions thereby gained considerable authority and financial resources.[6] As a result of this, the provincial leaders were often given similar authority to that of the federal president.

At the beginning of the 1990s regional assets were privatized. The regional administrations in many provinces were able to secure control over local enterprises and unite them into holding companies. Examples include the Financial Industrial Group Sistema in the city of Moscow, the FIG Doninvest in the Rostov area, the regional holding companies Tatenergo and Tatneft in the Republic of Tatarstan, and Bashernergo and

Bashneft in the Republic of Bashkortostan. The close interaction between the governor and the regional enterprises brought benefits to both sides. On the one hand, the firms received loans from the regional budget. They were guaranteed freedom from interference in their economic activity and a monopoly in the local market. On the other hand, the governors' victory in the regional elections was safeguarded and the creation of a potential opposition prevented. This established a certain status quo in the relationships between the two groups and underpinned the position of the governor in both the region and in negotiations with the federal centre.

The first attempts by large financial enterprises to expand into the regions took place between 1996 and 1998. They sought to acquire licences for the extraction of natural resources and take over regional businesses. This met with strong resistance from the regional leaders and the firms were often unsuccessful. It was not until the conclusion of informal agreements through which the companies were promised favourable conditions for the extraction of natural resources that the relationships between the representatives of the large businesses and the local leaders began to develop. However, the oligarchs remained in the shadows of political processes in the regions. The failure of this first attempt to expand was due to the weak position of the federal centre in the regions, the lack of necessary financial resources on the part of the large firms and their inefficient structure as holding companies.

At the beginning of the year 2000, the relationship between the oligarchs and the governors changed. The reasons for this can be found in the greater financial strength of the large firms after the financial crisis of 1998. At the same time, the governors' monopoly of political control at the regional level was weakened through the administrative reforms of 2000. This made the regions more attractive for further investment. The large companies put their hopes of expansion into practice and developed their own political strategies. They began to defend their interests in the regions through individual entrepreneurs and/or business associations. More importantly, between 1999 and 2003 many oligarchs became involved in regional gubernatorial elections. Some of them entered into close alliances with the governors and financed their elections. Others were able to take on the office of governor themselves. A number supported their own candidates in the parliamentary elections and positioned their own representatives in the regional parliaments. In this way, the oligarchs achieved political influence in several key economic regions and began to play an import role in the relationship between the federal centre and the regions (see Table 6.1).

Table 6.1 Representatives of large economic groups as governors

Name	Region	Economic group whose interest is being represented	Area of activity	Period of office
Yurii Evdokimov	Murmansk oblast	FIG Sistema	Telecommunications	1996–2000
Aleksei Lebed	The Republic of Khakassiya	Base Element	Metals	1997–2004
Roman Abramovich	Chukotka autonomous okrug	Oligarch who owns Millhouse/ RusAl/ Sibneft	Oil	2000–2005
Aleksandr Khloponin	Taimyr autonomous okrug	Interros/Norilsk Nickel	Metals	2001–2002
Boris Zolotarev	Evenkiya autonomous okrug	Menatep/Rosprom (Yukos)	Oil	2001–2005
Dmitrii Selenin	Tver oblast	Interros/ Norilsk Nickel	Metals	2004–2007
Aleksandr Khloponin	Krasnoyarsk krai	Interros/Norilsk Nickel	Metals	2002–2007
Oleg Budargin	Taimyr autonomous okrug	Interros/Norilsk Nickel	Metals	2002–2007
Viacheslav Shtyrov	The Republic of Sakha (Yakutiya)	Oligarch who owns the diamond concern Alrosa	Diamonds	2002–2007
Aleksei Lebed	The Republic of Khakassiya	Base Element	Metals	2004–2008
Boris Zolotarev	Evenkiya autonomous okrug	Menatep/Rosprom (Yukos)	Oil	2005–2007*

Source: Compiled by the author.
Note:*As part of the federal project 'On the amalgamation of regional entities' (ukrupnenie regionov) the Evenkiya autonomous okrug will be integrated into the Krasnoyarsk krai from 1 January 2007. The authority of the state organs of the autonomous okrug will be handed over to the corresponding organs of the krai.

As part of the continuation of the administrative reforms begun in 2003, the political and economic authority of the governors was distinctly reduced in favour of the federal centre. The regional administration could no longer set up special economic areas. Their ability to grant tax breaks was considerably limited. The tax authorities and the departments for internal affairs were subordinated to the federal centre. From 2005 the president was able to appoint and dismiss the governors. However, the governors are still trying to negotiate with the federal centre and exert influence on the large companies. The administrative reforms have brought no radical changes in this respect. Nevertheless, one can expect that the redistribution of executive authority in favour of the federal centre will create a new latitude for oligarchs to influence the regional legislative organs.[7]

Models of regional politics

The relationship between federal businesses and the representative of the regional administration has taken on very different forms in the various regions. A number of studies have tried to categorize systematically the relations between business and politics in the 89 Russian regions. Robert Orttung, an American political scientist, uses the question of which actors control the economics and politics of a region as the basis for his typology. He differentiates between the five following types:

1. *Corporate regions*, which are dominated by one firm. This group includes not only the small regions, which have few economic resources at their disposal (for example the Chukotka autonomous okrug, which was dominated by the oil firm controlled by Roman Abramovich, Sibneft), but also the financially strong regions (such as the city of Moscow, in which the FIG Sistema defines the rules of the market).
2. *Pluralist regions*, in which several enterprises compete for political influence. The example given by Orttung is Krasnoyarsk krai, where several big business groups, including Interros, Yukos and Base Element, have been active. The Khanty-Mansii okrug provides a further interesting example of this type: in this province a number of oil and gas companies, for example Yukos, Sibneft and TNK-BP, are active.
3. *State-controlled regions*, in which the economy is under the control of the regional administration. These include the Republic of Tatarstan, the Republic of Bashkortostan and Khabarovsk krai.
4. *Foreign-influenced regions*, in which the interests of foreign investors are given preference in the region's politics. This group embraces

Sakhalin oblast, in which several international companies are active in the production of oil and gas, and Leningrad, Moscow, Nizhnii Novgorod and Samara oblasts.

5. *Neglected regions*, which are of no interest to large companies. These regions are industrially underdeveloped and often have to rely on the federal budget, as in the case of the republics of the North Caucasus.[8]

A study by the World Bank also deals with the question of who shapes politics in the regions. It names, like Orttung, national and regional enterprises, federal and regional governments, as well as foreign investors, as possible contestants. However, the authors of the World Bank Study only identified about a dozen regions in which these groups really dominate regional politics (see Table 6.2). They concluded that regional enterprises and foreign investors are the most successful with regards to acquiring influence on the politics of "their region".[9]

Table 6.2   The dominant groups in Russian regions, 2000

Federal centre	The Republic of Sakha (Yakutiya), Belgorod oblast, Kurgan oblast, Nizhnii Novogorod oblast, Omsk oblast.
Regional administration	The Republic of Bashkortostan, the Republic of Tatarstan, the City of Moscow.
Regional private companies	The Republic of Mordoviya, the Republic of Tatarstan, Kaliningrad oblast, Moscow oblast, Perm oblast, Rostov oblast, Tula oblast, Tyumen oblast, Chelyabinsk oblast.
Federal private companies	The Republic of Kareliya, Krasnoyarsk oblast, Primorskii krai, Vologda oblast, Lipetsk oblast, Sverdlovsk oblast.
Foreign investors	The Udmurt Republic, Saratov oblast.

Whereas the two studies mentioned above focus on the dominant actors, an empirical study by Nataliya Lapina and Alla Chirikova attempted to draw up a typology of the interaction between state and economic actors. They developed four models: the patronage model, the partnership model, the model of "the privatization of power" and the model of "suppression" (or the "struggle of all against all").[10]

1. In the *patronage model*, the political leaders, in this case the governors, decide on the organization of the power structure in the region and the division and allocation of material and financial resources. Informal pacts are made between the governor in the role of patron and the economic actors. According to these agreements the latter accept the administrative rules set by the patron in return for privileges and budget resources. The economic actors do not have to reckon with competition

in the market, but rather with bureaucratic competition. This model characterizes the republics of Tatarstan and Bashkortostan, and Ulyanovsk Oblast (under governor Yurii Goryachev).

2. The *partnership model* develops in regions where an equal and constructive dialogue is conducted between politicians and economic actors. The characteristics of these regions are the successful introduction of market reforms and a highly developed level of enterprise. The governor plays the role of a guarantor for informal agreements between the different business groups. Some of the regions in which the partnership model can be seen are the Khanty-Mansii okrug, St Petersburg, Novgorod, Nizhnii Novgorod and Leningrad oblasts.

3. The *model of "the privatization of power"* developed in those regions in which the companies took over the monitoring functions of the central political authority. With this developed a consolidated economic elite which dominates the political actors and which independently presents itself as a power elite. This is the case in the republics of Kalmykiya and Khakassiya and the Yamal-Nenets and Chukotka autonomous okrugs.

4. The *model of "suppression"* or the *"struggle of all against all"* arises in those regions which only have limited economic resources at their disposal and are heavily dependent on the transfer of money from the federal centre. The regional political elite is too weak to steer the political decision-making process. The result is a conflict which not only takes place between economic elites and politicians, but also between competing groups in the political leadership and within the economic elite. This model is typical of poor regions such as Kirov.

In order to judge in concrete terms how far businessmen influence economic reforms and economic policy at the regional level, two case studies will be presented. The oil industry has been chosen because it unambiguously is one of the most influential economic actors in the country. Two contrasting regions, the Khanty-Mansii autonomous okrug[11] and the Republic of Tatarstan, were chosen. In the former the federal oligarchs occupy a strong position, but this is a case of Orrtung's pluralist region and the partnership model of Lapina and Chirikova; in the latter, the regional government is powerful, making this an example of Orrtung's state-controlled region and Lapina and Chirikova's patronage model. These cases demonstrate how differently the relationships between the representatives of the economy and regional political actors can develop and exert their influence.

Economic actors in the regions: two case studies from the oil industry

In both the Khanty-Mansii autonomous okrug and the Republic of Tatarstan, the oil industry has central importance for the development of the regional economy. Taxes on the extraction of oil and gas constitute 70 per cent and 60 per cent of the revenue of the respective regional budgets.[12] Consequently, in both cases regional political elites try to influence the development of this branch of the economy. This can take place through the distribution of subsidies or the acquisition of shares by the local and regional authorities. This is what happens in the Republic of Tatarstan and the oil firm active there, Tatneft. Alternatively, the regions can benefit from the companies' profits through tax payments and through the awarding of licences for the exploitation of natural resources and the licence fees connected with this. The economic importance of the oil industry for these extraction regions is not only determined by the production volume, but also through the share of the revenue in the regional budget yielded by the oil firms.

The case of the Khanty-Mansii Autonomous Okrug – Yugra

Around 60 per cent of the entire Russian oil reserves are in the Khanty-Mansii autonomous okrug (AO). Accordingly, the oil industry has a strong position in the province. Due to this fact, in 2003 the okrug was placed first in the ranking of Russian regions with regards to industrial production, second with respect to federal tax revenue and third for average income. The okrug administration commands a consolidated position within the okrug, supported by the representatives of the oil and gas companies. These businesses provide about 80 percent of the local production and are among the most important local taxpayers.[13]

In administrative terms, the west Siberian Khanty-Mansii AO[14] did not try to achieve independence from Tyumen oblast of which it was a part at the beginning of the 1990s. The regional political elite was far more interested in the creation of economic independence and cooperation with the oblast. At the end of 1992, Khanty-Mansii AO, Yamal-Nenets AO, Tyumen oblast and the federal centre signed a treaty through which the autonomous okrugs were declared to be equal subjects of the Russian Federation. Moreover, they aimed to obtain the right to decide freely what to do with the minerals and other resources on their territory. This, however, intensified conflict between the autonomous okrugs and the oblast. After long negotiations a compromise was found, which was incorporated into the Constitution of the Russian Federation of 1993.

According to the agreement, the autonomous okrugs were recognized as subjects of the Russian Federation, enjoying equal rights. This considerably extended their powers. However, they remained components of Tyumen oblast (the so-called "Matryoshka model" of federalism), able to elect the state organs of the oblast together with the rest of the region.[15] Despite the fact that several regional laws regulating the relations between the oblast and the autonomous okrugs had been passed, the relationship, especially in the economic field, remained complicated. The economically poor Tyumen oblast sought to establish control over the richer okrugs, which tried to maintain the independence they had won up to that stage. This destabilized the political situation in the region and led to open conflict.[16] Such conflict was brought before the Russian Constitutional Court in 1997. In its decision it declared that the autonomous okugs were federal subjects with equal rights, albeit as a part of Tyumen oblast.

In 2001 the speaker of the parliament of the Khanty-Mansii autonomous okrug, Sergei Sobyanin, was elected governor of Tyumen oblast. This fundamentally changed the relationship between AOs and oblast. In the same year these administrative units reached a new agreement. Within this framework, several regional decrees, including those on the coordination of taxation policy and the development of the regional infrastructure and industrial production, were passed.[17] However, the political situation in Khanty-Mansii okrug was shaken by a new project, the amalgamation of the Russian regions started by the federal centre in 2001. According to the federal project "On the amalgamation of territorial areas" (ukrupnenie regionov), Khanty-Mansii and Yamal-Nenets would be merged. With this, the political and economic authority of the autonomous okrugs would be abolished, and the state organs of the okrugs would be simplified and their powers transferred to the corresponding organs of Tyumen oblast.[18] With the centre's support, Sobyanin wanted to sign a treaty on the amalgamation of the three regions by 2005. Lengthy discussions were conducted on the question of political integration, but these ended without result. Only in June 2004, after the repeated personal intervention of the Russian presidential envoy in the federal okrug, did the three provinces sign a treaty defining their powers. In the treaty the administration of the oblast allowed the okrugs to retain important administrative powers, for example in the regulation of fiscal relations between the administration of the okrugs and the communes or the funding of education and health services, until 2009. In return, the okrugs undertook to pay 20 thousand million roubles into the Tyumen budget. Part of the proceeds was to be used for the implementation of joint development programs; the rest was to go into Tyumen oblast budget.[19]

However, in November 2005 the federal centre took an unexpected step by appointing Tyumen governor Sobyanin the head of the presidential administration in Moscow. His successor was Vladimir Yakushev, who had been Sobyanin's deputy. Yakushev was familiar with the political situation in the region; but most importantly for the federal centre, he has continued the policy started by Sobyanin of gradually bringing about the amalgamation of the three regions. In this way, the federal centre has achieved almost all the conditions for the unification of the three regions.[20] Increasingly, the original aim of economic integration has been replaced by a project of amalgamation forced through by the centre. The new Tyumen oblast will be one of the most oil- and gas-rich regions in Russia, with a transparent administrative and financial structure headed by a governor loyal to the president.

Two power groups have determined political life in Khanty-Mansii. The first group consists of the representatives of the regional administration headed by the governor. Many representatives of this administration began their careers as secretaries of regional and local committees of the Communist Party during the Brezhnev era in the mid-1970s. They are successful regional and local "insiders" on account of the fact that the majority of them came to work on the extraction of oil in the 1970s while they were Komsomoltsy. The friendships which they established at that time are still very important. A characteristic of administration in these regions is that while the autonomous okrugs have achieved a great deal of independence, there is still exchange of personnel between the okrugs and Tyumen oblast. A number of politicians from Yamal-Nenets AO and Khanty-Mansii AO have taken up important positions in Tyumen: the ex-governors Shafranik and Roketskii and the former speaker of the regional Duma Baryshnikov represent three prominent examples; the same is true of former governor Sobyanin and the parliamentary speaker Korepanov. Conversely, Neyelov, the governor of the Yamal-Nenets AO, comes from Tyumen oblast. In such cases, the arrival of administrators from outside did not change policy in the province: the governor from Tyumen sought to promote the interests of the Yamal-Nenets and the politicians from the autonomous okrugs sought to preserve the administrative unity of the oblast.

The chief figure in the administration has been Governor Aleksandr Filipenko. He was appointed under the Soviet system and then elected in 1996 according to the laws valid under Yeltsin. He received extensive authority through the regional charter,[21] including, for example, the development of regional financial and investment policy, the development of enterprise, the support of the regional bank and credit structures and the administration of the region's property. The governor and his government ensure that the holders of licences for the extraction of raw materials comply with the conditions of licensing and pay licence fees. They supervise

the observance of environmental legislation, develop conservation programmes and guarantee their implementation.[22] Filipenko has taken on
the role of guarantor of political and economic stability in the region. He
has facilitated the activity of the oil firms while also representing the
interests of the native inhabitants, the Khanty and the Mansii, among
whom he enjoys great popularity. His political flexibility and his ability
to find compromises in contentious situations between the oil companies
and the inhabitants of the region are highly regarded.[23] His success has
been acknowledged by both the Russian president and local politicians. In
February 2005, Putin reappointed him governor and the regional parliament accepted him without opposition.[24] In addition, Filipenko was
elected to the board of directors of a number of oil and gas companies,
including the oil firms Surgutneftegaz and TNK.[25]

The representatives of the large oil and gas firms form the second power
group in the province (see Table 6.3). These include, for example, the head of
the board of directors of the oil group Surgutneftegaz, Vladimir Bogdanov,
who is one of the Russian oligarchs. This group is directly integrated into the
political structure through their work as parliamentary deputies. As early as
the regional Duma elections of 1996, they were able to win nine of 23 seats
in the parliament. In 2001 the representatives of the oil and gas companies
came to form a majority with 60 per cent of the seats in parliament.

Table 6.3 The representatives of oil and gas companies in the Duma of the
Khanty Mansii Autonomous Okrug in the 2nd and 3rd legislative periods

Branch	Legislative period 1996–2001	In % (N = 23)	Legislative period 2001–2005	In % (N = 25)
Oil	7	30.8	9	36.0
Gas	2	8.8	4	16.0
Mixed companies	0	0	2	8.0
Total	9	39.6	15	60.0
Including:				
Gazprom	2	8.7	4	16.0
Lukoil	2	8.7	2	8.0
Yukos	0	0	1	4.0
Surgutneftegaz	2	8.7	3	12.0
Sibneft	0	0	0	0
Slavneft	1	4.3	1	4.0
Sidanko	1	4.3	0	0
TNK	1	4.3	1	4.0

Source: Compiled by the author after bringing together information on Duma for the 2nd and
3rd legislative periods, available at http://www.hmao.wsnet.ru/power/index.htm.

According to the regional charter, the regional Duma commands significant authority. It determines the procedure for the administration of the region's property and its privatization. In addition, it is responsible for the legal regulation of the exploitation and protection of natural resources.[26] The setting of taxes and duties on the basis of federal tax legislation and the procedure of levying them are the responsibility of the Duma. The governor has advisory rights in the parliament and either takes part personally or sends a representative. In this way, the regional parliament is the formal centre of negotiation between the economic and political elites.

Political and administrative relations in the region are characterized by a high level of integration between members of the oil and gas industry and the representatives of the regional administration. The representatives of the economy have developed a form of cooperative work with the political elites of the region thereby embodying an example of the partnership model. The results of this collaboration have been considerable tax benefits for the large-scale producers of raw materials and additional income for the regional budget. This trade-off was codified in laws passed by the regional parliament. During the 1990s, around 60 different laws on the regulation of the exploitation of mineral resources and regional taxation were passed. Above all, they provided for a complete or partial exemption from tax and license fees on the exploitation of natural resources. For example, the regional parliament passed a number of laws providing for exemptions from tax on oilfields while they were being explored and drilled. This allowed oil companies to bring the production of oil in these fields up to full capacity more quickly. A similar law was introduced for fields in which the depth of the oil deposits required the application of new technology to extract the resource. In the first three years in which such fields were operational they were taxed at the minimum level.[27] Consequently, between 1994 and 2003 more than 1.1 thousand million tonnes of oil were produced. In turn, taxes on oil production earned more than 14 thousand million roubles in revenue for the regional budget.[28]

Regional laws also opened the way for favourable tax decrees concerning the regional share of federal taxation and regional taxation. Partial or complete exemptions from tax on the extraction of raw materials and investment in the oil and gas industries were arranged in bilateral negotiations for every firm.[29] In 1999 a law was introduced for all oil and gas firms active in the region. They were allowed to decide which regional taxes they paid. The untaxed profits should, however, be reinvested in the extraction of oil.[30] In the same year, seven oil firms used these rules for 27 new oil fields and produced an additional 7.25 million tonnes of oil. As a result, the oil and gas firms reduced their tax payments considerably, invested more in the tapping of new oil sources and increased their production. In this way, an additional 6 million roubles poured into regional programs for social and economic development before the law was repealed in the year 2000.[31]

Putin's tax reform of 2000 considerably reduced the authority of the regions in the area of the exploitation of raw materials and taxation. In effect, the regional government could not give orders on the regulation of tax collection. It could only introduce a limited number of tax benefits on regional taxes and only on the condition that the company invest in the development of the regional economy. The political elite of the Khanty-Mansii AO opposed this law. A round table with representatives from the regional administration and the finance ministry was organized in order to discuss the problems created by the tax reforms. Filipenko criticized the tax reforms and the limitation of the authority of the regions connected with them. He also condemned the finance ministry's attack on the oil firms. He made suggestions of other possible solutions to the problems of tax payments, which the representatives of the federal centre accepted.[32] In this way, the regional government of the Khanty-Mansii AO was able in cooperation with the regional parliament to work out a program which created attractive conditions for further investment by oil companies. This safeguarded the firms' direct access to the new oilfields and increases in production. In addition, it guaranteed stable income for the regional authorities.[33] Therefore, the regional political and economic elite together defended regional autonomy against the federal centre and with it their leeway to make decisions.

However, at the end of 2003, as part of the Yukos affair, the federal centre again turned against elites in the region. An investigation was launched into allegations that the boss of Yuganskneftegaz, Yukos' main production firm, and the administrative heads of three communes in which the company was active had committed tax evasion and had been culpably granted undue advantage.[34] Moreover, Pyotr Latyshev, the presidential envoy in the federal district, initiated an inspection of the members of the AO parliament and administration. As a result, many members of the political elite lost their positions following accusations of illegally showing preferential treatment to oil companies. These included Vladimir Karasev, the deputy governor who was responsible for matters relating to the use of natural resources, and Veniamin Panov, who coordinated the department for oil and gas in the AO administration.[35]

These developments considerably weakened the position of Governor Filipenko. On the one hand, his room for manoeuvre with the oil companies was further limited. On the other, his position in the discussions over the amalgamation with Tyumen oblast became more difficult. At the same time, the pressure from the federal centre, by reducing the powers of the AO parliament in which the representatives of the oil and gas firms sit, has also restricted the companies' ability to take part in regional politics. Therefore the oil and gas companies were only passive bystanders in the amalgamation of the okrug and oblast. Moreover after 2006 considerable changes in tax legislation[36] and in the regulation of the exploitation of natural resources[37] are envisaged, which will transfer important powers over licensing to the federal centre. These will put to a severe test the model of cooperation between the regional administration and the private companies which developed under Filipenko.

The case of the Republic of Tatarstan

The Republic of Tatarstan is characterized by what is for Russia a very extensive degree of autonomy from the federal centre along with the rule of a strong political elite. In July 1991 Mintimer Shaimiev won the presidential elections in the republic.[38] From the beginning he strove towards greater independence from the federal centre. A referendum was held on the constitutional status of Tatarstan on 21 March 1992. Because the republic rejected the federal treaty with the Russian Federation, on 6 November 1992 the Supreme Soviet of Tatarstan passed a new constitution which declared the republic to be a "sovereign state" and a "subject of international law".[39] This event led to a political and economic confrontation with the federal centre.

After long negotiations a treaty on the demarcation of authority between the state organs of the Russian Federation and the Republic of Tatarstan[40] was signed on 15 February 1994. In it the federal centre confirmed the "special status" of the region. The regional political elite was allowed, in effect, to act independently of the federal centre. The Tatar government tried to acquire additional powers and authority. They were granted the right to determine the personnel policy not only of the Tatar authorities, but also of the federal agencies active on their territory. Further bilateral treaties between the centre and the regional administration led to the latter receiving ownership of the material resources and land in Tatarstan. It had at its disposal the oil and gas on its territory, possessed the right to levy its own taxes and the right to retain a large part of the proceeds from the export of these products.

The powers of the Tatar president, created by regional legislation, remained largely unlimited following the conclusion of the treaty. This led to the creation of a regime based on personal power, and is an example of the patronage model.[41] The Tatar president determines the character of the executive organs in the republic, from the head of the government to the individual ministers and the chairmen of relevant committees. He leads the activity of government and can repeal governmental decisions and orders which contradict the constitution. In the realm of the economy, he is responsible for budgetary, social and economic programmes. He can initiate laws on the introduction and revocation of taxes and on the granting of tax benefits for those taxes which go into the regional budget.[42]

Until 2002,[43] the Tatar parliament was formed through a process de facto determined by the president. Every candidate on the list had to be approved by him. By this means, a system was created which enabled the election to Parliament of leading members of the regional administration, which ensured their subordination to the president. In practice, the representative of the administration and that of the controlling organ could therefore be the same person. Of the 130 deputies in the Tatar parliament during the legislative period of 1994 to 1999, 52 were the heads of administrative institutions. Forty-five seats in parliament were occupied by leading economic functionaries, including the director of the oil firm Tatneft and the directors of important banks in the region. Following the regional parliamentary elections of 2000, 56 of the deputies represented the administration and 47 were economic functionaries. Table 6.4 shows a survey of the representatives of business in parliament.

Table 6.4   Representatives of the oil industry in the Tatar parliament, 1995–2004

	Legislative period 1995–1999	In % (N = 130)	Legislative period 2000–2004	In % (N = 130)
Total number of companies	45	34.6	47	36.15
Oil production	3	2.3	8	6.15
Petrochemicals industry	1	0.77	2	1.5
Together	4	3.1	10	7.7
Of which:				
Tatneft	3	2.3	8	6.15
Nizhnekamskneftekhim	1	0.77	1	0.77
Zavod SK in Kirova	—	—	1	0.77

Sources: These figures have been compiled by the author on the basis of the reports of the Central Electoral Commission of the Republic of Tatarstan, "Spisok Narodnykh Deputatov Respubliki Tatarstan izbrannykh 5 marta 1995 goda i zaregestrirovannykh Tsentrizbirkomom RT" of 9.3.1995, published in *Respublika Tatarstan* 11 March 1995, p. 3; "Spisok Narodnykh Deputatov Respubliki Tatarstan izbrannykh 19 dekabrya 1999 goda" of 24 December 1999, published in *Respublika Tatarstan* 28 December 1999, p. 3; and "Spisok Narodnykh Deputatov Respubliki Tatarstan izbrannykh pri povtornom golosovanii 29 dekabrya 1999 goda" of 31 December 1999, published in *Respublika Tatarstan* 6 January 2000, p. 3.

Alongside the formal institutions there are influential informal organizations which regulate access to political power in Tatarstan. It is characteristic of the regional elite that both politics and the economy are dominated by one group, centred on President Mintimer Shaimiev and his family. In Tatarstan key administrative positions and the control over regional resources have been given mainly to relatives of the presidential family or their friends. However, people who had obtained the respect of the family by performing a certain service or had successfully worked with them in the past could achieve important administrative posts. At the pinnacle of this hierarchy stood the president and his family, including distant relatives. The next level consisted of friends of the family, followed by a numerically large group of "socially intimate" high functionaries. On the whole, these are ethnic Tatars of rural origin or functionaries from Soviet times who could consolidate their position through their competence and their loyalty to their superiors.[44] According to one study of the ruling groups in Tatarstan, ethnic Tatars made up 80 per cent of the Republic's ruling elite in 2003. The majority of the governing politicians were of rural descent, between 40 and 60 years old and possessed a university education, mainly in the area of agronomy. Around 90 per cent of the members of the political elite came from the Soviet-era nomenklatura; 60 per cent of leading politicians even occupied the same position which they had held in the Soviet Union.[45]

Within the framework of the privatization process at the beginning of the 1990s, Tatarstan did not follow the federal example,[46] but rather developed its own "Tatar model". This was based on the strong control of economic processes by the administration. Through the introduction of their own checks on privatization and the exclusion of federal companies from regional auctions, the administration guaranteed its control over local firms.[47] At the beginning of 2000 about 65 per cent of the region's assets were in the hands of the ruling political elites.[48] In this way, the representatives of the administration also form the economic elite of the region.

The regional political elites' dominance is especially clear in the example of the oil firm, Tatneft. The government of Tatarstan holds 31.3 per cent of the shares in the company[49] and possesses a "golden share", which gives it the right of veto on certain decisions taken by the shareholders' meeting and the supervisory board. The regional administration actively supports Tatneft and its vertical integration and grants the company advantageous tax conditions and exemptions from fines for pollution. With the help of these tax breaks and exemptions, Tatarstan was able to extract an additional 44.9 million tonnes of oil (28.7 per cent of the entire production in the republic) between 1996 and 2000, at which point the federal tax reform was introduced. As a result of this, the regional budget received 13.5 million roubles in tax revenue, which in turn represented 40 per cent of the entire sum taken in tax in this region.[50]

Moreover, the regional government guaranteed Tatneft's monopoly of the regional retail market. Tatneft delivers fuel to both state-controlled and private petrol stations and to agriculture. The regional administration placed pressure on competing oil companies from "outside". The large Russian oil companies had barely any opportunity to operate in the region. A good example is the failure of Russia's biggest oil company, Lukoil, to gain access to Tatarstan's market. Lukoil tried to become active in Tatarstan at the beginning of the 1990s. The realization of a common project through the construction of a pipeline, a storage installation and petrol stations, did not take place. No agreement could be reached on how large the regional government's share in the project should be. Consequently, after unsuccessful negotiations only around 20 petrol stations were built by Lukoil. At the end of 2003, representatives of Lukoil announced that the firm would hand over its network of petrol stations to Tatneft because the conditions rendered economic activity in Tatarstan impossible for Lukoil. In return Tatneft would give Lukoil an equal number of its petrol stations in other parts of the Russian Federation.[51]

The corporation's management and the regional administration determine Tatneft's company strategy together. The economic interests of the regional administration, or rather the family of President Shaimiev, are given preference. Through the right of veto at the shareholders' meeting, the regional administration determines the composition of Tafnet's board of directors. The representatives of various ministries and the presidential apparatus of the republic occupy five out of fifteen seats on the board and also possess the right of veto. The prime minister of the Republic is the chairman of the board of directors. Moreover, the son of the president, Radik Shaimiev, was a member of the board of directors between 1998 and 1999; so too was Shaimiev's cousin Ilshat Fardiev, who at that time was in charge of the city administration of Almetsevsk, where Tafneft's headquarters are based.[52] Following criticism of the regional elite, Shaimiev's relatives left their posts at Tatneft and were replaced by representatives of Taif, which is controlled by Shaimiev's son Radik, and a bank with close ties to Taif. The regional administration was able to determine Tatneft's corporate strategy through their direct control over the management. In this way, Tatneft is an instrument of the region's economic policy. On the one hand, this can be seen in the fact that the revenue of the firm is used for the promotion of the regional economy. Between 1997 and 1998 the local government took out loans of US $230 million from western banks

for the implementation of regional development programs; these were cover-
ed through Tatneft's oil production.[53] On the other hand, Tatneft gave
loans for the financing of regional programmes, above all in agriculture
and supported the development of the regional petrochemical industry,
including the construction of the petrochemical firm NizhnekamskNPZ.
Tatneft invested around US $1.1 thousand million in the construction
and thereby achieved control over the company. Taif (with 7.5 per cent of
the shares) and the petrochemical firm Nizhnekamskneftekhim (25 per
cent of the shares) also took a stake in the project.[54] Following the opening of NizhnekamskNPZ in 2002 a conflict broke out between Tatneft and
Taif because Taif wanted to take control of the company. After long negotiations and the personal intervention of President Shaimiev a compromise
was reached in August 2005. Tatneft sold its shares to Taif and undertook
to build a new petrochemical company in the region. In this way, Taif
achieved absolute control over the regional oil-processing industry.[55]

The distribution of oil extracted by Tatneft, about 24 million tonnes per
year, is strictly controlled by the government. A third of the oil is exported
and the revenue from this is used to pay back loans taken out by the
regional government and Tatneft. Delivery abroad is conducted by the
Austrian firm Nira-Export, which was also founded by Radik Shaimiev.[56]
Another third of the oil was, in accordance with a governmental decree,[57]
sold to Taif. Taif's payments for the oil received went into the regional
budget at a very low price settled in a reciprocal settlement (*vzaimozachet'*)
with the Ministry of Finance. According to another governmental decree,[58]
Tatneft must deliver the last third of its oil to NizhnekamskNPZ for further processing at a fixed low price. For the most part, this arrangement
did not represent the interests of the company. The firm's debts rose to
US $990 million by the end of the 1990s. This almost led to Tatneft's
bankruptcy.[59] However, the firm's financial position was improved considerably as a result of the increase in the price of oil on the world market
after 1999. At this time Tatneft entered the regional petrochemical sector.
In the year 2000 the regional government gave the company the 34.39 per
cent of the ordinary shares which they owned in the large Russian tyre
manufacturer Nizhnekamskshina on the condition that Tatneft would
invest further in the oil industry. Moreover, it received the 77.06 per cent
of the ordinary shares held by the state in the petrochemical company
Zavod tekhnicheskogo uglevoda, which delivers the raw material to
Nizhnekamskshina. Through this increase in shares Tatneft gained control
over the oil-processing company NizhnekamskNPZ. In this way, Tatneft
came to manage all the facilities processing oil in the republic. Until the
end of 2003 the companies controlled by Tatneft made up a single

production process: from the extraction of the oil to the manufacture of car tyres.[60] Visible profits could again be made. Tatneft was unable, however, to work out an independent economic strategy.

From the beginning of 2001 regional legislation was changed in important areas. As a result of pressure from the federal centre, the conformity of regional laws with federal legislation was reviewed. The Supreme Court of Tatarstan declared void a number of laws dealing with the powers of the executive and legislative organs and the licensing and taxation of the oil industry. Changes in regional legislation had to be undertaken in order to make it conform with federal laws.[61] This was met with strong resistance from the regional elite in the region. They aimed to achieve both guarantees for the independence of the regional administration and as favourable regulations as possible for the regional oil industry. After several personal meetings between the president of Tatarstan and President Putin, the regional administration managed, despite the changes in the regional laws, to maintain a certain level of independence for the political elite from the federal centre. Together with the federal centre the regional government worked out a special social programme for 2001–2006. The most important aim of the programme is to promote the further development of the regional oil industry. The resources for the implementation of the programme were partially guaranteed from the regional budget (13.8 per cent of the predicted expenditure) and from Tatneft's own income (37.74 per cent). In order to enable the company to put this sum together, it was granted special tax benefits. The federal contribution (19.87 per cent) was almost entirely financed by federal tax levied in Tatarstan, which in this way went back into the region.[62]

In 2006, new legislation on taxation was to come into force. The regional elite sought to interfere in the negotiations between the federal government, the ministries and the Russian parliament through its representatives at the national level, hoping to achieve special taxation mechanisms for oil production. This would allow the region to maintain oil production and the profits resulting from it at the present level. The relevant law should have been passed by the Duma in 2005, but at the time of the submission of this chapter the draft law was still in preparation. It is still unclear when the final version will be passed.[63]

Conclusion

The Khanty-Mansii autonomous okrug provides a good example of the partnership model described by Lapina and Chirikova in their typology. Economic actors, in this case the representatives of the oil and gas industries, take up formal political posts in the regional legislature and work out the economic policy of the region together with the political elite represented in the regional executive. The result of this cooperation is a coalition of interests which brings advantages for all those involved. The firms receive privileges, especially in licensing and taxation, and the political elite is assured of considerable revenue. This not only guarantees economic development and political stability, but also the political elite's own grip on power and personal income. These coalitions of interest are so strong that together they try to prevent and avoid the limitation of their powers by the centre.

The Republic of Tatarstan, on the other hand, is an excellent example of the patronage model. Both the political and the economic actors are subordinated to the president. Political actors take on roles in the economy in order to direct it in their interests. The example of Tatneft clearly shows that in Tatarstan the political elite profits from the support of business: not only through regional development and budget revenues, but also in the maintenance of their own power and self-enrichment. In contrast to the Khanty-Mansii autonomous okrug, the economic actors cannot assert their own interests. Economic actors from outside who could not be controlled by the government, such as Lukoil, were refused entry into the regional market. The political elite around the president of Tatarstan felt itself strong enough to combat the intervention of the centre in regional economic policy.

The two case studies therefore provide a differentiated picture with regard to Hellman's thesis that the early beneficiaries of the reform process obstruct drastic economic reforms. In Tatarstan, where the economic actors cannot act independently, both the implementation of economic reforms and economic development are slower than in the Khanty-Mansii autonomous okrug, where the economic actors, as Hellman puts it, have "captured" politics. One must note that the Khanty-Mansii autonomous okrug is in two senses an exception. On the one side, the local economy is completely orientated towards the oil and gas businesses, so that other economic interests barely play a role. In a more complex economy, the representation and development of other interests would probably suffer through the dominant role of the oil and gas companies. On the other side, the region is not dominated by one large firm. Consequently, the regional elites must first agree on a common position. The political elite was able to use the necessity of negotiation to build a partnership model. If a single large business had dominated, one could expect the model of the privatization of power instead, as is the case in Chukotka autonomous okrug.

In conclusion, it is possible to say that under certain conditions economic actors, even in the case of the Russian oligarchs (who according to Hellman are the typical obstructers of reform on the national level), can be constructive and can intervene in politics in the interest of general economic development. An assessment of their role in economic policy must therefore always be specific to each case. The same is true for the political elites. As the example of Tatarstan shows, their influence can obstruct economic reforms just as persistently as that of economic actors. It is also possible to find parallels here with the national economic policy of President Putin. While the oligarchs increasingly value a market-orientated and long-term development of their businesses and have, for example, considerably improved their corporate governance[64] and delegated their exertion of political influence to a great degree to their business associations, the political elite around Putin is increasingly trying to gain control over the economy. In this way the situation approximates to the patronage model described above. This could lead to a guided economy, subordinated to the president, which would affect political and economic development both in Russia as a whole and in its individual regions in a negative fashion.

Notes

1 I am grateful for the comments on a draft of this article by Christopher Gilley, Heiko Pleines and Hans-Henning Schröder.

2 Joel S. Hellman, "Winners take all. The politics of partial reform in postcommunist transition", *World Politics* 50, 1, 1998, pp. 203–34. See also Heiko Pleines, *Wirtschaftseliten und Politik im Russland der Jelzin-Ära (1994–99)* (Münster: LIT, 2003), pp. 69–71.

3 Hans-Henning Schröder, "El'tsin and the oligarchs: the role of financial groups in Russian politics between 1993 and July 1998", *Europe–Asia Studies* 51, 6, 1999, pp. 957–88; Peter Rutland (ed.), *Business and State in Contemporary Russia* (Boulder: Westview, 2001).

4 For more on this see D.E. Hoffman, *The Oligarchs: Wealth and Power in the New Russia* (New York: Public Affairs, 2002); Stefanie Harter, Jörn Grävingholt, Heiko Pleines and Hans-Henning Schröder, *Geschäfte mit der Macht. Wirtschaftseliten als politische Akteure im Russland der Transformationsjahre 1992–2001* (Bremen: Edition Temmen, 2003); Hans-Henning Schröder, "Die Jukos-Affäre", *Russlandanalysen*, 6, 2003; "James Nixey, "The Conflict Surrounding the Russian Oil Company Yukos", http://www.riia.org/pdf/research/rep/BNNov03.pdf; Heiko Pleines and Hans-Henning Schröder (eds), "Die Jukos Affäre. Russlands Energiewirtschaft und die Politik", *Arbeitspapiere und Materialien der Forschungsstelle Osteuropa*, 64, 2005.

5 Margarete Wiest, *Russlands schwacher Föderalismus und Parlamentarismus. Der Föderationsrat* (Münster: LIT, 2003).

6 Irina M. Busygina, "Die Gouverneure im föderativen System Rußlands", *Osteuropa* 47, 6, 1997, pp. 544–56 (pp. 550–3); Andreas Heinemann-Grüder, 'Der asymmetrische Föderalismus Russlands', Hans-Hermann Höhmann and Hans-Henning Schröder (eds), *Russland unter neuer Führung. Politik, Wirtschaft und Geselschaft am Beginn des 21. Jahrhunderts* (Münster: Agenda, 2001), p. 81.

7 For more on this see Rostislav Turovksii, "Gubernatory i oligarkhi: istoria otnoshenii", *Politeia*, 5, 2001, pp. 118–23; Nataliya Zubarevich, "Izmeneniya roli i strategii krupnogo biznesa v regionakh Rossii", in Nataliya Lapina (ed.), *Regional'nie protsessy v sovremennoi Rossii: Ekonomika, politika i vlast* (Moscow: INION, 2002), pp. 72–88; Robert W. Orttung, "Business and Politics in the Russian Regions", *Problems of Post-Communism* 51, 2, 2004, pp. 48–60; Peter Reddaway and Robert Orttung (eds), *The Dynamics of Russian Politics: Putin's Reform of Federal–Regional Relations* (Lanham: Rowman & Littlefield, 2004).

8 Orttung, "Business and Politics", pp. 54–6.

9 The World Bank, "From Transition to Development: A Country Economic Memorandum for the Russian Federation, April 2004", April 2004, http://www.worldbank.org.ru/ECA/Russia.nsf/bef4f7b517099c0a85256bfb006e03e0/fe49ab3fb21ae703c3256e6f00410397/$FILE/Country%20 Economic%20 Memorandum%(English).pdf.

10 Nataliya Lapina and Alla Chirikova, *Regional'nye elity RF: Modeli povedeniya i politicheskoi orientatsii* (Moscow: INION, 1999); Nataliya Lapina and Alla Chirikova, *Strategii regional'nykh elit: Ekonomika, modeli vlasti, politicheskii vybor* (Moscow: INION, 2000) pp. 79–93.

11 Through a presidential decree of the Russian Federation, the Khanty-Mansii autonomous okrug was renamed the Khanty-Mansii autonomous okrug – Yugra. See "O vkluchenii novogo naimenovaniya sub'ekta Rossiiskoi Federatsii v statiyu 65 Konstitutsii Rossiskoi Federatsii", 25 July 2003, *Sobranie Zakonodatelstva RF*, 30, 2003, St. 3051.

12 "Finansy Khanty-Mansiiskogo avtonomnogo okruga", available at http://www.admhmao.ru/economic/econom/12_2003ut/Finans.htm; Anna Rakipova, "Effektivnye nalogi – stabil'naia ekonomika", *Respublika Tatarstan* 21 November 2003, p. 2.

13 The tax payments of the oil and gas firms in 2003 were distributed among the different companies in the following way: Surgutneftegaz – 35 per cent, Yukos and Lukoil 20 per cent each, TNK – 15 per cent, other producers – 10 per cent; on this see "Khanty-Mansiiskii avtonomnyi okrug – kreditnyi reiting, Standard & Poor's. Analiz i Kommentarii vom 29.9.2004", available at http://www.sandp.ru/p.phtml/analysis?idcontent=1462.

14 The Khanty-Mansii national okrug was founded in 1930. In 1944 it was integrated into Tyumen oblast. In 1977 it received the status of an autonomous okrug, but remained a part of Tyumen.

15 For more see Gary N. Wilson, "'Matryoshka Federalism" and the Case of the Khanty Mansiysk Autonomous Okrug', *Post-Soviet Affairs*, 2, 2001, pp. 167–94.

16 For more on this see Nikolai Petrov, Aleksei Titkov and Aleksandr Glubotskii, "Tyumenskaia oblast", in Maikl Makfol and Nikolai Petrov (eds), *Politicheskii Almanakh Rossii*, 2, II (Moscow: Moskovskii Tsentr Karnegi, 1998), pp. 938–52;

Peter Glatter, "Federalization, Fragmentation and the West Siberian Oil and Gas Province", in David Lane (ed.), *The Political Economy of Russian Oil* (Lanham: Rowman & Littlefield, 1999), pp. 143–60; Pete Glatter, "Continuity and Change in the Tyumen' Regional Elite 1991–2001", *Europe-Asia Studies* 55, 3, 2003, pp. 416–20.

17 The agreement "Soglashenie ob osnovnykh napravleniiakh soglasovannoi politiki v sotsial'no-ekonomicheskoi sfere organov gosudarstvennoi vlasti Tyumenskoi oblasti, Khanty-Mansiiskogo avtonomnogo okruga", of 15 February 2001, is to be found at the internet site: http://www.hmao.wsnet.ru/pravo/flame.htm.

18 For more on this see Sergei Ivkin and Irina Perminova, "Panikhida po matreshke", available at: http://www.mfit.ru/lokalpub_4_191.html, D.Pol Gud [Georg Paul Good]: Rossiya pri Putine: ukrupnenie regionov, available at http://www.ruthenia.ru/logos/number/46/06.pdf/, Julia Kusznir: Die russische Territorialreform. Die Zusammenlegung von Regionen im politischen Kontext, *Russlandanalysen* 90, 2005, available at: www.russlandanalysen.de

19 Vitalii Sotnik, "Tainaya vecherya", *Uralpolit*, of 12 July 2004, available at: http://www.uralpolit.ru/polit/?art=6091.

20 Sergei Makarkin, "Sergei Sobianin-rukovoditel administratsii prezidenta", *Politkom.ru*, 13 December 2005, available at: http:www.politkom.ru/2005/amalit280.php.

21 Articles 37–44 of the Charter of Khanty-Mansii autonomous okrug of 26 April 1995, available at http://www.hmao.wsnet.ru/pravo/fame_2.htm.

22 Articles 45–58 of the Charter of Khanty-Mansii autonomous okrug.

23 Iliya Verkhovskii, "Kommentarii po rezultatam ekspertnogo oprosa 'Samye vliyatel'nye lyudi Rossii – 2003' v Khanty-Mansiiskom avtonomnom okruge", *Samye vliyatel'nye lyudi Rossii* (Moscow: Institut Situatsionnogo analiza i novykh tekhnologii, 2003), pp. 676–82.

24 Filipenko is one of the first governors to have been appointed by the president following the new administrative reforms introduced on 1 January 2005. For more on this see Vitalii Sotnik, "Bez 5 Minut naznachenets Filipenko", *Uralpolit*, 21 February 2005, available at http://www.uralpolit.ru/hmao/art=18674.

25 Filipenko was a member of the board of directors of the oil company TNK until its merger with British Petroleum in the middle of 2003. For more, see http://saint-petersburg.ru/print/24638/.

26 Articles 37–44 of the Charter of Khanty-Mansii autonomous okrug.

27 Law of the Khanty-Mansii autonomous okrug "O nedropol'zovanii", 18 April 1996, available at http://www.hmao.wsnet.ru/pravo/flame.htm; the regional law "O razrabotke mestorozhdenii uglevodov na territorii avtonomnogo okruga", 26 June 1998, available at http://www.hmao.wsnet.ru/pravo/flame.htm.

28 "Neft i Gas Yugry, Analiticheskii obzor", *Neftegazovaia Vertikal* 13, 2004, available at http://www.ngv.ru/magazin/view/hsql?id=1608&mid=71.

29 Law "O nalogovykh lgotakh v Khanty-Mansiiskom avtonomnom okruge", 12 December 1997, with the amendment "O nalogovykh lgotakh v Khanty-Mansiiskom avtonomnom okruge", 25 December 2000, available at http://www.hmao.wsnet.ru/pravo/flame.htm; the law "O razrabotke mestorozhdenii uglevodov na territorii avtonomnogo okruga, 26 June 1998, available at

http://www.hmao.wsnet.ru/pravo/flame.htm; the law "O podderzhke investit-sionnoi deyatel'nosti organami gosudarstvennoi vlasti avtonomnogo okruga na territorii KhMAO", 8 October 1999, available at http://www.hmao.wsnet.ru/pravo/flame.htm.

30 Law "O stimulirovanii uskorennogo vvoda v razrabotku neftegazovykh mestorozhdenii v predelakh litsenzionnykh uchastkov nedr na territorii KhMAO", 9 April 1999, available at http://www.hmao.wsnet.ru/pravo/flame.htm.

31 For more on this, see Valerii Karasev, "Gosudarstvo vse vremya pytaetsia izymat mificheskie sverkhpribyli", *Neft i kapital* 6, 2000, pp. 34–8; Vitalii Sotnik, "Duma prinyala okolo 60 zakonov, posvyashchennykh probleme VMSB", 17 May 2004, available at http://www.uralpolit.ru/hmao/news/?art=3932; Aleksandr V. Malovetskii, *Investitsionnaia politika neftianykh korporatsii* (Surgut/Moscow: URSS, 2002), pp. 120–9.

32 Sergei Pravosudov, "Syrevye regiony kritikuyut pravitelstvo", *Nezavisimaya Gazeta*, 1 February 2001, p. 4.

33 "Neft i Gas Yugry"; Valerii Nikolaev and Nikolai Sotnikov, "Kupite sebe neftyanuyu skvazhinu", *Uralpolit*, 19 November 2003, available at http://www.uralpolit.ru/hmao/?article_id=8329.

34 These were the head of the city administration of Nefteyugansk, Viktor Tkachev, the head of the city administration of Pyt-Yach, Valerii Vesnin, and the head of Nefteyugansk raion, Aleksandr Klepikov. See Larisa Rychkova, "Byvshego direktora 'Yuganskneftegaza' neubreditelno opravdali", *Kommersant*, 18 August 2005, and Vitalii Sotnik, "Yugra: schastlivchiki i neudachniki sezona", *Uralpolit*, 3 August 2005, http://www.uralpolit.ru/hmao/?art=25702.

35 Dmitrii Vasilev, "Sud osvobodil obviniaemogo s boliu v serdtse", *Kommersant*, 17 August 2005, and Sotnik (Yugra).

36 Whereas the regional budget in the 1990s received about 60 per cent of the revenue from taxes on the exploitation of raw materials, after the tax reform of 2000, only 20 per cent of the revenue went to the regional budget. Thereafter this fell to 13.4 per cent in 2004 and 5 per cent in 2005. According to the next stage of the federal tax reform, from 2006 tax revenue from the extraction of mineral resources will go directly to the federal budget and then be equally distributed among all regions. This means that the extraction regions will receive no direct income from the extraction of oil. For more on this see Tatyana Stanova, "Nalogovaya evolutsiya", *Politkom*, 14 April 2004, available at http://www.politcom.ru/2004/zloba3986.php, and "KhMAO zainteressovan v korrektirovke byudzhetnogo i nalogovogo kodeksov", available at http://www.infoil.ru/news/print/4576.

37 According to the draft law "On the subsoil", the regions will lose their authority over the regulation of the exploitation of strategically important mineral resources such as oil and gas to the federal centre. For more on this see Alena Kornysheva, "Ubili nedra", *Kommersant-Vlast*, 49, 2004, pp. 30–6; Alena Kornysheva, "Mikhail Fradkov odobril natsional'izatsiyu nedr", *Kommersant* 18 March 2005, available at http://www.kommersant.ru/doc.html?docId=555656; William Tompson, "Re-writing Russia's subsoil law: from sovereignty to civil law?", *Russie.Cei.Visions*, 3 May 2005, available at http://www.ifri.org/files/Russie/Tompson_anglais.pdf.

38 Mintimer Shaimiev has been elected president three times. In March 2005, President Putin proposed him as the republic's presidential candidate for the next five-year term. The following month, the regional parliament confirmed the nomination. See Yurii Nikolaev and Nataliya Alekseeva, "Shaimievu dobavili srok. Samyi nepokornyi iz glav regionov stanovitsya naznachentsem", *Izvestiya*, 18 March 2005.

39 "Konstitutsiia respublika Tatarstan", 30 January 1992", F.M. Mukhametshin and R.T. Izmailov (eds), *Suverenyi Tatarstan* (Moscow: CIMO, 1997), pp. 201–40.

40 The treaty between the Russian Federation and the Republic of Tatarstan "O razgranichenii predmetov vedeniia i vzaimnom delegirovanii polnomochii mezhdu organami vlasti Rossiiskoi Federatsii i organami gosudartsvennoi vlasti Respubliki Tatarstan", 15 February 1994, can be found in Mukhametshin and Izmailov, *Suverenyi Tatarstan*, pp. 33–9.

41 For more on this see Valentin Mikhailov, "Tatarstan: Jahre der Souveränität. Eine kurze Bilanz", *Osteuropa* 4, 1999, pp. 366–86; Mary McAuley, *Russia's Politics of Uncertainty* (Cambridge: Cambridge University Press, 1997), pp. 82–108; N. M Moukhariamov, "The Tatarstan Model: A Situational Dynamic", in Peter J. Stavrakis (ed.), *Beyond the Monolith: The Emergence of Regionalism in Post-Soviet Russia* (Washington: The Johns Hopkins University Press, 2000); Kimitaka Matsuzato, "From Ethno-Bonapartism to Centralized Caciquismo: Characteristics and Origins of the Tatarstan Political Regime, 1990–2000", *The Journal of Communist Studies and Transition Politics*, 17, 4, 2001, pp. 43–77; Midkhat Farukhshin, "Tatarstan: Syndrome of Authoritarianism", in Cameron Ross (ed.), *Regional Politics in Russia* (Manchester: Manchester University Press, 2002), pp. 193–207.

42 Articles 106–115 of the Constitution of the Republic of Tatarstan of 30.11.1992, in Mukhametshin and Izmailov, *Suverenyi Tatarstan*, pp. 201–40, and Articles 89–98 of the Constitution of the Republic of Tatarstan of 10 May 2002, available at http://www.tatar.ru/?DNSID=bc97005d5514f2567b 36caf8cb9967d1&node_id=222.

43 The new Constitution of 2002 changed the system of elections to the regional parliament. Half of the 100 parliamentary seats were now to be directly elected in constituencies and the other half through party lists. In order to receive seats through the party list, parties or electoral alliances had to receive at least 7 per cent of the votes cast. See Articles 67–88 and Articles 89–98 of the constitution of the Republic of Tatarstan of 10 May 2002, available at http://www.tatar.ru/?DNSID=bc97005d5514f2567b36caf8cb9967d1&node_id=222.

44 Alexander Salagaev and Sergei Sergeev, "Kommentarii po rezultatam ekspertnogo oprosa 'Samye vliyatel'nye lyudi Rossii – 2003' v Respublike Tatarstan", *Samye vliyatel'nye lyudi Rossii* (Moscow: Institut Situatsionnogo analiza i novykh tekhnologii, 2003), pp. 164–76; see also Midhat Farukshin, "O samykh vliyatelnykh lyudyakh Tatarstana", *Zvezda Povol'zhya*, 3–9 July 2004, p. 2; and Sergei Micheev, "Shaimievu i Putin ne pomekha", available at http://www.politcom.ru/2002/p_region10.php.

45 Salagaev and Sergeev "Kommentarii po rezultatam", pp. 164–76; see also Farukshin, "O samykh vliiatelnykh liudiakh Tatarstana", p. 2.

46 The federal privatization programme drawn up by Egor Gaidar was rejected by the indigenous political elite of Tatarstan. Tatarstan's long-standing president

Shaimiev gave the following reasons for this in an interview: "One can be a backward province in an economically leading country, but at the same time one can be a flourishing region in an economically weak country. Even Russia as a whole has a great economic policy, that doesn't guarantee success for the enterprise of Tatarstan because competitive benefits are established at the regional level"; cited in Arbakhan Magomedov, *Regional Ideologies in the Context of International Relations* (Zürich: Eidgenössische Technische Hochschule, Working Paper No.12, 2001), pp. 29–30.

47   After the end of the privatization of the most important regional companies in 1997, the Tatar government had control of 392 regional firms in the fuel, oil extraction and processing industries. For more on this see Igor Denisov, *Vzaimodeistvie praviashchikh i ekonomicheskikh elit v regionakh Rossii* (Kazan, 2003, Manuscript), available at http://polit.mezhdunarodnik.ru/archives/denisov_vzaimo.pdf.

48   Interview between the author and Professor Midhat Farukshin, the Dean of the Department of Political Sciences at the University of Kazan, 10 June 2004.

49   5 per cent of these belong to the son the Republic's president, Radik Shaimiev, and 7 per cent to the joint venture Taif. The American – Tatar company Taif contains 23 different firms which are active in important areas of the economy of Tatarstan. Radik Shaimiev is at the same time a member of the board of directors and advisor to the leader of this group. Taif also has shares in Nizhnekamsknefekhim (about 10 per cent) and NizhnekamskNPZ (7.5 per cent). On this see "Genprokuratura RF initsiirovala proverku odnoi iz krupneishchikh kompanii respubliki – OAO 'Tataro-amerikanskie investitsii i finansy'" (TAIF), available at http://gazeta.etatar.ru/news/view/10/5221.

50   Renat Muslimov, "Tatarstan's Oil and Gas Policies: Why Fix it if it Ain't Broken?", *Oil and Gas Eurasia*, 10, 2003, p. 14.

51   Akhmet Ivanov, "Respublika Tatarstan v dekabre 1996 goda", available at http://www.igpi.ru/monitoring/1047645476/1996/12967/16.html; "'Lukoil' i 'Tatneft'" menyayutsya benzozapravkami", available at http://www.neftemarket.ru/info-press-view.htm?id=937&month=09&year=2003.

52   Following his dismissal as a member of the board of directors in 1999, Fardiev became head of the energy supply firm Tatenergo, which has a monopoly on the regional market.

53   John Thornhill and Clay Harris, "Tatarstan used front to borrow from foreign banks", *The Financial Times*, 9 September 1999, and "Kak Tatarstan ispol'zoval kompaniyu 'Tatneft'", *Zvezda Povol'zhya*, 6 October 1999, available at http://dpcom.narod.ru/199939/ddddd.htm.

54   In the middle of May 2005, NizhnekamskNPZ sold their shares to Taif, which made it the second largest shareholder in NizhnekamskNPZ. For more on this, see Tatyana Korneeva, "Obezdolennyi zavod", *Kommersant-Kazan*, 24 August 2005, available at http://www.kommersant.ru/region/kazan/page.htm?year=2005&issue=157&id=12664

55   See Anon., "Kovarstvo l lubov. Uchrediteli Nizhnekamskogo NPZ snova ne mogut dogovoritsya", Neft i Kapital, 11/2003, pp. 21–5; and Korneeva, "Obezdolennyi".

56   Anatolii Kovalev, "O klane Shaimieva zamol'vite slovo. Komu Duma dala shans na beskonechnoe pravlenie", *Novaya Gazeta*, 18 December 2000.

57   Governmental decree "O poriadke vzaimozachetov mezhdu AO 'Tatneft' i AO 'Taif' ", 19 August 1998, *Pravovaia Sistema 'Garant'*, 20 June 2004. According

to this, Taif paid Tatneft 300 roubles per tonne in the form of bills of exchange; in addition, the Republic's government paid 50 roubles per tonne out of the regional budget. See Vera Postnova, "Chernaya dyra. 20 tysiach neftianikov Tatarstana ostanutsya bez raboty", *Nezavisimaya Gazeta*,16 March 2002; Midkhat Faroukshine, "Tatarstan's Oil has Already been Divided Up", *Russian Regional Report*, 13 November 1997, p. 12.

58 Governmental decree "O vzaimopostavkakh syria i produktsii predpriyatiyami neftekhimicheskogo kompleksa respubliki na 2000 god", 17 December 1999, *Pravovaya Sistema 'Garant'*, 20 June 2004. See Postnova, "Chernaya dyra".

59 Thornhill and Harris "Tatarstan".

60 Gulnaz Sharafutdinova, "Concentrating Capital Helps Tatarstan Leaders in Battle with Putin's Centralization", *Russian Regional Report*, 17 October 2001, pp. 4–5.

61 For more on this, see Sergei Sergeev, *Politicheskaya oppozitsiya v sovremennoi Rossiiskoi Federatsii. Federalnye i regionalnye aspekty* (Kazan: Kazanskii gosu-darstvennyi universitet, 2004), pp. 312–38.

62 Governmental regulation of the Russian Federation, "O federalnoi tselevoi programme sotsial'no-economicheskogo razvitiya Respubliki Tatarstan do 2006 goda", 24 August 2001, available at http://www.tatar.ru/?DNSID=0968aacb270b8c164d5727849eb6ad9a&node_id=2565&lid=567.

63 Kovalev "O klane Shaimieva"; Ekaterina Vorobeva and Irina Rybalchenko, "Prezident Rossii vstal na storonu Tatarstana", *Tattsenter. Delovi Tsentr RT*, 27 December 2004, available at http://www.neft.tatcenter.ru/market/22040.htm.

64 For more on this, see Andrei Yakovlev, "Evolution of Corporate Governance in Russia: Government Policy vs. Real Incentives of Economic Agents", *Post-Communist Economies*, 16, 4, 2004, pp. 387–404.

7
Russia's Northern Periphery in Transition: Regional Fragmentation of the Far North?

Daniel Göler

As earlier chapters have demonstrated, the distribution of power in Russian federalism has been changing. Following the Yeltsin period, when the power of the centre seemed to be waning in the face of increased assertiveness from within many of the Russian republics, under Putin the centre has been able to reassert some of the control that had been lost and, in the process, cast some doubt on the continued federal nature of the system. Within many of the federal units there has also been change. The most important aspect of this has been the relationship between the political authorities and business interests. The stabilization of this relationship has in many cases produced a regime in which political and economic power has become almost fused into a form of rule with profoundly anti-democratic implications. These two processes, the centralization of power and the consolidation of local rule through the combination of political and economic power, have also occurred in peripheral regions of Russia.

Introduction

Regional disparities are one of the main features of current development trends in Russia. There are great differences between the European and the North-Asiatic parts of the country, between urban and rural as well as between central and peripheral areas. These contrasts continue on the sub-national or sub-regional levels, with most of the Russian regions (i.e. the 89 federal territorial units) showing the same patterns of dissimilarity. These disparities existed during communist times. In fact, the historical patterns are deeply rooted in the current spatial structures of the Russian Federation. As a result of uneven economic development during the transition period, these historical disparities have been on the rise since the beginning 1990s, with a tendency to increase even more in the twenty-first century.

This has been to the disadvantage of the large periphery of the north-eastern part of the Russian Federation.

Most of the main political and theoretical concepts have failed in enabling us to understand these regional effects of post-socialist transition. Theories of regional development have generally relied on economic growth, with crisis on a larger scale, no matter how temporary or regionally limited, not expected. Such a crisis, however, has dominated recent developments in the Russian Federation, especially in the Far North.[1] This area is defined as the territory of the Republic of Sakha (better known as Yakutiya) in the Russian Far East and the northern parts of Irkutsk oblast and Krasnoyarsk krai in Eastern Siberia. This chapter seeks to put recent development trends in this area into a higher geographical framework and provide a better understanding of the transition process in peripheral areas.[2]

History and the current situation

Under the centralized planned economy of the socialist period, the northern regions of the Soviet Union were considered an area with great prospects. The so-called Far North had a special status in spatial planning, with the result that, until the 1980s, the North was the target of enormous investments. In many places new settlements were erected for the first time. Most of them were mono-functional, "urban settlements" with 5,000 and only sometimes up to 15,000 inhabitants each (Russian: *posyolok gorodskogo tipa*).[3] The only purpose of such settlements, which were fully equipped from an infrastructural point of view and inhabited all year round, was to exploit the abundant resources of the Far North (fossil energy sources, ores, diamonds and others). In terms of the conditions and spatial dimensions, the Soviet achievements were enormous from a development point of view, but cost–benefit considerations were of only minor importance.

In the post-Soviet period, however, the Far North has been characterized by a profound change. For the North the collapse of the Soviet Union meant the loss of its financial basis. And with the breakdown of the socialist system, the basic organizational structures disappeared, too.[4] It did not take long for the negative consequences to become apparent. Depopulation and dramatic economic problems appeared in most parts of the North, especially outside the locations of the oil and gas industry in Western Siberia. In the course of the socioeconomic transition during the 1990s, the Far North has changed from a boom region to an area characterized by crisis conditions in its structural, economic and social aspects. To a significant degree, these developments were characteristic of the extreme northern and the most peripheral regions of Russia in Eastern Siberia and the Far East. But they were exacerbated by what, some decades ago, the Soviet planner Slavin listed as "northern factors": the harsh climatic conditions, a low population density, remoteness and the high costs of living and construction compared to other parts of the country.[5]

Under the new conditions of a market economy, the effect of these northern factors was heightened. Parshev has calculated the "costs of the cold":[6] prices for housing and transport have been rising exorbitantly, supply shortages have resulted in decreasing living standards, living conditions have reached a remarkably low level, especially in the arctic and subarctic regions. These regions have more in common with the situation known from developing countries than with a former superpower. The lack of prospects for their future has led to mass out-migration by the population.[7] Some federal territorial units in the extreme north-eastern periphery of Siberia and the Far East, like Chukotka autonomous okrug or Magadan oblast, had a decline in their population of more than 40 or 50 per cent during the intercensus period 1989–2002 (Figure 7.1). The decay of both the physical (in terms of settlement structures) and cultural infrastructures has been evident throughout the region. This withdrawal from the Northern Periphery and, in some parts, the step to derelict landscapes,[8] which is a specific problem of mono-structured locations, has three aspects.

Three dimensions of the withdrawal from the Northern Periphery: precondition for a new beginning?

The withdrawal of the population

The most remarkable sign indicating the current withdrawal from the Northern Periphery is the out-migration of the population. Most of the small and medium-sized "urban" settlements in the region had a decline of more than 50 per cent of inhabitants. A large number of unoccupied blocks of flats as well as destroyed or burnt-out buildings are evident within the town precincts. Meanwhile many settlements have been completely abandoned. In Yakutiya, for example, one out of five settlements has been "liquidated". This development was especially common in the second half of the 1990s. Liquidation in the given context means that the settlement was closed by official decree. The inhabitants were evacuated and resettled, mainly in other parts of Russia. In most cases this is the best result for the people who had been living in the North, because they received financial and organizational support from the Russian state.

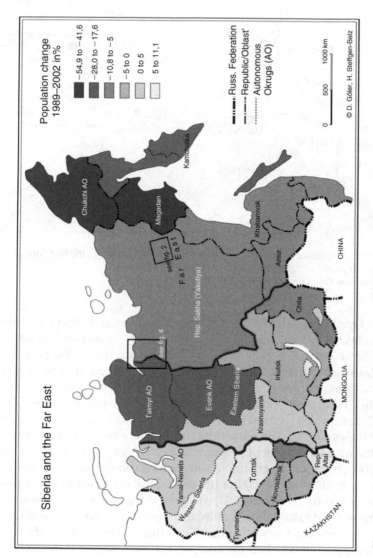

Figure 7.1 Population change in Siberia and the Russian Far East between 1989 and 2002
Source: Calculations according to Goskomstat Rossii 2001 and www.gks.ru.

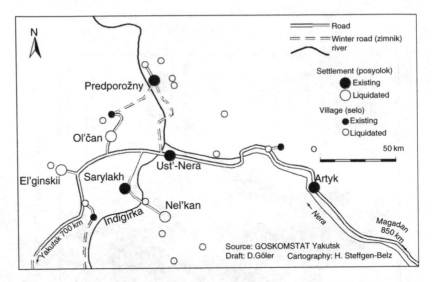

Figure 7.2   Liquidations and changes of the settlement structure in the Oymyakon district, Republic of Sakha/Yakutiya
(*Note*: the map shows the northern part of the district)

The Oymyakon district (Figure 7.2) is among the regions that have been most affected by liquidations. There almost every second settlement has been abandoned. For some periods of time since the 1940s, prisoners (GULag-detainees) were used for gold mining in the region. In later years the locations have been further expanded in line with the complex (social-ist) method of development. Some of the younger mining settlements like Olchan, which received town status only in 1977, have ceased to exist since the late 1990s. The remaining inhabitants were evacuated in con-nection with a resettlement programme in 1997–98. The costs amounted to €5,000 per person, an enormous sum for local conditions.[9] Gold mining, however, is still continued: after the mining had decreased by about two-thirds in Yakutiya between 1991 and 1998,[10] the partial privatization of the state-owned YakutZoloto enabled many private artels to obtain digging licences. These small private companies of shareholders work on the basis of enormous individual efforts and personal risks. Today, such artels are profitable businesses because they are no longer responsible for the expen-sive infrastructure (including settlements) and world-market prices have been rising (as at 2001). Due to the limited size of the deposits, the out-dated mining technology, rising wages and the dependency on world-market prices, the current usage is very likely to run out in the medium term. The effects on the settlement structures are, as seen in the example in Figure 7.2, not so much a total withdrawal *from*, but a withdrawal *within* the northern periphery. As in other regions,[11] the smaller settlements of minor importance are generally the ones liquidated, while some "central places" continue to exist.

The withdrawal of economy

The current depopulation is in most cases the result of a total breakdown of the local economic basis. There have been several sites, for example, of coal, tin and gold mining in Yakutiya, begun between the late 1930s and the beginning of the 1980s. In the course of socioeconomic transition during the 1990s, most of the resource-based extracting industries (except the oil, gas and diamond sectors) in the Russian North went more or less directly into bankruptcy. In the case of a coal mine in Sangar, situated on the river Lena about 300 km north of Yakutsk in the Republic of Sakha/ Yakutiya, work began during communist times to expand the mine even further. After an enormous increase in mining costs in the 1990s and the disappearance of state subsidies, the state-owned mine was closed in 1997 and Sangarskaya Shakhta finally liquidated. Settlements other than those whose locations depended on raw materials were also affected in this way. Cherski (Nizhnekolymsk district, Republic of Sakha), a settlement near the mouth of the river Kolyma that was well known in Soviet times as an important base and port for transhipment on the Northern Sea Route, has undergone an almost total marginalization during the 1990s because of the closing down of the combine for building materials. Table 7.1 shows some selected indicators that are proof of the socioeconomic decline within the region: apart from the production of alcohol (*sic!*), all other figures are decreasing. Another alarming factor is that the number of both employees and inhabitants has shrunk due to migration, while the number of pensioners, however, is relatively constant. The reason is that many pensioners, sometimes only because they cannot afford a flight ticket to central Russia, are not able to undertake migration. To some extent such settlements can be described as "trap towns".[12] So, after the crash of the local economy most of the mono-functional settlements seem no longer to be viable. Under conditions of market economy, their partial or total abandonment is a logical consequence.

To complete the picture, it has to be mentioned that traditional economies and ways of living have also taken a negative turn. In Sakha, for example, the livestock of reindeers has declined by 53 per cent (see Figure 7.3) during the 1990s, a clear sign of a substantial crisis.[13] The thesis of a rising "neo-traditionalism"[14] has proved wrong and quite the reverse

194

Table 7.1 Nizhnekolymskii Ulus – Selected parameters of socioeconomic change

Socioeconomic indicators	1990	2001	change in %
Total population	13,800	7,700	−44
Urban population (Cherski)	11,300	5,600	−50
Rural population	2,500	2,100	−16
Number of employees	7,800	2,900	−63
pensioners	1,700	1,613	−5
Agriculture and manufacturing; stock of ...			
reindeers	35,100	15,300	−56
pigs	1,174	275	−77
cattle	134	51	−62
Production of ...			
meat (t)	999	109	−89
milk (t)	117	52	−56
fishery products (t)	1,739	409	−76
full-cream milk products (t)	780	16	−98
vodka and liqueur (unit)	0	8.3	—
electric energy (mio. kwh)	40.0	6.0	−85
Traffic and transport			
Handling of goods (1,000 t)	927	23	−98
Transport of goods (1,000 tkm)	23,647	171	−99
Building activities ...			
Investments in new buildings (Mrd. roubles)	29.8	0	−100

Source: GOSKOMSTAT Respubliki Sakha (Yakutiya) 2003.

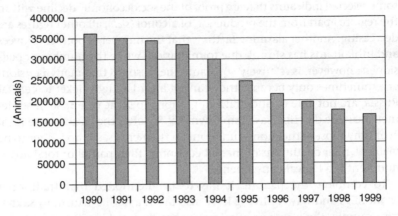

Figure 7.3 Development of reindeer livestock in the Republic of Sakha during the 1990s
Source: GOSKOMSTAT Respubliki Sakha [Yakutiya] 2000.

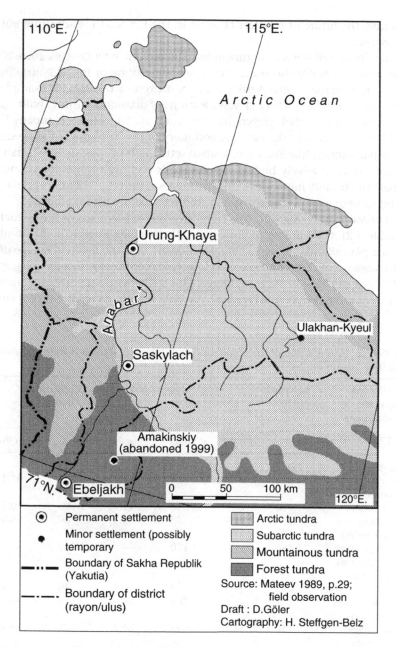

Figure 7.4 Anabar district, Republic of Sakha
Source: Modified and supplemented according to Mateev (1989: 29).

is true: the future of reindeer farming in the Far North is anything but positive.

But, beside all the abandonment and the regressive tendencies, there is, on a smaller scale, also some progressive development in the Northern Periphery. In the Anabar district in the northwest of Yakutiya for example (Figure 7.4), are a number of new locations of diamond mining, built up by one of the global players in that industry, the Alrosa company.[15] Although located in the extreme periphery of the Russian Far East, such company-towns like Ebelyakh, a small settlement of roughly 900 inhabitants, have relatively high living standards and high wages for young, male and healthy miners, working in long-term shifts (i.e. 12 hours per day and sometimes the whole summer mining season without a break).

Ebelyakh differs significantly from the other settlements of the district (Table 7.2): the number of employees, the average wage (the diamond mine pays slightly above €1,000 per month), and the low percentage of pensioners, invalids or people with low wages contrasts with a completely different situation in Yuryung-Khaya. This settlement is mainly inhabited by indigenous people (the Dolgans) and only slightly above 30 per cent are

Table 7.2   Comparison of the population and the living standards in the Anabar district (figures for 2000)

Settlement (year of foundation)	Saskylakh (1930)		Yuryung-Khaya (1930)		Ebelyakh (1984)	
	Total	(in %)	Total	(in %)	Total	(in %)
population	2,062	—	1,108	—	870	—
working population	612	29.7	328	29.6	541	62.2
pensioners	410	19.9	218	19.7	93	10.7
working pensioners	110	26.8	75	34.4	80	86.0
average level of pensions (in Rbl.)	1,150	—	1,150	—	1,150	—
invalides	93	4.5	38	3.4	10	1.1
low wages (families)	279	—	264	—	12	—
low wages (people)	1,116	54.1	899	81.1	38	4.4

Source: Data of the Saskylakh administration, Anabarskii Ulus, Republic of Sakha/Yakutiya.

employed, the percentage of people with low wages lies at over 80 per cent. In this context it has to be kept in mind that the income from reindeer farming for example is €40 and only slightly more than the medium pension level.

The withdrawal of the state

In nearly every settlement visited during research in these remote areas, empty administrative buildings were evident. To some extent this is an indicator of the withdrawal of the state. This is for two main reasons. First, this is a consequence of the dramatic loss of population and, as mentioned above, of economic marginalization. But second, this is also a result of the deregulation of state sovereignty. The public sector in most of the prospering locations of diamond mining, for example, is shrinking. Things like infrastructure, the supply of goods, and the transport system are guaranteed mainly by private institutions (such as the local mining company).[16] As well as Yakutiya, this is the reality in most of the resource-based peripheries in Russia (like Western Siberia, Noril'sk and Sakhalin, for example). The consequence on the one hand is the reliability of supply systems, but on the other hand also a higher degree of dependency and control by the company, which has not been rejected by most of the inhabitants and especially by the working staff.

Thus it is clear that the whole of the Northern Periphery has been affected by massive withdrawal tendencies, but this phenomenon does not include a total abandonment as living and economic space. Indeed, it can even be stated that the partial abandonment has to be seen as the foundation of a future regional development adjusted to the market-economic conditions of a global economy.

Fragmenting development in Russia's Northern Periphery

These contradictory developments can generally be considered a typical feature of the peripheries of a society undergoing transformation. The current development in Russia's Far North (in terms of population, settlements and economy) is characterized by regressive and progressive tendencies taking place at the same time. Regional development within the Northern Periphery is clearly marked by fragmenting tendencies. Therefore, regional fragmentation needs to be explored as a key trend to further understanding the inconsistent, heterogenous developments there. The main influences on the currently fragmenting regional development in the

Northern Periphery are listed in Figure 7.5. The fragmented Northern Periphery can be explained as a flashpoint of three main factors:

1. Post-socialist transition processes and the effect they have go back to the change of the legal, social and political system that emerged following the fall of the Soviet Union. These processes led to far-reaching socioeconomic change, in most cases with negative effects for the Northern Periphery (as shown above). Protagonists in that area must not only cope with economic disadvantages, but also with the loss of normative institutions and familiar, daily routines.
2. Transition, in the sense of the process which is commonly described as globalization, also means that the markets of the former Soviet Union are further opening up, for example, to foreign direct investments (internationalization by FDI); capital or profit maximization are gaining increasing influence on regional development and the formation of spatial disparities in Russia both on the national and regional levels (for example in the Northern Periphery); and investments are concentrated in locations with the highest profit expectations. The increasing integration of one region is opposed by the marginalization of another region.

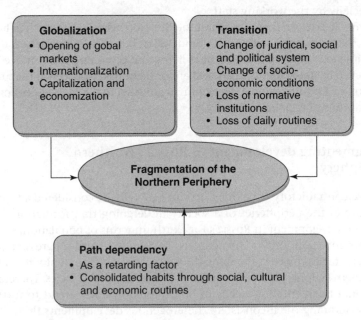

Figure 7.5   Factors of fragmentation of the Northern Periphery

3. A third, rather conservative element, is so-called "path dependency".[17] This factor has been ignored far too often, especially in early post-Soviet research; indeed, this was one of the big errors of scientific geographical research at the beginning of the 1990s. Path dependency assumes that traditions, social rules and structures acquired over a long period of time are retained even during the course of profound change. That means that the transition processes (as well as the influence of globalization) in particulars depends to a high degree on the former situation. As these elements are rigid for a long time in the future, they understandably react to changes only very sluggishly. Path dependency stands, therefore, to some extent, as a retarding element in transition process.

As mentioned above, regional fragmentation is a typical feature of the transition process in the periphery. The underlying model of global fragmentation – in German geography, for example, discussed by Scholz[18] – was originally meant to describe and explain the regional effects of ongoing globalization, with special respect to developing countries. Apparently, the fragmenting tendencies on a global level continue on a smaller scale as well.

A model of peripheral fragmentation

Against this background, I propose a model of "northern" or "peripheral fragmentation" (Figure 7.6), as an attempt to take into account the situation of deep crisis, marginalization and social exclusion as well as the more

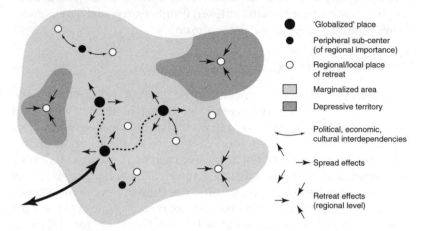

Figure 7.6   Spatial patterns of fragmenting development in the Northern Periphery

positive developments there. The structural differentiation ranges between a few globalized places which are highly integrated into the global economy (like the resource-based settlements) or sub-centres with a certain regional importance (e.g. concerning administrative matters), and the huge marginalized regions or depressed territories which have entirely lost the basis of their livelihood. Other locations have been integrated in former (socialist) times, now however, due to the process of transition, most of these are places of retreat. That is particularly the case with depressed territories which have lost almost all of their economic and cultural interdependencies to other settlements within or outside the Northern Periphery, and are thus increasingly cut off from external influences. Their share of the economic value added is very limited, although, for example, Sakha formally ranks among the wealthy republics of Russia. This wealth, however, is mostly generated at some globalized places and only from there certain spread-effects are noticeable, but merely into the immediate regional neighbourhood.

The consequent pattern of post-socialist spatial development (seen as a result of the socioeconomic transition process) is thus not a complete withdrawal or an abandonment of the Northern Periphery as a whole. In fact, it is a withdrawal within the Northern Periphery. Some areas are characterized by marginalization and abandonment, but others are characterized by ongoing integration, economic growth and prosperity. As at the global level, on the regional and local levels the power of the market economy and capitalism can be identified as a mechanism of these economic changes. They function as a kind of engine for fragmenting regional development by increasing the disparities of regional development. In all peripheral areas in the Russian Northern Periphery, regional development shows a noticeable economic determinism.

Concluding remarks

In conclusion three aspects concerning the thesis of regional fragmentation of the Northern Periphery are of particular interest. First (and basically), it always has to be kept in mind that the model of global fragmentation stems from research on developing countries, so its applicability to other fields should not be accepted without argument. According to international statistics, Russia is considered neither an extremely developed nor a less developed country. The Human Development Index rank shows a medium level of human development,[19] while in terms of per capita GDP, Russia is number 54 out of 180 countries in the world.[20] But in spite of that, quite a high percentage of the population lives in poverty. This is particularly the case on the periphery, and especially among pensioners and indigenous people with a traditional source of income. The resource-based regions in the North, like the Republic of Sakha or especially Tyumen oblast for instance, are indeed, in comparison and at least statistically, among the richest regions in the Federation.[21] But the northern territories are also the regions with the highest share of the population living at the subsistence level; most of the population is apparently excluded from any kind of prosperity. So, to some extent, *peripheral transformations* are at the same time *peripheral fragmentations*.

Second, in research as well as in regional policy concerning the post-Soviet Northern Periphery during the transition period, not enough attention has been paid to the social situation of the people living in the Far North. Today, in terms of the present state of retreat, migration plays a dominant part. Apparently, for the majority of the non-native population (i.e. ethnic Russians, Ukrainians etc.) out-migration appears to be the easiest and most obvious way to deal with their problems. But with a decreasing population, the stayers' living conditions and supply of goods are put at risk. So there is an important task for the future: to deal with the deplorable state of "daily geography" on the Northern Periphery, in other words with the critical living conditions that are present there. Out-migration and evacuating inhabitants can only be part of a solution. But those problems also mean that the achievements of Soviet times, which are the starting point for post-Soviet development, are also called into question.

Third, the fragmentation of the post-Soviet Northern Periphery, especially its economic and political elements, to some extent calls into question two trends evident nationally, the strengthening of central control and the consolidation of local power. While both of these may be characteristic of much of the country, they also apply in those parts of the Far North experiencing the withdrawal of the population, economy and the state, but in another form. Beside the vast and more or less abandoned territories (there is no need for state control any more), local power seems to be also strengthened, but highly patronized by the local, regional, national or global economy, meaning that peripheral regions will underlie new dependencies in the future.

Notes

1   H. Klüter, "Der Norden Russlands – vom Niedergang einer Entwicklungsregion", *Geographische Rundschau* 52, 12, 2000, pp. 12–20; and Daniel Göler, "Raumstruktureller Wandel im sibirisch-fernöstlichen Norden. Regionale Fragmentierung der nördlichen Peripherie Russlands", *Geographische Rundschau* 55, 12, 2003, pp. 26–33.

2   This is based on empirical study of socioeconomic aspects of the post-socialist transition period in Russia's northern periphery undertaken by the author between 1999 and 2004. Daniel Göler, *Rückzug aus der nördlichen Peripherie Russlands? Jungere raumliche Entwicklungen im Hohen Nordern Ostsibiriens und des Fernen Ostens – ein Beitrag zur peripheren Transformationsforschung* (Leipzig: Institut für Länderkunde, 2005).

3   In the Soviet Union, a functional way of describing urban settlements was used for regional planning. The decisive factor to categorize settlements as urban or rural ones is not so much their size, but their non-agricultural economic structure. That means that small or medium-sized settlements can be described as towns, although they have no major centrality concerning administrative or supply functions.

4   Klüter, "Der Norden Russlands", p. 12.

5   S.V. Slavin, *The Soviet North. Present Development and Prospects* (Moscow, 1972).

6   A.P. Parshev, "Pochemu Rossiya ne Amerika. Kniga dlya tekh, kto ostayetsya zdes", http://www.parshev.r52ru/book/index.phtml 2004; See also Fiona Hill and Clifford Gaddy, *The Siberian Curse. How Communist Planners Left Russia Out in the Cold* (Washington, DC: Brookings Institution Press, 2003).

7   Documented, for example, by A. Bond, "Outmigration, Economic Dislocation, and Reassessment of Labour Resource in the Russian far North", *Post-Soviet Geography*, 35, 5, 1994, pp. 299–308; T. Heleniak, "Migration from the Russian Far North During the Transition Period" (Washington, DC: Social Protection Discussion Paper Series, No. 9925, 1990); Daniel Göler, "Migration und Bevölkerungsentwicklung an der nördlichen Peripherie Russlands", F. Swiaczny and S. Haug (eds), *Bevölkerungsgeographische Forschung für Migration und Integration* (Wiesbaden: BiB, 2004, Materialen zur Bevölkerungswissenschaft, vol. 112), pp. 131–149; and Göler (Ruckzug).

8   P. Knox and S. Marston, *Places and Regions in Global Context: Human Geography* (Upper Saddle River: Prentice Hall, 1998), p. 235.

9   P.E. Alekseev and A.M. Stolyarov, *Staratel'skaya dobycha zolota v usloviyakh rynka* (Yakutsk, 2000), p. 29.

10 Alekseev and Stolyarov, *Staratel'skaya*, p. 29.

11 J.O. Habeck, *Seßhaftwerdung und Seßhaftmachung sibirischer Rentiernomaden. Siedlungsstruktur und Siedlungsgeschichte im Ewenkischen Autonomen Kreis* (Münster: Berichte aus dem Arbeitsgebiet Entwicklungsforschung, Heft 30, 1998).

12 N. Wein, "Bevölkerungsbewegungen im asiatischen Russland. Migrationsströme in Sibirien und im Fernen Osten nach dem Zusammenbruch der Sowjetunion", *Osteuropa*, 49, 9, 1999, p. 914 (following S.V. Soboleva,"Nastoyashchee i budushchee narodonaselenya Sibiri", in V.V. Kuleshov (ed), *Sibir na poroge novogo tysyachiletya* (Novosibirsk, 1999), p. 99.

13 GOSKOMSTAT Respubliki Sakha/Yakutiya, *Ulusy i goroda za 1990–1999 gody* (Yakutsk, 2000), p. 41.

14 A. Pika, "Neotraditionalism in the Russian North. Indigenous Peoples and the Legacy of Perestroika" (Seattle: Circumpolar Research Series 6, 1999).

15 Abbreviation for "Almazy Rossii Sakha", a closed-type joint-stock company which was founded 1992 as successor to the former state-owned YakutAlmaz. Alrosa contributes 75 per cent of the total budget of Yakutiya, rendering it the main pillar of the economy of the Republic of Sakha.

16 A similar argument is used by Rautio with regard to mining towns situated on the Kola Peninsula in the Northwest of Russia serving as an example. V. Rautio, *The Potential for Community Restructuring – Mining Towns in Pechenga* (Saarijarvi: Kikimora Publications, 2004), p. 82.

17 David Stark, "Path Dependency and Privatization Strategies in East Central Europe", *Eastern European Politics and Societies*, 6, 1,1992, pp. 17–54.

18 F. Scholz, *Geographische Entwicklungsforschung (Studienbücher der Geographie)* (Berlin, Stuttgart: Borntraeger, 2004), pp. 215ff; and F. Scholz, "The Theory of Fragmenting Development", *Geographische Rundschau International*, 1, 2, 2005, pp. 4–11.

19 UNDP, *Human Development Report 2005.* http://hdr.undp.org

20 A.G. Aganbegyan, "Sotsial'no-ekonomicheskoe razvitie Rossii", *EKO* 1, 2004. http://econom.nsc.ru/eco/arhiv/ReadStatiy/2004_01/Aganbegian.htm.

21 Göler, *Rückzug*, p. 53.

Conclusion: Democratization and Regional Politics?

Graeme Gill

The course of politics in the Russian regions will continue to be shaped by the development of those two factors which have been so central up until now, the relationship with the centre mediated in part through the federal structure, and the disposition of power at the local and regional levels. Any attempt to look at the possible future course of politics in the regions, including the prospects for democratization, must therefore consider these two issues.

Central–regional relations

Earlier chapters have shown how the reforms introduced into the federal structure by Vladimir Putin have changed the balance of power in favour of the centre and perhaps, as Oksana Oracheva and Andreas Heinemann-Grüder argue, undermined the federal model. The centralizing tendencies evident in such changes have been matched by what many observers have seen as the shift of the political system in an anti-democratic direction. The consolidation of presidential power and the marginalization of the legislature, the state takeover of leading media outlets and the narrowing of press freedom and independence, the pressure on leading independent businessmen culminating in the arrest and jailing of Mikhail Khodorkovsky, the law on political parties reducing the capacity of small groups to organize effectively as parties, and the 2006 law requiring the registration of non-governmental organizations (NGOs) and the tightening up on foreign funding of their activities, have all been pointed to as indicating a reduction in the freedom of political forces to organize and act effectively in Russia. This claim has significant merit, and although it deals principally with the central political arena in Moscow, what happens there has important ramifications for politics throughout the country.

Any strengthening of authoritarian rule in the centre would be bound to have direct effects on the course of politics more broadly. But such changes at the centre would need to be accompanied by changes to the way in which the relationship between the centre and the regions was structured if a new authoritarian regime was to become consolidated.

The consolidation of authoritarian rule across Russia would require the construction of an institutional framework through which such rule could be exercised. Is there any evidence of such a framework being established? The Putin reforms have involved a combination of reducing the scope for leading regional politicians to play an active and independent role in politics at the centre with creation of a new institutional structure for central–regional relations. The reform of the Federation Council and the creation of the State Council as an advisory body were clearly means of limiting the room for regional activism at the centre. The establishment of federal districts with presidential envoys, and the introduction of presidential power to appoint regional governors constitute the basis for a new institutional structure for central–regional relations. As well as these alterations to the institutional structure of the state, the Putin elite has also tried to establish a political party which would unite the governors into a formal political machine that potentially could have exercised some control over them. When United Russia was created in 2002, it was an amalgam of Unity and Fatherland-All Russia. Fatherland-All Russia was itself an amalgam of two groups: Fatherland, a movement centred mainly around Moscow mayor Yurii Luzhkov and designed principally to further his presidential ambitions, and All-Russia, headed by Yevgenii Primakov and composed of an alliance of the governors of some of Russia's largest and most economically powerful regions. Unity was the political organization established in 1999 by people around President Yeltsin to block the challenge that Fatherland-All Russia seemed to pose in the forthcoming Duma elections and, when Putin ran for the presidency, to support him. Following the respective performances of Unity and Fatherland-All Russia in the 1999 Duma election, it was decided to merge these groups under the Kremlin's auspices, thereby creating the new entity, United Russia. This body sought to build on the regional basis Unity brought and co-opt leading regional figures into its ranks. One clear intent in establishing the party was to bring those leaders into a political machine loyal to the president, and thereby integrate the country through an extra-constitutional institutional mechanism; one commentator has likened it to the Communist Party of the Soviet Union, in that it is meant to act as a ruling party, but one which is "a political machine based on principles of subordination and corporative loyalty" rather than a clear political ideology.[1]

But have these developments produced an effective political machine answering to the president and projecting his power throughout the country? At the centre, the consolidation of power in the presidential apparatus at the expense of the legislature has been maintained, substantially assisted in the period immediately after the 2003 election by United Russia's dominance of the lower chamber. Although the majority in the lower house has not acted simply as the instrument of the president, proceedings in this body have not been generally hostile to his interests or wishes. Similarly the Federation Council has been a tame body, while the State Council has been publicly lauded by Putin for the positive contribution it has made to the working out of policy, an encomium consistent with it acting broadly in accord with the president and his wishes.[2] Furthermore, the field of civil society remains one in which there is little evidence of the creation and development of a sustained opposition to the president and those around him. The independent and critical voices that remain show no sign of coalescing into a powerful movement that could pose a major threat to the continued maintenance of what has widely been called "managed democracy".[3]

Turning to the institutional mechanisms linking centre with regions, the first of these is the federal districts and presidential envoys. The creation of these offices to exercise general oversight of the governors has not made for an effective means for the centre to exercise close control over developments at lower levels. The federal districts are very large entities which would be very difficult to micro-manage from one centre. Furthermore, the powers of the presidential envoy are poorly defined and remain puny compared with those of the governor. The envoys have many fewer economic and administrative resources at their disposal than the governors, they seem to have less freedom of policy room than the governors, and they lack the firm local footing possessed by the governors, with the result that they are generally considered to have significantly less power than the governors.[4] Nor is it clear that the position of the governors has been made much less secure by the creation of a presidential power to remove them. While many new appointments to gubernatorial positions have been based mainly on considerations of loyalty to the centre rather than competence, this has not meant large-scale renewal; of 32 governors appointed between January and September 2005, 23 were the incumbents re-appointed.[5] Priority has clearly been given to stability in regional rule over the creation of a loyal political machine. Furthermore, the attempt to create an extra-constitutional mechanism of rule including the governors through United Russia has not succeeded. Historically the governors had been somewhat promiscuous in their party affiliations, often associating themselves with more than one party at the same time.[6] This trend does not seem to have been replaced by a wholesale public commitment to United Russia; even after United Russia's 2003 Duma election victory and Putin's re-election to the presidency, both of which were associated with the rallying of gubernatorial ranks around the electoral standard of the president, few governors actually ran for re-election under the banner of United Russia.[7] The party does not therefore seem to have developed as an effective institutional home for the gubernatorial elite or a means of tying them to the presidential elite. Thus by the middle of Putin's second term, if his intent had been to create an institutional machine for projecting his power throughout the regions, there was still considerable work to do to make that a reality.

The limitations evident in institution-building are also present in shortcomings in the other ways in which Putin has sought to modify the federal arrangements he inherited.[8] Despite the pressure for "harmonization" of laws and constitutional provisions, a large number of cases of regional provisions contradicting those of the centre have remained. The legal provisions under which the centre could initiate the removal of a governor prior to the change at the end of 2004 proved largely ineffective. A range of financial measures designed to regularize and equalize the financial relationship between individual regions and the centre proved to have little effect. The attempt by the centre to exercise influence in the appointment of people to posts in the regional branches of federal institutions, especially in the law enforcement area, seems to have had little practical effect. And generally the centre was not always able to achieve the electoral outcome it desired in the regions. Thus in all of these areas, the practical effect of central measures has been much less than a literal reading of them might suggest, and the relationship between centre and regions retains something of that quality of bargaining and compromise evident in the behaviour of Tatarstan analysed by David Cashaback.

The limited success the centre has had in both creating a new institutional structure of centre–region relations and reshaping the processes of those relations does not mean that these measures have not thrown into question the continuing viability of the federal system as inherited by Putin. Clearly the measures he has introduced have sought to fundamentally reshape the balance of power in that system in favour of the centre, and to the extent that this involves the loss of power by the regions, it may be seen as constituting a form of de-federalization. But it may just as easily be seen as readjustment within the federal system, which is the implication of Cashaback's notion of "hegemonic federalism". It is a matter of judgement how far readjustment can go before it involves transformation of the federal structure into a unitary structure (and therefore de-federalization), and the power to appoint regional leaders seems to go substantially in that direction. But what should cause pause here is that the practical effects of the changes seem at this stage to have been limited. However, it remains early days in this process, and the constraints upon that process, reflected chiefly in the limited turnover of regional officials, are not deeply embedded in the constitutional or legal system; it has not been constitutional or legal restraints but the political preference of the centre not to produce substantial turnover that has led to relative stability among the ranks of the governors. Should that preference change and there was the sweeping replacement of incumbent governors by new ones whose chief political resource was loyalty to and support for the centre, the political system would appear significantly different from what it does now, and its federal nature would be seen as being more problematic. Crucial in this is, of course, the question of the presidency and whether Putin will seek to engineer his re-election and, if not, who will replace him and the view that that person will take towards the regions and the federal structure within which they are embedded. In the meantime this means that the governors remain as significant autonomous actors in the system, and the political systems of the regions retain a high level of importance for the Russian political system as a whole. Indeed, the configurations of power at the regional level may continue to constitute a significant barrier to the exercise of central power, particularly if the centre was to seek to exercise that power more vigorously than it has done in the past. But this would be less because of the formalities of the federal structure than because of the dynamics of power at the regional level.

Regional power disposition

Regardless of whether a governor is appointed by the president or elected by a regional constituency, if the governor is to bring about effective regional government, he will have to be able to get along with the other political forces in the region. Unless some form of regularized and stable system of interaction can be established between the different forces in the region, the capacity of the regional administration to function effectively is likely to be substantially undermined, although as Daniel Göler has shown, in some regions this capacity is under threat due to the operation of processes of fragmentation. In the case of those regions where a democratic regime has been established, the institutional structures provide a means for mediating between the different actors in the region in a way that holds out the prospect of lending stability to the structure and thereby consolidating its democratic features. Non-democratic regimes must also develop a structure that will contain the interactions between actors in the region and promote political stability. The forms in which such interaction may be systematized have been noted earlier in this volume by Kerstin Zimmer, Rostislav Turovsky and Julia Kusznir. The question is whether the non-democratic regimes, which Andreas Heinemann-Gruder argues are unstable, will be able to stabilize themselves and blunt any pressures for democratization.

Putin's reforms may, as Gordon Hahn argues,[9] have stimulated some elements of democratization in some of the regions. Pressures for "harmonization" led in some regions to discussion of questions of institutional design, which in turn led to changes involving the reduction of executive power both over the legislature and more generally, increased scope for autonomous action by local government, the democratization of some electoral laws, and the demand for greater protection of citizens' rights and for judicial protection. But such developments have not substantially altered the fact that the overwhelming majority of political systems in the regions retain significant democratic deficits. And it is not clear that in many of these regions there is a civil society emerging that will be sufficiently robust and powerful to be able to bring about early political change. The capacity for popular organization and mobilization along political lines remains restricted, and as long as the ruling authoritarian political machines retain their capacity for control, the opportunities for the development of local opposition will remain limited. This is even more the case given the post-Orange Revolution measures in Russia to cut independent organizations off from foreign sources of finance and support. But how secure is the control enjoyed by these regional regimes?

Crucial in understanding this is the financial relationship a particular region enjoys with Moscow. Notwithstanding the effects of the changes to the federal system noted above, those regions which are net donors to the federal budget[10] are much better placed than those which are net recipients. The relative, and in some cases absolute, economic weakness of the latter makes them much more vulnerable to pressure from the centre than those regions which are not directly reliant on Moscow to make ends meet. If federal budgetary transfers are the economic lifeline, the capacity to resist federal pressures will be reduced; for example, the simple expedient of tying funds to particular policy positions is one way in which the centre can make use of the economic weakness of a particular region. This does not mean that these financially-dependent regions are the mere handmaidens of Moscow, as the history of federal relations in the

Yeltsin and Putin periods has shown. But it does mean that their capacity to pursue an autonomous course of action may be more limited than those regions with effective financial autonomy from the centre.

Those regions which are net donors to the federal budget, and therefore may enjoy a potentially greater degree of autonomy from the capital, are those which have major natural resources or operating production facilities under their control. In the cases of the federal cities, Moscow and St Petersburg, these resources reside in the broad infrastructure of both cities and the roles they play in the national economy. In the other cases, the regions have substantial reserves of natural resources available for both domestic consumption and for export, with oil and gas being the most important of these. It is in such economically self-sufficient regions that big business has emerged as a major player in regional politics. As illustrated earlier in this book, the course of regional politics in all regions, but especially in those where major economic actors are to be found, will be determined in large part by the sort of relationship that exists between political elites based in the regional politico-administrative structure, and economic elites based in the major companies operating in the region.

International experience shows that alliances between such elites can be stable and long-lasting, at both the national and the regional levels. However, such stability could potentially be upset by changes of four types:

1. Changed perceptions of any party (or even any major individual) about either their place in the alliance or about how best to realize their interests. In principle, such alliances can have three different configurations: political dominance and business subservience, business dominance and political subservience, or approximate equality between the parties. Further complicating this picture is the fact that neither political nor economic actors may be unitary; there may be different political groups (sometimes called "clans") and there are likely to be different economic interests active in the region. In the context of these alternatives, it is conceivable that any party may wish to change the prevailing balance of influence within the alliance, and in seeking to bring that about, bring on significant change in the local regime. A struggle for power between political and economic elites is the most extreme form of this, but it could also involve competition between different economic or political forces. For example, electoral politics may be structured as much by the preferences of major economic groups as it is by democratic considerations; this was the situation in the September 2002 gubernatorial election in Krasnoyarsk krai following the death of governor Aleksandr Lebed which saw the

candidate of Norilsk Nickel (and behind that, Interros), Aleksandr Khloponin, opposed to the candidate of RusAl and former speaker of the regional legislature, Aleksandr Uss.[11] Such a situation could be brought on by changing perceptions about how best to realize their interests. Ultimately, an alliance at regional level is based on the partners to that alliance getting something out of that arrangement: business seeks certainty and a boost to its operating capacity through privileges provided by the political elites (such as tax breaks, lower costs, and incentives of various sorts) while the politicians seek support for their political ambitions and possibly personal financial returns; improved performance of the regional economy is also desired, in part for benefit of the local populace/electorate. If any partner seeks to change the distribution of benefits coming from the alliance, and this involves unacceptable reductions in benefits for any of the other parties, a disruption to the alliance is likely.

2. The changed situation of the economic elite. The position of the economic elite in the regional power structure could be changed as a result of changes to the circumstances under which the particular company is operating. Whether the economic performance of the company has improved or deteriorated could be an important factor, with improved performance bolstering the company's position in the local economy and a lowering of performance having the opposite effect. Performance can be affected by market factors – for example, the opening of new export opportunities, the loss of markets, increased competition – but it can also be affected by political decisions; the imposition of new taxes, the withdrawal of privileges and concessions, decisions to devalue the currency, and political moves like those against Khodorkovsky in 2003 are the sorts of political decisions that can have significant implications for a company's standing. This can also be shaped by resource considerations; the drying up of existing sources of natural resources or the discovery of new sources of such resources can both have direct and significant implications for the health of individual companies.

3. The changed situation of the political elite. The regional political elite needs to ensure the continuing solidity of its local base if it is to fend off potential challengers to its position. As long as its political machine can continue to dominate politics in the region and exclude potential challengers from gaining any opportunity to mount an effective challenge, and it can maintain unity within the elite itself, that machine can go a long way towards stabilizing the rule of the regional elite. A dangerous time for the regional elite can be if the governor dies, thereby removing the lynchpin of the whole structure, especially if that

elite is formed around a family as is the case in Tatarstan. There can also be changes to the position of the elite from outside the region. The sorts of considerations discussed earlier in terms of Putin's federal reforms constitute the best instance of this. Should the president choose to move against a governor and remove him, as he did in the case of Yevgenii Nazdratenko in Primorskii krai in 2001,[12] the ruling regional political machine can be brought crashing down. It is this power of the centre that is the most dangerous for the governor, and which can be the most potent factor in rapidly recasting the nature of politics in individual regions.

4. The entry of new players into the regional arena can alter the dynamics of the regional political system. Such players could be political in nature; for example, the presidential envoy taking a closer interest in developments within a particular region, presidential appointment of a new governor, or the establishment of new party branches in a region. But the more common form this has taken has been new economic players. Sometimes, companies based in other regions seek to expand their operations into neighbouring regions. But the more important form this has taken has been the post-1998 expansion of major national companies into the regions. The extent of this expansion has been significant,[13] and where it has occurred it has disrupted existing power arrangements and led to the development of new patterns. Such national companies usually bring with them resources that far exceed those available to most regionally-orientated groups.

These four potential sources of disruption to a regional ruling machine can all bring about the internal weakening, perhaps even dissolution, of that machine. Furthermore their origins all lie in the dynamics of elite relations and do not rely on the strengthening of civil society or the mobilization of democratic forces. Fuelled by personal perceptions and ambitions, stimulated by competition in a marketplace far removed from the scene of regional politics, or structured by the political priorities of a president worried about his future, these sorts of developments can lead to significant changes in the structure of politics within individual regions. Shifts in power in the regional power structure can bring about major alterations in the way in which regional politics are played out and could lead to the growth of democracy in the Russian regions. This possibility would be strengthened were Moscow to take an active lead and promote democracy in the regions. However, the main trends of the Putin presidency do not seem favourable to such a development, and in this context, the prospects for democratization in the regions remain at best uncertain.

Notes

1 Nikolai Petrov, "The 2003 Duma Elections and the *Unified Russia* Phenomenon", in Geir Flikke (ed), *The Uncertainties of Putin's Democracy* (Oslo: Norwegian Institute of International Affairs, 2004), pp. 98–99.

2 Although it did vigorously reject attempts by Putin in 2002 to make it easier for the centre to remove governors, thereby ensuring that there was no weakening of the established position. Elena A. Chebankova, "The Limitations of Central Authority in the Regions and the Implications for the Evolution of Russia's Federal System", *Europe-Asia Studies* 57, 7, November 2005, p. 938.

3 For this term, see Timothy J. Colton and Michael McFaul, *Popular Choice and Managed Democracy. The Russian Elections of 1999 and 2000* (Washington, DC: Brookings Institution Press, 2003).

4 See the discussion in Chebankova, "Limitations", pp. 943–5.

5 Chebankova, "Limitations", p. 946.

6 Henry E. Hale, *Why Not Parties in Russia? Democracy, Federalism, and the State* (Cambridge, Cambridge University Press, 2006), pp. 133–4.

7 Ibid., p. 136.

8 This is based principally upon Chebankova.

9 See the argument in Gordon M. Hahn, "The Impact of Putin's Federative Reforms on Democratization in Russia", *Post-Soviet Affairs* 19, 2, April–June 2003, pp.114–53. Although Hahn also acknowledges that in some instances executive power has been enhanced at the expense of the legislature.

10 On the basis of the share of transfers coming from the federal budget in 1999, the following were donor regions (ie. they received no such transfers): the cities of Moscow and St Petersburg; Moscow, Lipetsk, Samara, Perm and Sverdlovsk oblasts; Khanty-Mansii and Yamalo-Nenets AOs; Komi, Tatarstan and Bashkortostan republics; and Krasnoyarsk krai. Cameron Ross, *Federalism and democratisation in Russia* (Manchester: Manchester University Press, 2002), p. 84.

11 Khloponin was also the former governor of Taimyr AO. Andrew Yorke, "Business and Politics in Krasnoyarsk Krai", *Europe-Asia Studies* 55, 2, 2003, pp. 256–7.

12 Formally Nazdratenko was not removed but resigned and took up a post in Moscow as head of the federal fisheries service, but there is little doubt that it was central pressure that led to his resignation.

13 For details of the presence of major companies in the different regions, see Robert W. Orrtung, "Business and Politics in the Russian Regions", *Problems of Post-Communism* 51, 2, March–April 2004, pp. 52–4.

Index

214